TELEVISION HISTORY,
THE PEABODY ARCHIVE,
AND CULTURAL MEMORY

THE PEABODY SERIES IN MEDIA HISTORY

SERIES EDITORS

Jeffrey P. Jones, *University of Georgia*
Ethan Thompson, *Texas A&M University, Corpus Christi*

TELEVISION HISTORY, THE PEABODY ARCHIVE, AND CULTURAL MEMORY

EDITED BY **ETHAN THOMPSON,
JEFFREY P. JONES,
AND LUCAS HATLEN**

THE UNIVERSITY OF GEORGIA PRESS | ATHENS

© 2019 by the University of Georgia Press
Athens, Georgia 30602
www.ugapress.org
All rights reserved
Designed by Kaelin Chappell Broaddus
Set in 10.75/13.5 Garamond Premier Pro Regular
by Kaelin Chappell Broaddus

Most University of Georgia Press titles are
available from popular e-book vendors.

Printed digitally

Library of Congress Cataloging-in-Publication Data

NAMES: Thompson, Ethan, editor. | Jones, Jeffrey P., 1963– editor. |
    Hatlen, Lucas, 1988– editor.
TITLE: Television history, the Peabody Archive, and cultural memory /
    edited by Ethan Thompson, Jeffrey P. Jones, and Lucas Hatlen.
DESCRIPTION: Athens : University of Georgia, [2019] | Series: Peabody
    series in media history
IDENTIFIERS: LCCN 2019021675 (print) | LCCN 2019981523 (ebook) |
    ISBN 9780820356181 (hardback) | ISBN 9780820356204 (paperback) |
    ISBN 9780820356198 (ebook)
SUBJECTS: LCSH: Television archives—United States. | Peabody
    Collection—Archives.
CLASSIFICATION: LCC PN1992.16 .T45 2019 (PRINT) | LCC PN1992.16
    (EBOOK) | DDC 026.79145/0973—dc23
LC record available at https://lccn.loc.gov/2019021675
LC ebook record available at https://lccn.loc.gov/2019981523

CONTENTS

This volume is the product of a multiyear collaboration between the Peabody Awards program and public historians and media scholars. Its goal is to uncover, explore, and analyze historical television programming contained in the Peabody Awards Collection at the University of Georgia. The Peabody archive houses the programming (and large collections of ancillary materials) submitted to the awards program since its beginning in 1940. That means the collection includes not just the annual award winners but also a vast treasure trove of programs that have largely been forgotten, much of which was produced at the local level owing to the nature of American broadcasting for a large part of this time.

This scholarly effort looks both wider and deeper than the well-known canon of U.S. broadcast history that dominates popular memory of the relationship of television to American society. It examines a wide array of programming that has largely been unexplored in television studies scholarship. But what are the Peabody Awards, how did they come into being, what do they recognize, and why have television (and radio) producers submitted their programming for adjudication in the first place?

The Peabody Awards are the oldest and most prestigious broadcasting awards in the world. Founded in the Grady College of Journalism at the University of Georgia in 1940 (under the auspices of the National Association of Broadcasters), the award began as the Pulitzer of radio. As broadcasting technology changed—through the advent of television, cable, streaming and digital programming—the award kept pace by recognizing ever-changing media platforms. And from the award's beginning, it has recognized programming across multiple genres, including news, documentary, and entertainment as well as children's and public service programs.

There has never been a fixed set of criteria for what constitutes a winning program. What has stayed constant is the fundamental recognition, first and foremost, of storytelling that serves the needs of viewers as citizens. The award is not, then, just a tip of the hat to the craft of media production or the media industry that produces it. It is the story itself that the award celebrates, recognizing stories that contribute in some way to an engaged citizenship. Owing to this central purpose, the award has at times been seen mistakenly as primarily a "journalism" award. Yet from the beginning, the Peabody jurors have consistently understood that entertainment programming can be as powerful a tool for inspiring empathy and understanding as forms of reportage.

That the Peabody Awards sit outside of the media industry has proved significant for an award that many consider the most prestigious in television and radio. The award cannot be lobbied or campaigned for, as is the quite costly norm with the Television Academy's Emmy Awards, where networks routinely spend millions of dollars yearly in advertisements, DVD mailers, billboards, and so on, to sway the academy's twenty-two thousand voting members. The Peabody Awards, by contrast, are determined by a relatively small board of jurors (currently eighteen members), who meet in face-to-face deliberations, choosing winners through a unanimous vote.

The board is composed of scholars, television critics, journalists, television and radio producers and executives, and former government officials. In the board's early years, members included such publishing luminaries as Alfred A. Knopf and Bennett Cerf and later such distinguished political, journalistic, and entertainment media stalwarts as Barbara Jordan, Newton Minnow, Kitty Carlyle, John Daly, Ron Nessen, Charlayne Hunter-Gault, and Marcy Carsey.

The number of awards the organization has handed out over the program's seventy-eight years has varied. The greatly expanded landscape of media channels and networks in recent years has expanded the number of submissions, which currently stand at approximately twelve hundred per year, thirty of which receive awards in any given year. In 2016, the program also began recognizing thirty additional nominees. The winning programs over seventy-eight years truly constitute a canon of great American storytelling and a pantheon of master storytellers. But what of the vast majority of programming in the archives that did *not* win a Peabody? It encompasses items such as local children's shows, talk shows directed to minority populations, low-budget documentaries, global music specials, atypical public affairs programming, scripted shows from one-season runs, and much more. The archive is thus a distinctive repository of cultural memory, much of which not only is not part of the canon that typically dominates our understanding of who and what we are as a nation but also is not reflected in accounts of American cultural history offered by television studies.

This project therefore asks what we might find if we look to the archive for what's been forgotten. How might these programs change our understanding of television's past and impact the ways we think about television's present and future? How might our understanding of gender, class, sexual, racial representation, and citizenship shift as a result of witnessing programming that stands outside the canon that often defines such thinking? What can be learned about the approaches and assumptions of production and intended audiences? In short, what new questions can we ask and what new approaches should we take as a result of seeing and experiencing this programming?

To address these questions, two conferences were held. In October 2015, the contributors to this volume traveled to Athens, Georgia, to view an assortment of clips selected from the Peabody archive by Ethan Thompson in consultation with Lucas Hatlen and Jeffrey Jones. The participants then had one year to pursue a research project related to the Peabody archive before they were scheduled to meet again to share their work. Those 2016 presentations were then turned into the chapters of this book. All of the chapters deal with television (and in one case, radio) programs housed in the archive, some exclusively so. None of the chapters, however, deal only with programs selected and screened for them at the first conference.

What follows are the fruits of this scholarly exercise. It is our hope that this project will raise as many new questions as it answers, and that it will inspire others to begin exploring the rich cultural history that this archive contains. This book is also the first volume in a series through the University of Georgia Press dedicated to research on the Peabody archive specifically and television and broadcast history more broadly.

What this volume and series suggest, then, is that the Peabody Awards should not be seen as just yearly awards that recognize contemporary stories that matter but should also be seen as a collection of the ways a vast array of storytellers have made sense of their world, advocated for change, represented their communities, expressed their art, demanded justice, and attempted to inspire citizens through the power of television. For ultimately, it is stories such as those represented and reflected on in this volume that shape how we see and know ourselves and how that mediation is configured in popular memory.

JEFFREY P. JONES

ACKNOWLEDGMENTS

This book is the product of a multiyear collaborative effort by not just the editors and authors listed on the contents page but also a number of other scholars who participated in the project at various stages, as well as the supporting staff of the Peabody Awards Program, the Walter J. Brown Media Archives, and the Hargrett Rare Book and Manuscript Library, all at the University of Georgia. The hard work of many people made this book possible.

In particular, major thanks are due to Ruta Abolins, Mary Miller, and the rest of the staff of the Walter J. Brown Media Archives, whose work to preserve and catalog the Peabody Awards Collection makes this and future scholarship possible. Aside from their long-term maintenance and organization of the collection, the staff fielded lots of questions and tirelessly facilitated many requests to make screenings available for our group symposium and independent research projects.

Thank you to the scholars who contributed to this book for their long-term commitments to our project: Christine Becker, Susan J. Douglas, Herman Gray, Jonathan Gray, Heather Hendershot, Eric Hoyt, Deborah L. Jaramillo, Derek Kompare, Susan Murray, Allison Perlman, and Lynn Spigel. Additionally, Michelle Hilmes, Victoria Johnson, Quinlan Miller, Jason Mittell, Khadijah White, and Mark Williams also attended our symposiums and took part in our discussions about how the Peabody collection might impact our understanding of television history. This book bears their influences as well.

ACKNOWLEDGMENTS FROM ETHAN: I was privileged to spend a semester in residence in Athens, getting to know the holdings of the Peabody Awards Collection as best I could. This was possible because 1) Jeffrey P. Jones and the Peabody program invited me to do so; 2) my home institution, Texas

A&M University, Corpus Christi, allowed me to take a semester's absence; and 3) most importantly, my wife Maria graciously agreed to tend to three kids and two dogs while I was away! All three deserve and have my genuine gratitude.

When I got to Athens in August 2015, I realized my most pressing charge was to put together a collection of screenings that would inspire the scholars attending our symposium to engage the collection for their own research projects. This meant watching a lot of TV that hadn't been watched in many years, and also making a lot of requests for viewer copies of archival programs when none were available. I am exceedingly grateful for the graciousness and expeditiousness with which the archive's staff made these available. Sometimes it meant digitizing video so it could be viewed remotely; sometimes it meant getting 16-mm film equipment repaired; sometimes it meant sending off two-inch videotape for conversion. I don't think I ever had a request turned down. I like to think that the scholarship in this collection will justify that labor and expense. So, a big thank you again to Ruta Abolins and Mary Miller and the rest of the staff at the Walter J. Brown Media Archives. I also want to thank Jermaine King and the employees and student workers at the media desk in the main library, where the existing viewer copies from the Peabody collection are held. The staff quickly adjusted to my habit of letting myself into the stacks to fill my backpack with VHS tapes to take home to watch. They never once tackled me on my way out the door. Lynh Tran and the staff of the Peabody program not only supported my work but made Athens feel like a home away from home.

I am thankful to my fellow editors for everything they did in addition to coediting this book. Thanks to Jeff for inviting me in the first place, and thanks to Shana and Andrew for welcoming me and my family into their home. Thanks to Lucas, whose work with the collection meant that I already had a jump start when I got to Athens. The screenings, the discussions, the individual projects, and ultimately the chapters in this book would not have been possible without Lucas.

ACKNOWLEDGMENTS FROM LUCAS: I would first like to thank Jeffrey Jones for the opportunity to work as an editor and contributor to this book, and for the opportunity to work with the Peabody collection more broadly. It has been a once-in-a-lifetime opportunity, and one for which I will be eternally grateful. If not for his vision and planning, this book would not exist. I am immensely grateful to everyone at the Walter J. Brown Media Archives for facilitating this research by providing an exceptional level of access to the collection. I would like to offer particular thanks to Ruta Abolins and Mary Miller, who were always willing to share their knowledge of the archive with me and always seemed to be able to answer any question I had with alarming speed. Thanks so much to Lynh Tran and Molly Williams, who were instrumental in the success of the symposiums. I am so grateful for their involvement and contributions throughout this entire process. Thanks to my friends, family, and my partner Gloria Jen for all their encouragement and support. Finally, thanks to Ethan, who always kept this book on track, and who helped to guide me through the process of editing a book for the first time. Many of the programs referenced and discussed throughout this anthology were discovered as a result of Ethan's time in the archive and his curation of screenings for the symposium, so his role in the production of this book is difficult to overstate.

ACKNOWLEDGMENTS FROM JEFF: The two conferences from which this book is drawn were made possible by the generous gifts of Lessie and Charles Smithgall. Mrs. Smithgall and her husband's gift enables the Lambdin Kay Chair for the Peabodys, and this scholarly research is a product of their legacy. Mrs. Smithgall was a contributing founder of the Peabody Awards in 1939 and is still alive today at 108 years old. She is one of the few humans who can say that all of the programming discussed in this volume appeared in her lifetime.

I too greatly appreciate the efforts of Ruta Abolins, Mary Miller, and the staff at the Richard Russell Special Collections Library. This book is a scholarly celebration of materials that they painstakingly tend and manage daily and the first attempt by the Peabody Awards Program to mine these rich resources for their lasting impact on American culture and society. Likewise, many thanks to Lisa Bayer, Walter Biggins, and the staff at the University of Georgia Press for greenlighting this project and for their recognition that scholarly research of one of the richest collections of media programming in the world deserves public attention. Thanks too to the Peabody program staff, Lynh Tran, Molly Williams, Margaret Blanchard, Wes Unruh, Christine Drayer. The two conferences would never have been as successful without their superb professionalism and smart attention to detail.

Finally, most appreciation is reserved for Ethan Thompson and Lucas Hatlen. This book would never have happened without the vision, leadership, planning, thinking, and hard work both put into making this goal of a serious scholarly examination of the Peabody archive a reality. Ethan's deep curation and love of these materials is evident on every page of this volume, and Lucas's willingness to support every step of planning and execution was invaluable.

TELEVISION HISTORY, THE PEABODY ARCHIVE, AND CULTURAL MEMORY

LYNN SPIGEL

INTRODUCTION

THE PEABODY AWARDS COLLECTION,
THE ARCHIVE, AND LOCAL TV HISTORY

Like television itself, the television archive is an apparatus that promises to make the world visible, holding out the hope of bringing the distant (or even recent) past nearer, collapsing the space between the "now" and "then," the "near" and "far." But archives never really deliver a transparent "window on the world"; instead they offer partial views. Archives give order to television's ephemeral past by preserving, selecting, filing, and arranging the leftovers of the vast amount of audiovisual materials that TV transmits on a daily basis to people around the world.

To be sure, television archives offer rich research opportunities for anyone interested in understanding the past. But archives are themselves deeply historical spaces. In *The Archaeology of Knowledge*, Michel Foucault observes that history (as a narrative form and discursive mode) makes the archive. Rather than assume there is a preexisting collection of facts waiting to be accessed, Foucault posits that the archive is preceded by a discursive formation that selects, acquires, and arranges words and things. And, as John Tagg argues with respect to the history of crime photography, archives are rooted in modern techniques of filing, which are themselves beholden to larger systems of cultural power (such as police records).[1] In this respect, scholars go to the television archive in search of the past, but the past they find depends on the logic of the filing system itself.

In the television archive we find, for example, the historical procession of recording technologies on which television programs have been shot and restored (kinescopes, film, various tape formats, and digital files); the economic and legal practices (such as ownership and copyright laws) that regulate access and use; the human traces of metadata (such as search terms and file descriptions) that facilitate but also circumscribe our choices about what to retrieve and why to retrieve it; the constraints of space and funding; and the design practices (building types, shelving, vaults, study areas, and viewing settings) that affect the ways we literally *re-view* TV outside of its everyday habitat (which historically was primarily the home). Television archives transform TV from its status as an everyday, even mundane practice, into a historical document.

As a cultural form constituted by what Raymond Williams famously calls "flow," television is a particularly unwieldy object that poses challenges for archivists and researchers.[2] In a fundamental sense the paradox of television archives is that they really don't save television—*as an experience*—at all. While television (especially TV of the classic commercial broadcast era) was typically experienced as a flow of entertainment, information, commercials, promotional materials, title art, and related interstitials that aired across the TV schedule, archives arrest the flow of television, acquiring, saving, and cataloguing television as programs (or singular works of art akin to books, films, or paintings). In this respect, the television archive operates through techniques of redaction, and the historian is left trying to piece together the larger televisual context in which particular programs appeared. Because of the sheer amount of television produced and its episodic or serial nature, the historian likewise faces the daunting task of figuring out which bits of archived material to watch. (The whole series? An award-winning episode? Does the archive have original broadcasts with commercials and title art intact? Or is the program missing advertising and graphic elements that viewers from the period would have seen?) And given the fact that much of early live television was not recorded, how are we to theorize the gaps in the record? Even in the late 1950s and 1960s, when videotape became a more common production practice, technicians often taped over videos as a cost-cutting strategy (thereby erasing many programs). In this sense, television archives always operate on a paradox of scale—they offer too much (hours and hours of television programming) and too little at the same time.

Acts of preservation are also deeply cultural, bound up in television's status as a form of mass culture and the taste biases against commercial TV since its rise in the 1950s. In fact, even while the Library of Congress now holds historical collections of commercial, educational, and public television, in the medium's first two decades there was no national archive for television. The Library of Congress isolates several practical factors that led to what it calls its "eclectic" and "uneven" collection practices in the early period, including live television's ephemerality and the fact that early television producers did not often seek copyright registration for their programs.[3] But it also admits its cultural bias: "There was an attitude held by Library of Congress acquisitions officers toward television programming which paralleled that of the scholarly community in general. The Library simply underestimated the social and historical significance of the full range of television programming. There was no appreciation of television's future research value. So before the mid-1960s, few programs were acquired for the collection."[4]

While the Library of Congress was slow to collect TV, other institutions did envision TV libraries and museums in the early days of broadcasting. Most prominent were the Museum of Modern Art (which first envisioned an archive in 1952), the Television Academy of Arts and Sciences (which began plans for a television library in 1959), and the never built Hollywood Museum (an elaborate scheme for a museum of film, radio, TV, and the recording arts that was envisioned by Hollywood luminaries and the city of Los Angeles in the early 1960s). As I have argued at length elsewhere, none of these plans worked out exactly how their visionaries imagined, but these institutions did create rationales for collecting TV that helped set an agenda for future archives.[5] Most important for my purposes here, all of these cultural institutions were located on the coasts, and all had synergies with the television industry. By 1976, the coastal logic and industry forces at the heart of these early archive visions came together with the opening of the Museum of Broadcasting in New York, founded by CBS chair William S. Paley (and now known as the Paley Center for Media, which has branches in both Manhattan and Beverly Hills). Given their connections to the television industry, it is not surprising that television's first archivists focused on network programs, which became central to the logics of the television archive in years to come. The national bias of historical collections is compounded by the fact that local stations did not usually save their programs, which leaves the historical record spotty at best.

Indeed, much of what remains from the early broadcast period reinforces this emphasis on network television programs produced mainly on the coasts and, by the mid-1950s, increasingly by Hollywood studios.[6] The Television Academy's collection, which is constituted mostly of programs nominated for prime-time Emmys, was first put on loan at the UCLA Film and Television Archive in 1966 and remains on permanent loan there today. The Paley Center's historical television collection is populated by a catholic mix of mostly network genres. Although UCLA, the Paley Center, and Chicago's more modest Museum of Broadcast Communications do hold collections of local programming pertinent to their own urban locations, they do not offer a broad cross-section of local television programs from across the country.[7]

The Walter J. Brown Media Archives and Peabody Awards Collection is unique among peers because it contains much local programming culled from Peabody Award entries.[8] First opened to the public in 1995, the Peabody Awards Collection contains entries for the awards starting in 1940 for radio and 1948 for television, and the library houses programs by local, national, cable, and (in recent years) international producers and internet-only providers. As of 2017, roughly 37 percent of the programs hail from local commercial and educational/PBS affiliate stations. Programs span a range of genres from news, documentary, and entertainment to educational and children's programming, and the collection also contains accompanying materials such as station ephemera and viewer mail. For most of its history, the Peabody Awards charged an entry fee, but standards have been loosely defined over the years, with elastic criteria such as "excellence on its own terms" or "stories that matter."[9] The collection, therefore, provides examples of programs that broadcasters thought represented their best efforts each year. As several authors in this volume suggest, despite the Peabody's flexible criteria, the collection demonstrates what broadcasters deemed quality TV within the context of wider taste standards of an era. Moreover, given the fact that many entrees in the collection are public affairs programs, they in particular satisfy expectations of localism and public service that the FCC established for broadcast stations. In this regard, like all archives, the Peabody Awards Collection is representative rather than comprehensive. Nevertheless, the programs and related station materials in the collection help to flesh out a more nuanced picture of television culture around the nation.

Drawing on the collection, the essays in this book demonstrate how television history, which has traditionally focused mainly on network programs, can be significantly reconceptualized and enhanced by attention to local productions. And because the Peabody Awards Collection offers a wide range of programs from local stations and national broadcast networks, as well as educational, public, and cable venues, this volume provides a comparative framework that accentuates local TV while analyzing it alongside television's other programming frameworks. Taken together, the essays highlight how particular forms of television materialized within the general institutional parameters of the U.S. broadcast and cable systems between the 1950s and 1980s (the period generally considered as the three-network TV era). In light of the Peabody's own practices of collection and arrangement, the book also asks questions about archives and historical interpretation. In the remainder of this introduction, I explore issues historians confront when studying local television, and I examine the opportunities that the Peabody Awards Collection affords.

ACCENTUATING THE LOCAL

How is it possible to use television to understand the specificities of place in networked cultures? In the context of an increasingly globalized and mediatized world, television has contributed to changes in the ways people experience their lived environments. Television has been central to the patterns of what David Harvey calls the "space-time compression" of the modern world, which ideally can result in greater access to cultural exchange but which also contributes to the economic and cultural homogenization of place.[10] Or as Marc Agué suggests, the postindustrial networked world has upended the traditional anthropological sense of place, creating a series of "nonplaces"—supermarkets, air terminals, freeways—places we pass through rather than inhabit. Nonplaces depend on the "invasion of space by text"—signposts, billboards, and importantly for our purposes, TV or computer screens.[11] In a similar vein, taking TV as her central object, Margaret Morse argues that television is bound up in the history of a whole architecture of everyday life that operates through simulation, distraction, and the "derealization" of the actual physical sites and communities in which we live. Specifically, Morse sees television (along with freeways and shopping malls) as paradigmatic "nonspaces" of postwar U.S. life.[12] While such accounts of television and related aspects of the built environment do help explain the disorientation and alienation often felt in postindustrial mediatized places, these theories operate at such a "macro" scale of abstraction that they wind up evading the "micro" analyses of local cultures in those places. For example, they say nothing about local media production cultures. And they ignore how audiences use local TV (or radio or podcasts) as a political, educational, or spiritual resource (as with public affairs programs or religious shows) or as a source for fan cultures and other forms of personal and community pleasure. In this regard, macro theories of nonplace could benefit from a history lesson on local TV.

That said, my point is not that local TV offers a more authentic (or direct) sense of past experiences just because its scale is smaller than that of network programs. Indeed, local programs often use highly conventionalized forms of presentation and representation (the cast of chatty anchors is a daily ritual, whether in Tulsa or LA). Nevertheless, by exploring local programs historians can discern "accents" not registered in prime-time network fare. For example, cultural affairs programs produced by local stations demonstrate how different parts of the country deal with—or fail to deal with—issues of importance to their local communities and/or the nation and world. Programs in the Peabody Awards Collection can help derail the big city bias of Hollywood or New York production, and the often untested (or even unconscious) assumption that programs produced in major metropolitan areas such as Boston, New York City, or San Francisco are always more politically "progressive" than local programs produced, say, in Little Rock or Des Moines. Moreover, as Susan Douglas demonstrates in this volume, social activists (such as the 1970s gay and lesbian activists she explores) sometimes made themselves heard on local TV *before* they found a place on the networks. Research on local programs can therefore challenge received wisdom about historical change and progress on television. In addition, a focus on local production can reveal long forgotten genres and production practices. In this collection, for example, Ethan Thompson explores "fake news" shows that reenacted past events or speculated on impending disasters (such as nuclear war or environmental blight). More generally, research on local programs can complicate well-rehearsed theories and histories of television's aesthetics, revealing outliers—those programs or moments in programs that seem not to fit into our memories and histories of what TV was at a particular time.

Pioneering (if still scarce) historical scholarship on local television by historians such as Gayle Wald, Mark Williams, and Meenasarani Linde Murugan has demonstrated the value of moving past the emphasis on the networks. This body of work often points to counterhistories and counterpractices not visible or audible (and in some cases censored) on network programs. Along these lines, Wald's *It's Been Beautiful* (2015) considers the black power program *Soul!* that was broadcast on New York City's public Channel 13 (WNET) between 1968 and 1972. Wald finds alternative perspectives on blackness, activism, pleasure, art, and community than are found in histories that focus on the networks' depiction of the civil rights movement. Williams and Murugan have each analyzed strains of midcentury "orientalism" in the early television performances of Korla Pandit (an African American musician who donned the identity of an Indian mystic on KTLA's *Adventures in Music* between 1948 and 1951). They explore the intersections of race and gender on early local TV, showing how Pandit's "exotic" performances helped forge one of the first fan communities for television (in this case composed mainly of women in the LA area).[13] The essays in this book continue this work, recovering surprising new histories of local programming by examining a range of aesthetic, cultural, and political issues.

For example, several contributors to this volume use the Peabody Awards Collection to reconsider television's relation to U.S. racial politics. As Allison Perlman argues, by exploring programs outside of the mainstream (white-dominated) networks, scholars can "rescript" the "relationship between television history and the long-standing struggle for civil rights in the United States." With this in mind, Perlman explores Ozzie Davis and Ruby Dee's 1965 series *History of the Negro People* produced by National Educational Television (NET) and *With Ozzie and Ruby*, first broadcast on the Dallas public station KERA-TV in 1981–82. Examining the programs in the context of Davis and Dee's longer history of activism and artistic interventions, Perlman shows how they used NET and KERA-TV as a stage for articulations of black voices, authorship, and resistance via the presentation of African American arts, culture, and history.

Other authors in this volume use a comparative framework. Focusing on the racism of the "war on drugs" in the Reagan and Bush eras, Deborah Jaramillo examines how nine local stations depicted drug use in their communities. Comparing Peabody-submitted local programs to each other as well as to network and HBO entries, Jaramillo considers what the stations thought made their "war on drug" programs Peabody-worthy "quality TV" that fulfilled the FCC mandate (and Peabody nomination category) of public service. But, at the same time, she unpacks the complex deployment of terms like "public service" and "quality TV" by showing how the programs often racialized the war on drugs, defining the local public as "white" people threatened not just by drugs but also by people of color (who were variously depicted as drug dealers, gang members, and crack mothers). Also using a comparative framework, Heather Hendershot uses the Peabody Awards Collection to explore coverage of the 1970s urban crisis and civil rights struggles in New York. Comparing local to national formats, Hendershot finds that live local radio shows often contained a broader set of community voices (especially with respect to race and ethnicity) than did scripted public affairs TV or talk shows (which often focused on the charismatic image of Mayor John Lindsay). Finally, concentrating on special event TV, Christine Becker and Lucas Hatlen compare local and network coverage of the 1976 bicentennial. This national event allows Becker and Hatlen to consider how different stations across the country used a common frame of national symbols to celebrate America. However, they argue, the stations deployed these symbols in a range of different ways, using them to salute American exceptionalism as well as to evoke more critical countermemories of slavery and the struggle for civil rights. Here, as elsewhere, attention to local productions allows for a rich understanding of television's role in orchestrating national conversations and yields new insights into the varied dimensions of television history, beyond the network frame.

But even while local programs can productively disrupt the network bias of television history, we should not replace one bias—"the national"—with another—"the local." Broadcast television was historically founded on the dialectic between localism and nationalism, not only because of its affiliate structures and regulation policies but also due to its textuality and scheduling flows. The voice of the local station has always made itself heard, literally in the voice of station announcers and figuratively in the daily flow of local news, morning shows, station breaks, and fringe-time pleasures (like midnight movies). In the classic TV era, when broadcasting was not a round-the-clock affair, the local station greeted viewers in the morning and put them to bed at night with sign-ons and sign-offs (and the latter were typically followed by the station's local iteration of the national anthem). As an experience, U.S. television broadcasting is therefore really neither local nor national but rather both at once.

Local television fragments television's national "cultural forum" with intimate connections to particular places. Local stations maintain audiences through affective ties that speak to hometowns (or at least individual broadcast markets). Along these lines, local TV is often connected to childhood memories. The goofy horror hosts, chummy weathercasters, the clowns on children's shows, and fast-talking car dealers who appear on local stations become part of our personal itineraries and resonate through time. More broadly, insofar as they are licensed on the condition that they serve the public interest, local stations—especially through public affairs and news programs—have helped define community boundaries, both including and excluding viewers. The diverse holdings in the Peabody Awards Collection allow researchers to compare articulations of television, offering opportunities to think about TV's role in the formation of imagined communities, citizenship, and identity—issues that various authors in this book engage.

Throughout broadcast history citizenship and community have always been intricately imbedded in consumerism. As Derek Kompare observes in this volume, the concept of the local in broadcast history is vexed in this regard. Broadcast stations were based on the markets their signals covered (and related practices of market research and ratings) rather than preexisting organic communities or neighborly ties. Therefore, Kompare argues, even while stations seeking Peabody Awards have often nominated programs on the basis of their public service to their communities, historians need to unpack what terms like public service and community mean in relation to the consumer infrastructure of a broadcast market.

In a related fashion, the Peabody Awards Collection provides opportunities to consider the tensions between education and commercialism in the U.S. broadcast system. Susan Murray, for example, considers these tensions with regard to programs created by medical professionals, many of which were produced by and/or aired on local TV stations in the 1950s. Despite the programs' educational mission, TV critics at the time reviled the gory nature of some of the more graphic surgical shows seen by home audiences. Murray demonstrates how the mandates of good taste for commercial broadcast TV were at times in conflict with the educational goals of local broadcasters and medical professionals. Similar conflicts between commercialism and education have, of course, been especially pronounced in the history of debates about children's programs. Addressing these debates, Jonathan Gray looks at program tie-ins for children's educational shows, including items like flash cards, books, and toys (materials that broadcasters included with their Peabody program entries). While acknowledging that tie-in objects have often been part of the commercialization of childhood, Gray nevertheless argues that they also have played a positive role in the life worlds and education of children. More generally, he contends, historians need to take these objects seriously as "paratexts" that should be analyzed as symbolic forms and not just as exploitation.

While the topics in this book vary, the common project of exploring local television opens up methodological and theoretical issues regarding scale—or the relationship between general forms of knowledge about television and the particular examples that an archive like the Peabody, with its focus on local TV, affords. Mining the archive, numerous authors scale down by paying close attention to textual forms, analyzing, for example, modes of narration, costume, staging, or music used in a program. At the same time, many authors also scale up by considering what local TV can tell us about broader questions regarding media institutions, aesthetics, politics, culture, and historical change. Most explicitly here, Eric Hoyt approaches the relationship between the general and the particular by using a computational quantitative method of metadata analysis, which allows him to aggregate general trends in the kinds of programs that local stations nominated for Peabody Awards between 1948 and 2013. In addition, in order to determine *why* programming types changed over time, Hoyt pairs his quantitative approach with qualitative methods that zoom in on the history of one particular local station. In Hoyt's case, the issue of methodological scale is directly related to geographical scale—and to his own "local knowledge" because the station he explores is situated in his hometown of Madison, Wisconsin. Here as elsewhere, the focus on localism has an anthropological dimension that reminds us that broadcast stations are not just local industries but also venues through which people come to know—and are oriented in—the places in which they live.

In all of these ways, this book is much more than a survey of an archive and its holdings. Instead, the authors use the Peabody Awards Collection as a resource for reconsidering how to write about television history itself.

THE ARCHIVE AND THE HISTORIAN

I want to end with some historiographical questions about the pleasures, practices, and interpretative dimensions of television history and the archive. Like all historians, media historians find joy in digging through the remains of the past. The pleasures of the archival search are enhanced by the scarcity of local programs and especially the promise they hold for telling us something new about television's past, or at least different from the knowledge generated by the network or nationally syndicated series that usually form the corpus of TV history. This is especially so in the contemporary media environment, where network series have lost some of their historical mystery as they circulate in seeming endless rotation on DVDs, nostalgia networks like TV Land, or through streaming services like Netflix. In this new media context of vintage TV abundance, network series have lost what Carolyn Steedman calls the "dust" of the archive.[14] With downloads on demand, there are no long journeys to far-off places that store boxes and bundles of long-forgotten things. The romance of the archive (as a space of memory, daydreams, and speculation) gives way to the mundane practices of ordinary TV viewing. All we have are the same endless stream of digitized "classics" that just about anybody (with access to fast-speed broadband and cable) can retrieve with the stroke of a hand. I am speaking hyperbolically, of course. In reality, the new media environment is not a substitute for the brick and mortar archive (which contains programs, commercials, and interstitials that do not circulate elsewhere). Nor is it a replacement for the archivists' knowledge, skills, creativity, and labor. Nevertheless, DVDs, cable, and streaming networks—as well as digital archives like the Smithsonian's Internet Archive or unofficial archives like YouTube—have all become an important supplement to the traditional TV archives.[15] The proliferation of vintage TV and our ability to store it ourselves transform the purposes and pleasures of archival research.

With its strong focus on local programs, the Peabody Awards Collection allows the contemporary TV historian to rediscover the romance of the dig for lost treasures in the age of TV abundance. Certainly, this volume is testimony to the pleasures of hunting for TV materials that heretofore remained relatively untouched by historians' hands. This book is all about that project of recovery. Still, the desire to recover a lost or occluded past is, as the editors and authors in this volume demonstrate, never as simple as it seems. Instead, as I suggested at the outset, the television archive is a filing system that is based on a specific organization and selection of the past and provides a particular apparatus of access to it.

Speaking of such issues, Jacques Derrida writes, "Today, we can at least pretend (in a dream) to archive everything, or almost everything. . . . But because it is not possible to preserve everything, choices, and therefore interpretations, structurations, become necessary." And for this reason, "whoever is in a position to access this past or to use the archive should know concretely that there was a politics of memory, a particular politics, that this politics is in transformation, that it is a *politics*."[16] For Derrida, archives are not just places of historical recovery. Instead, as he argues in *Archive Fever*, they are riddled with loss, absence, trauma, and even a "radical evil" that erases histories, such as the histories of people forced from their homelands. (Derrida's book was first delivered as a lecture at the Freud Museum in London, which was also the home in exile to which Freud escaped in the Nazi era.) The archive is not just an empirical holding place but also a "spectral" space haunted by ghosts neither fully absent nor present in material terms.

In a more materialist fashion, Foucault approaches the archive as a technical apparatus (or *dispositif*) that stores the "positivities" of the past—things that are said and recorded, as opposed to everything or everyone. While archives may indulge the historian's positivist dream of completion (the desire to find every artifact), in a counterintuitive move Foucault argues that the archive exposes the "rarity" of statements it was possible to speak in the discursive formations of their times.[17] Even if we were able to find every single television recording ever made (the ideal TV archive), that archive would still be founded on the principle of rarity. As discursive systems, TV and its archives give voice only to what is "speakable"—and, I would add, only what is "recordable" and "savable"—in the context of their social, industrial, technological, political, historiographical, and institutional parameters. Paradoxically, in this respect, the archive preserves absence. In the TV archive we find, for example, a relative lack of TV directors and writers of color in the early period of broadcast TV. But we also find the rare conditions under which their bodies and statements became visible. Historians, therefore, need to consider what is not in the archive and to track those pasts that did not necessarily materialize or proliferate as documents. This is where the archive ends and historical interpretation starts—in the ethereal pasts we can imaginatively find only in the gaps left behind.

In recent years, archives have become increasingly interesting to media and cultural historians such as Ann Cvetkovich, Sean Vogel, and Marsha Gordon and Allyson Nadia Field, who use the term "archive" not only to mean a physical or digital means of storing media but also with respect to theoretical concerns regarding the relationship of media to memory, trauma, absence, rarity, and loss—and with respect to people whose lives were not recorded in official archives.[18] In much of this work the archive is something the researcher creates through a bricolage of traces, affects, and clues left behind—things not necessarily recorded in the metadata of traditional archive filing systems or searchable in the newer online systems. In this vein, Cvetkovich traces a history of lesbian culture through an "archive of feelings" and trauma that she finds in ephemeral performance art, videos, films, music, poetry, and photographs. Gordon and Fields explore the experience of 1960s Watts through the eyes of a young girl, Felicia, as she is recorded in a rare sixteen-millimeter educational film of that title. Although much of this work focuses on home mode and nontheatrical film and media (home movies, educational films, home videos, snapshots), some of it also attends to more widely distributed films, video, literature, and musical recordings. Such scholarship proposes models of interpretation capable of grasping the diversity and multiplicity of media and its publics, as opposed to work that traces only dominant teleologies (of either progress or decline). Local TV can be a useful source for this type of historical inquiry and interpretation because it provides insights into a larger range of cultural practices—and performers—outside of the network TV circuit.

In this volume, for example, Herman Gray considers the politics of race and representation on local TV programs of the 1950s and 1960s, critiquing the standard historical accounts of racial representation as a progressive move toward "legibility" and inclusion on the airwaves. Drawing on the work of postcolonial scholar Édouard Glissant, Gray instead argues for an interpretive approach that embraces programs (or moments in programs) that demonstrate "opacity," a refusal to be "read" and "known" as a raced body or singular sociological type through the lens of TV's white hegemony. Although Gray is careful to avoid embracing local programs as entirely utopian or "resistant" texts, the Peabody Awards Collection offers him an opportunity to consider representational practices and counterpractices on local stations. Even while the programs he and other writers here explore may be one-off local "specials" or short-lived series, their methods and theoretical questions offer broad reassessments of the way scholars read TV more generally. Such modes of research and history writing are highly interpretative—and intentionally so. Not all historians may agree on methods or analysis. Indeed, for any historian, television's status as a "document" opens up a whole set of questions about interpretive methods that numerous essays in this book take on, either explicitly or implicitly, in a variety of ways.

In the most fundamental sense, when using TV as a document, historians need to understand the places in which it is saved. The television archive is itself a historical formation whose cultural attitudes toward TV, synergies with the industry, practical concerns (such as copyright, funding, donations, and storage space), institutional agendas, and relationship to the broader taste cultures surrounding TV, help establish what remains (or does not remain) behind. Television archives respond to transformations in the media (and media research) environment, and archival practices of selecting and arranging TV programs can change over time. The television archive is a complex archeological layering of shifting notions of what TV is. Today, at a time when TV has become a more ubiquitous, mobile, and global experience, television historians are increasingly interested in the local programs of the older national broadcast system. Perhaps the "nonplaces" of digital streaming networks make us more aware of—and even a bit nostalgic for—the local as a historical formation of television. As this book demonstrates, the Peabody Awards Collection offers researchers an opportunity to relocate the sites of television and to reconsider the multiplicity of its historical practices and cultural forms.

NOTES

1. John Tagg, *The Burden of Representation: Essays on Photographies and Histories* (Minneapolis: University of Minnesota Press, 1988).

2. See Raymond Williams's chapter on flow in his *Television, Technology, and Cultural Form* (1975; reprint, New York: Routledge, 2003).

3. See "Television in the Library of Congress," loc.gov/rr/mopic/tvcoll.html.

4. Ibid. By 1966 the library expanded its television collections, but it was not until the passing of the Copyright Act of 1976, "which gave the Library the awesome responsibility for establishing the American Television and Radio Archives," that a national center was created to "house a permanent record of television and radio programs (William T. Murphy, *Television and Video Preservation 1997: A Report on the Current State of American Television and Video Preservation*, vol. 1 [Washington, DC: Government Printing Office], 13).

5. Lynn Spigel, "Our TV Heritage: Television, the Archive, and the Reasons for Preservation," in *The Television Companion*, ed. Janet Wasko (London: Blackwell, 2005), 67–102. Rationales for preservation included everything from enlightenment ideals of education (which all of these institutions embraced) to saving TV as art (as with MoMA's attempts to save TV in the context of the fine arts and its already existing film library) to saving TV as part of a project of encouraging urban tourism via appeals to nostalgia (as with the Hollywood Museum Commission's elaborate designs for a media research library nestled inside a Hollywood tourist attraction and with William Paley's later success with the Museum of Broadcasting in 1976).

6. Note that because networks, Hollywood studios, and Hollywood producers continued to donate programs to archives over the decades, collections continued to skew toward national network programs (or, to a lesser extent, nationally syndicated fare). Most prominently here, in 1986 the NBC network donated eighteen thousand programs to the Library of Congress.

7. For example, the UCLA Film and Television Archive holds the KTLA Newsfilm Collection; the Paley Center for Media holds New York local programs, particularly from the CBS flagship WCBS station; and Chicago's Museum of Broadcast Communications specializes in Chicago broadcast history.

8. Horace Newcomb, former George Foster Peabody Awards director and groundbreaking TV scholar, explains that "the overall collection, which is built from entries, not just winners, is probably the best collection of local programming in

the country, but that's the overall collection. Unlike UCLA or even the LOC, which lean toward network collections, local stations and multi-system owners have always known Peabody would look closely and also would archive the work" (personal email from Horace Newcomb to Lynn Spigel, August 26, 2017).

9. According to Jeffrey Jones, George Foster Peabody Awards director, there was not a formal submission process or fee in the earliest years, and "the board simply recognized that which was on the airwaves" (personal email from Jeffrey Jones to Lynn Spigel, August 20, 2017). Speaking more specifically about shifting terms of judgment, Horace Newcomb claims, "As for criteria, the early years leaned toward public service, but children's, entertainment, educational, etc., were always present. The definition of 'entertainment' shifted over the years. . . . Certainly after the Lear shows and the MTM shows came along, it was easier to go toward prime time. When I was on the Peabody Board, 89–95, we did more and more entertainment." He also notes that after he became director in 2001, the board of jurors "used 'excellence' as a catch-all criterion, but as one of our British judges said, and as I used [to] comment, it was 'excellence on its own terms,' meaning something with poor production values might be judged excellent because of content, etc." (personal email from Horace Newcomb to Lynn Spigel, August 26, 2017).

10. David Harvey, *The Condition of Postmodernity: An Enquiry into the Origins of Cultural Change* (London: Wiley-Blackwell, 1991), 147.

11. Marc Agué, *Non-Places: An Introduction to Supermodernity* (London: Verso, 2009), 76–80. Agué borrows the idea of nonspace from Michel de Certeau, but he takes the concept in a different direction.

12. Margaret Morse, "An Ontology of Everyday Distraction: The Freeway, the Mall, and Television," in *Logics of Television: Essays in Cultural Criticism*, ed. Patricia Mellencamp (Bloomington: Indiana University Press, 1990), 196. Morse's concept of nonspace is similar to Augé's nonplace; however, Morse cites a range of other postwar artists, architects, and critics when explaining the concept.

13. Gayle Wald, *It's Been Beautiful* (Durham, NC: Duke University Press, 2015); Mark Williams, "Entertaining 'Difference': Strains of Orientalism in Early Los Angeles Television," in *Living Color*, ed. Sasha Torres (Durham: NC: Duke University Press, 1998); Meenasarini Linde Murugan, "Exotic Television: Empire, Technology, and Entertaining Globalism" (PhD diss., Northwestern University, 2015). Other histories of local TV focus on issues of policy and community activism. See, for example, Steven Classen, *Watching Jim Crow: The Struggles over Mississippi Television, 1955–1969* (Durham, NC: Duke University Press, 2004), and Allison Perlman, *Public Interests: Media Advocacy and Struggles over U.S. Television* (New Brunswick, NJ: Rutgers University Press, 2016).

14. Carolyn Steedman, *Dust: The Archive and Cultural History* (New Brunswick, NJ: Rutgers University Press, 2002).

15. Note that unofficial archives like the TV collections on YouTube have numerous examples of local television, often uploaded by people who recorded them off the air. However, as Kompare notes in this volume, these local materials tend to be clips from special TV moments, such as local footage taped off air of 9/11 or unin-

tended recordings (such as a local commercial someone taped off the air in the course of taping a network program). In other words, they are not the kinds of materials found in the Peabody Awards Collection.

16. Jacques Derrida and Bernard Stiegler, *Echographies of Television: Filmed Interviews* (London: Polity Press, 2002), 62–63.

17. Michel Foucault, The *Archaeology of Knowledge*, trans. A. M. Sheridan Smith (New York: Pantheon, 1972), 118–31. For an illuminating discussion of Foucault and the *dispositif*, see Giorgio Agamben, *What Is an Apparatus?*, trans. David Kishik and Stefan Pedatella (Stanford, CA: Stanford University Press, 2009).

18. Ann Cvetkovich, *An Archive of Feelings: Trauma, Sexuality, and Lesbian Public Cultures* (Durham, NC: Duke University Press, 2003); Ann Cvetkovich, "In the Archives of Lesbian Feelings: Documentary and Popular Culture," *Camera Obscura* 17, no. 1 (2002): 107–47; Sean Vogel, "Closing Time: Langston Hughes and the Queer Poetics of Harlem Nightlife," in *The Scene of the Harlem Cabaret: Race, Sexuality, Performance* (Chicago: University of Chicago Press, 2009); Marsha Gordon and Allyson Nadia Fields, "The Other Side of the Tracks: Nontheatrical Film History, Pre-Rebellion Watts, and *Felicia*," *Cinema Journal* 55, no. 2 (2016): 1–24.

PART 1

CONSIDERING PEABODY
MEDIA TEXTS, PARATEXTS, AND METADATA

UNDERSTANDING AND WORKING WITH THE PEABODY AWARDS COLLECTION

In 1971, WCKT, the NBC affiliate in Miami, submitted "Television Repair Series" to the Peabody Awards program for consideration.[1] The weeklong exposé of television repair shops opens with a question from reporter Dick Benedict: "It seems few craftsmen can challenge the tube and transistor man from last place in the public's heart. But is the reputation deserved?" After the station's chief engineer intentionally blows a vacuum tube, the crew delivers the otherwise functional set to successive shops to see how timely and honestly the problem will be diagnosed and the set repaired. Back at the station, the crew reopens the set to see what work was actually done and to compare to known costs of replacement. At the end of the week, an anchor delivers a summary commentary: "The art and craft of television repair obviously is not taught in the Boy Scouts. Certainly 80 percent of the service performed for us would hardly qualify for a merit badge in integrity."

Like many programs in the Peabody archive, there's nothing that seems immediately excellent or exemplary about "Television Repair Series" as an example from television history. And, indeed, it didn't win a Peabody.[2] The segments feature a local news team doing investigative work on behalf of its audience, work that (the submission form noted) led to two criminal convictions. Exemplary or not, "Television Repair Series" reminds us of one way in which "television" has changed as a technology. What was once a household appliance that required routine maintenance—the replacement of tubes, not to mention the repositioning of an antenna—is now cheaply replaced and upgraded. Even media scholars might need reminding that the TV set once required regular upkeep.

WCKT's Dick Benedict investigates local television repair.

But more than that, WCKT's "Television Repair Series" is an example of a local station making television programming that attempts both to serve the interests of local viewers and be *interesting* to those viewers. That is, it promises to uncover those who might cheat the audience and to expose them on-screen in an entertaining—even suspenseful—way. The "Television Repair Series" offers a rich example of 1971 television culture (and fashion, too!). But if we contextualize it as an example of a holding of the Peabody archive (rather than as an example of 1971 television or of local news more broadly), it offers, for our purposes, a productive way to begin to demonstrate the range and depth of the Peabody holdings.

The Peabody Awards have long been recognized as the most prestigious awards in American broadcasting. While the award is well known, there is a wealth of programs considered for the award that were not honored and, thus, have largely been forgotten yet hold the potential to reshape our understanding of American television history. This edited volume aims to draw attention to these programs, which are archived in the Peabody Awards Collection at the University of Georgia. By the design of the editors and the inclinations of the contributors, the chapters investigate television produced all over the country rather than the network programming that has typically been the subject of television historiography. Plenty of broadcast and cable network programs have been submitted for Peabody consideration, and plenty have won.[3] But by virtue of the awards criteria and the preservation practices associated with the submissions, the Peabody archive constitutes a unique national archive of local programming. Housing over ninety thousand programs submitted to the Peabody Awards since its inception in 1940, the archive contains programming from local, national, and international producers. Its curation derives from what producers deemed their "best" work—that is, what they believed was award worthy. Items from local broadcasters, in particular, carry special value not just because they are centrally collected at Peabody but because producing organizations rarely saved these materials; Peabody houses the only remaining copies.

This chapter attempts to provide both an overview of the archive's holdings, with special attention to the range of submissions in award categories over the years, as well as an "up-close" (if cursory) look at specific programs that convey the range of programs (and program-related materials) available; we hope this provides an enticing glimpse that will encourage scholars to explore the Peabody archive, as well as some useful information about how to get started doing so.

LOOKING AT THE COLLECTION: TOP DOWN AND UP CLOSE

The Peabody Awards Collection contains most—but not all—of the radio, television, and web submissions to the Peabody Awards. From the earliest days of the award, submissions required the inclusion of a copy of the program, which was to be kept by the Peabody Awards for the purposes of research, scholarship, continuing education, and instruction. In some cases, however, programs were returned to the submitting station or institution. In the early years, programs were most frequently returned at the request of CBS and to a lesser extent NBC.[4] Additionally, some entrants, such as a local CCTV station in New York that produced material designed to educate students and community members, could not easily submit representative media. In these instances, extensive scrapbooks with a description of the program and the mission are all that exist in the archive.

The Peabody holdings include radio entries dating from 1940, television entries dating from 1948, and webcasts dating from 2000. These entries can be searched using the Peabody database, which contains more than seventy-three thousand titles.[5] Programs are submitted to the Peabody Awards and then entered into the database in categories that include children's (first entered in 1944); documentary (first entered in 1978); education (first entered in 1942); entertainment (first entered in 1942); news (first entered in 1942); and public service (first entered in 1940). Several categories were only temporarily in existence or have been discontinued: promotion of international understanding was in use from the 1940s to the 1970s, bicentennial only existed for the year 1976, and special was discontinued as a category in 1975. Additionally, there are entries for individual/personal awards, which recognize the contributions of individuals and institutions, such as Walter Cronkite in 1980, the John D. and Catherine T. MacArthur Foundation in 1990, and Oprah Winfrey in 1995.

Due to the sheer number of entries each year, the database is continually being added to, and not every entry includes the same level of information or detail. Additionally, some programs in the collection do not appear in the database, in part because for programs submitted prior to 1975, the archive only has a record if the entry was a winner or if there is media held for it.[6] Information about programs that were submitted or won Peabody Awards but are not held in the archive can be found through the use of digest entries, which catalogue each entry, by category per submission year, and include a brief description of the program taken from the entry form.[7] These digests were produced until 2013, when the sheer number of entries as well as the more automated submission and cataloguing process rendered their creation both overwhelming and unnecessary. Thus, a researcher can determine what programs were submitted for consideration, even if there isn't an entry in the database.

Researchers who work with the archive have an opportunity to look at much more than the television or radio programs themselves. Physical materials associated with the Peabody holdings also constitute a remarkable collection documenting the production and reception of media texts. Every program in the collection is submitted with an entry form that briefly describes the entry, usually offering some brief explanation of what makes it worthy of consideration. Many submissions come with more extensive presentations, including records of how programs were conceptualized and produced and how they were made sense of by members of the public and critics. These papers are made available to researchers at the Hargrett Rare Book and Manuscript Library within the Special Collections Library.[8] For some entries, the only papers contained in the archive are the corresponding entry forms. These entry forms provided an opportunity for the submitters to describe the program and to briefly explain why the program was deserving of a Peabody Award. Many submissions include additional supplementary material, ranging from press kits and newspaper clippings to scrapbooks and promotional items. In some cases, particularly from the earlier years of the awards, these materials are all that remain of the submissions.

Initially, the programs submitted to the awards were held by the University of Georgia's Grady College, the institution responsible for administering the award. Individuals at Grady College had briefly considered giving the Peabody collection to the Library of Congress, but because the collection was the property of the university, they decided that the materials should stay at Georgia, under the auspices of the libraries.[9] Grady College continues to administer the award while the libraries now handle the collection, which has continued to grow by approximately twelve hundred entries each year since 2008. By 1974, all of the materials had been transferred to the libraries, and efforts to preserve the materials and facilitate public access to the archive commenced.[10]

An important step toward increased access was taken in 1974, when the library began making copies of the programs it received available immediately. This vastly expanded the number of programs available for in-person viewing, and visitors can still watch programs in person using analog copies at the main library of the University of Georgia. Today roughly 65 percent of the collection has an analog copy available for in-person viewing.[11] The Walter J. Brown Media Archives and Peabody Awards Collection was formally constituted as an archive in 1995. As an archive, it has carried on the missions of preservation, protection, and access to media materials of historical significance, with the Peabody Awards Collection representing the flagship collection of the archive.[12] Peabody materials were moved to a newly created special collections building in 2011, and this became the access point for these materials by 2012.[13]

These various stages in the stewardship and collection of data related to the submissions help in part to explain the varying levels of detail present in the database at different points in the collection's history. The database is less comprehensive for programs prior to the mid-1970s, when the libraries assumed stewardship over the archives. From the mid-1970s to the early 2000s, the database is more consistent, although there remain a few years where details are sparse. After the migration to digital submission forms in 2000, the database becomes far more detailed and consistent, as is to be expected given the automated inclusion of metadata. In 2013, the Peabody Awards started to ask that all media entries be submitted digitally, which should result in greater access to media materials.[14] However, the size and scope of these digital submissions provide storage and preservation challenges in their own right.[15]

Even though the information in the database can be inconsistent, a great deal can be learned from looking at broader trends in submissions to the Peabody Awards. For much of the history of the collection, there were more submissions from local stations than from national broadcasters, and the collection contains an impressive array of programming from local stations throughout the country. Because many stations have been shuttered or consolidated over time and because many stations had neither the budget nor the inclination to meticulously preserve and catalogue their programming, many entries in the Peabody archive are likely the only extant copies of the programs in existence. The archive is undoubtedly one of the most comprehensive collections of American local broadcasting history.

Throughout the 1980s and 1990s, local commercial submissions remained fairly steady, but by 2000 they dropped sharply. In fact, since 2000 entries from public or not-for-profit broadcasters have consistently outpaced those from local commercial broadcasters. By the late 1980s, the total number of programs submitted each year had ballooned, in part owing to the stark rise in the number of submissions from broadcast and cable networks, which greatly surpassed those from local channels. In 1972, there were 234 television submissions. By 1997, that number had grown to just over 1,100.

Submission trends in the categories submitted to the archive have changed over time as well. For the first several decades, education, news, and public service programs regularly topped the yearly entries of television programming. Once documentary was added as a category in the late 1970s, it rapidly became the most popular category for submissions and remains the most popular category as of this writing in 2018. Entertainment programming has also seen a surge in popularity as a submission category. For much of the history of the award, entertainment program submissions trailed behind public service programming entries, but by 1996 entertainment programming entries began regularly outpacing public service submissions by triple digits. By the turn of the century, entertainment programming was firmly established as one of the top three entry categories; from the 1990s on, there have been hundreds of submissions each year in the documentary, news, and entertainment categories. Although some other categories occasionally spike into triple digit entries (1995 saw 129 entries in the children's category), the children's, public service, education, and individual/institution categories have rarely seen a hundred submissions per year for the entirety of the award.

The numbers of and shifts in submissions convey the scope of the Peabody holdings, but there's simply no substitute for spending time searching through the database. Those looking for particular titles in the archive can check for them easily enough. However, due to the particular nature of the Peabody submission process, there are strategies that can help users find titles they didn't know they were looking for—the real archival prizes.

One strategy is to search for a particular station's submissions. For example, if we found "Television Repair Series" interesting, we could search the producing station's call letters to see what else they submitted. Entering "WCKT" into the Peabody catalogue search, we find 211 program records, ranging from 1957's "Whispered Menace," an entry in the public service category with the subject heading "sex offenders," to 1982's "Behind the Front Line," an hour-long documentary about south Florida's drug war. If, encouraged by this impressive number of submissions, we check PeabodyAwards.com to see if WCKT ever won a Peabody, we find it won three institutional awards: in 1960 ("for locally produced programs"), 1974 ("for a superb series of investigative reports which brought considerable response and change"), and 1975 ("for compiling an envious record of outstanding investigative reporting"). But not all of WCKT's submissions were straight news or educational programming. Other programs submitted from the year of the first institutional award include "Concert Omnibus" (1960), which "broadcast once each month on an irregular schedule to provide serious music in a manner acceptable to everyone" and *Mary Jane and Melvin* (1960), which was "a morning half-hour feature designed to entertain preschool children daily on the set. The children were taught worthwhile things, were shown cartoons, and were served refreshments." In between its institutional awards, WCKT produced some captivating television. Its 1964 "St. Augustine: Fountain of Dissent" was one of a number of programs on various stations that year awarded "for inescapably confronting the American public with the realities of racial discontent."[16] Among other harrowing scenes, the program includes footage of an irate hotelier tossing chemicals into a pool while children and adults jump in and swim, attempting to integrate it. Most of WCKT's submissions were news investigations of social issues, such as discriminatory hiring practices, and nearby political struggles in the Caribbean. But WCKT had fun, too: in the bicentennial year, the news team, including Wayne Farris, who narrated "St. Augustine: Fountain of Dissent," dressed up in colonial costumes on July 4, 1976, to report the news of July 4, 1776.[17]

If "Television Repair Series" instead piques our interest in the subject of television about television, we can do a keyword search to try to dig up other examples of how submissions to the Peabody Awards have represented, even interrogated, television. There's an episode of *The Open Mind*, a public affairs program from NBC's owned-and-operated WRCA in New York titled "Television: Its Impact on American Life" (1958) that features host Richard D. Hefner leading a conversation among Stockton Helfrich, NBC director of continuity acceptance (or, as Hefner says, "chief

An episode of the NBC public affairs program *The Open Mind* in 1958 featured intellectuals and industry professionals discussing TV's impact on American life.

censor to put it less politely"), CBS executive (and future longtime head of CBS News) Richard S. Salant, and University of Chicago professor and author of *The Astonished Muse* (and coauthor of *The Lonely Crowd*) Reuell Denney.[18] In 1966, another NBC owned-and-operated station, WMAQ in Chicago, produced *The First Television War*, a documentary about U.S. involvement in Vietnam. As the title suggests, the focus is not what is happening in the war, though it does include footage of Ron Nessen, reporter and future press secretary in the Ford administration (and *Saturday Night Live* guest host), getting hit by shrapnel, but "the organization of TV coverage of the war" and its "impact and effect on the American public."[19] In 1974, ABC submitted an episode of its flagship documentary series *Close-Up* titled "Prime-Time TV: The Decision Makers," which examines the process by which prime-time network programs were chosen. In it, Paul Klein explains his famous "least objectionable programming" theory that people flip the dial not to find a program they like but just one that is tolerable, because the alternative, he says, "is to do nothing or use another medium such as read or talk to your family."[20] Then there is *Television Believers* (1986), an exposé produced by Simmons Cable in Long Beach, California, that revealed how televangelist Peter Popoff "miraculously" connected with needy members of his audience via a wireless microphone system in his ear.[21]

Searching for more examples in the Peabody collection of how television represents the uses and potential impact of television yields, for instance, "Justice on Television" (1978), a series of news reports from KABC in Los Angeles that examine the first time TV cameras were allowed in a California courtroom.[22] We also find *The Place: Youth News*, from WRC in Washington, DC, in 1973, a half-hour monthly show "for, about, and by young people." Among the segments is one on the influence of television advertising on kids.[23] Youth news reporter Niki Tollett interviews kids who uniformly dismiss such concerns—though they do complain that commercials can be boring and take up too much time. Keep digging, and there's "Rock 'n Reality Special II" (1984), an episode of *Eve-*

KYW's "Rock 'n Reality" hybridized specials combined locals dancing in music videos with "man in the street" interviews.

ning Magazine from KYW in Philadelphia that goes behind the scenes of the making of its "Rock 'n Reality" segments, a hybrid of music videos and "man in the street" interviews.[24] Executive producer Jim Anderson (a ringer for "Weird Al" Yankovic) explains: "We're going at least one step further than MTV; we're adding content, we're adding people's opinions, people's points of view. It's not just pretty pictures, it's saying something, too." The episode shows us the extensive preparation that goes into a segment set to Pat Benatar's "Love Is a Battlefield," starring a cast of dancers doing their best *West Side Story* impression in 1984 garb.

After watching "Rock-n-Reality II" and many other Peabody submissions, one will undoubtedly find oneself asking, "What were they thinking in submitting *this*?" That is the unique power of the Peabody collection, because we know that they were indeed thinking something was special, atypical, significant, even excellent about that program. If their reasons for submitting don't register with us, that's a signal we need to look more closely.

SITUATING PEABODY EXCELLENCE

As Lynn Spigel and Derek Kompare both note in this book, it is vitally important to consider how the holdings of any particular media archive relate to the broader media landscape. What is the "television" of this television archive? Who put it there, and why? The Peabody Awards, by definition, do not go to typical television, and so no scholar ought to turn to the Peabody archive because he or she is looking for material that will enable them to generalize about television or American culture. It would be unwise to pull a program from the archives, be it a network drama, a local news story, or a documentary that aired on cable, and claim that it is "typical" television of its time. For while there have never been standardized guidelines for judging what deserves a Peabody Award, by virtue of being submitted for an award, these programs were considered exceptional by those who submitted them.

Those submitting programs range from successful network showrunners who believed a particular episode was their best to local news directors who picked out their best public service stories of the year to independent documentary makers who hoped to draw further attention to what they saw as an important story. In addition, the submissions "categorize" television's cultural role as entertainer, as educator, as facilitator of public discussion, and so forth. Judgment of what constitutes exceptional television by the Peabody board or anyone else can't be separated from what the *uses* of television are thought to be. That is, Peabody winners are not merely "good" but the very best examples of what TV is "good for." The yearly accumulation of so many individual judgments of what constitutes exceptional television amounts to an unparalleled repository of television culture.

Though each program in the Peabody archive was thought to be an example of programming excellence by the submitter, the vast majority fell shy of the standards of the Peabody board at the time, and when they are viewed today, the justification for their claim of excellence is often far from self-evident. It thus may be productive to replace the idea of excellence with that of significance when we think about the submissions and the formation of the Peabody archive. Excellence is difficult to separate from judgments of quality that come and go according to who is making them and at what time, but significance can be more objectively assessed. The Peabody Awards Collection is an archive consisting of television (and radio and new media more recently) that significantly differs from typical television culture. That is, it is an archive of significant television.

Many scholars of popular culture will take offense at the suggestion that some television is more significant than other television. Let us clarify: all television is significant in the sense that something can be learned from studying it. As scholars, we pick and choose what we deem to be worthy of study, to be significant enough to us, according to our preferred methods, critical concerns, and theoretical guides, to turn our time and attention to. In doing so, we as scholars produce a body of what we argue is "significant television," much as popular critics or fans list "best" shows or episodes. In contrast, the Peabody archive is, to borrow a term from internet culture, a crowd-sourced body of significant television already constituted, awaiting scholarly explication (and subsequent assignment to additional bodies of significant TV). It would be glib and inaccurate to say that the Peabody archive consists of materials thought either excellent or significant by just anyone. These programs have been submitted by the media producers themselves. We mean "producers" in the broadest sense: producers, news directors, and station managers as well as, in the case of the big networks, employees specifically tasked with applying for awards. Whatever the case, these are programs deemed significant by media workers, not academics or critics. We do know that there have been cases in which members of the Peabody board encouraged producers of a program to submit, and surely in the history of Peabody Awards, critics or scholars reached out to a particular station, producer, or executive to encourage him or her to submit a program. But these would be rare cases in relation to the enormous number of entries.

While it is true that one thing that makes the Peabody archive unique is that the standard for inclusion is overwhelmingly made by media workers, we should be careful about overstating the extent to which it collects "best work." Peabody submissions occur annually, not retrospectively. That is, media workers can't look back over the course of a series and decide what to substitute from various seasons. Episodes submitted for particular series or by particular producers or networks offer glimpses in time: this represents our most-Peabody-worthy work this year. Additionally, the number of episodes submitted for a particular series can vary dramatically from year to year, seemingly as a strategy for garnering attention, rather than signifying a bounty of quality in a single year versus another. For example, *House, M.D.* submitted one episode in 2004, nineteen in 2005 (the year it won a Peabody), three in 2006, four in 2007, two in 2008, one in 2009, then nineteen again in 2010. Sometimes attention is drawn to a particular episode, and sometimes the Peabody program is expected to sift through nineteen episodes to find it. On top of that, producers are sometimes unaware their programs were even submitted, much less did they themselves pick out what they thought was their best. Before David Chase won Peabody Awards in 1999 and 2000 for *The Sopranos*, his short-lived drama *Almost Grown* was nominated by CBS, completely unbeknownst to him, in 1989.[25] So while it's true the Peabody archive contains many examples of what media producers believed was their best work, they cannot be individually designated as "the best." They are ongoing selections, and they are often made by people other than those we might identify as the key creative forces behind the shows.

CONCLUSION

Every television program produced in a given year is thought to embody excellence by somebody, somewhere. And every year since 1948, a very few select television programs have been awarded a Peabody for embodying excellence in broadcasting—for being, to borrow the most recent slogan of the Peabody program, Stories That Matter. The Peabody archive is rich not just for holding those winners but for being home to so many more programs deemed excellent, or at least significant or atypical, enough to be submitted for Peabody consideration. For scholars in search of media culture worth thinking about and working with, this makes the Peabody Awards Collection a unique resource. This is especially the case because it is an archive of programming produced and submitted not just by the big networks in New York or Los Angeles but by stations and media producers across the nation and, more recently, around the world. The contributions in this volume corroborate this, offering a dramatic range of approaches that demonstrate how scholars can productively engage the archive's media and physical holdings to examine and reconsider television history.

NOTES

1. WCKT, "Television Repair Series," 1974, 71011 NWT 1 of 1, Peabody Awards Collection, Walter J. Brown Media Archives and Peabody Awards Collection, University of Georgia (hereafter PAC), http://dlg.galileo.usg.edu/peabody /id:1971_71011_nwt_1. The show is viewable online.

2. Although WCKT didn't win for "Television Repair Series," it did do the segment again and submit it in 1978. It didn't win then either.

3. The interested reader can go to www.peabodyawards.com/awards, click on a year, and read the citations for every program awarded that year and can also search for a particular program, person, or keyword, which might suggest follow-up searches in the archives for programs, people, and topics of interest for that (or other) years.

4. Mary Miller, PAC, conversation with Lucas Hatlen, April 2018.

5. The archive search tool is available at Peabodyawards.com and at www.libs.uga .edu/media/collections/peabody/index.html.

6. Mary Miller, PAC, conversation with Lucas Hatlen, April 2018.

7. As of this writing, the digests are available with the Peabody viewing copies in the media collection at the main UGA library, as well as through the George Foster Peabody Awards Records in Hargrett.

8. To search for physical materials associated with Peabody entries, go to the main page for the Hargrett Rare Book and Manuscript Library: www.libs.uga.edu /hargrett/index.shtml. In the first collection search box (historical manuscripts and university archives) enter "ms3000*". The resulting page provides links to the various finding aids, separated by years covered and whether they are radio or television entries.

9. Mary Miller, PAC, conversation with Lucas Hatlen, April 2018.

10. Ibid.

11. Ibid.

12. In addition to the Peabody Award Collection, the Walter J. Brown Media Archives include the WSB Newsfilm Collection, the Andrew Avery Home Movie Collection, the Kaliska-Greenblatt Home Movie Collection, the Georgia Folklore Collection, and the Foxfire Collection, all of which contain many valuable cultural artifacts.

13. "About," PAC, https://bmac.libs.uga.edu/pawtucket2/index.php/About/Index.

14. Mary Miller, PAC, conversation with Lucas Hatlen, April 2018.

15. Because grants and funding have been provided to the archive to catalogue and preserve particular types of submissions, like public programming, some categories may be overrepresented in the database relative to the whole. For instance, in 1998, the Peabody Awards Collection received a $96,590 grant from the National Endowment for the Humanities Division of Preservation and Access. This grant allowed the archive to catalogue, preserve, and provide access to more than eleven hundred television programs dating from 1949 to 1996 that document African American history and culture. More recently, in 2017, the National Historic Publications and Records Commission awarded the archives $216,280 to digitize and make available online 3,477 public radio and television programs (approximately four thousand hours). Independently of the National Historic Publications and Record Commissions grant, a growing number of other programs have been made available for viewing online. As of 2018, 8,193 unique titles, across radio and television, are accessible online to users on the University of Georgia campus, while 1,255 of those programs are available to users worldwide.

16. WCKT, *Outlook*, "St. Augustine: Fountain of Dissent," May 9, 16, 1964, 64010 NWT 1 of 1, PAC, http://dlg.galileo.usg.edu/peabody/id:1964_64010_nwt_1, http://dlg.galileo.usg.edu/peabody/id:1964_64011_nwt_1.

17. See Thompson, "Events Described Are Not Occurring," in this volume.

18. WRCA, *The Open Mind*, "Television: Its Impact on American Life," September 21, 1958, 58056 PST 1 of 1, PAC, http://dlg.galileo.usg.edu/peabody/id:1958 _58056_pst_1.

19. WMAQ, *The First Television War*, March 27, 1966, 66009 NWT 1 of 1, PAC, http://dlg.galileo.usg.edu/peabody/id:1966_66009_nwt_1.

20. ABC News, *Close-Up*, "Prime-Time TV: The Decision Makers," September 2,

1974, 74277 EDT 1 of 1, PAC, http://dlg.galileo.usg.edu/peabody/id:1974_74277_edt_1.

21. Aron Ranen, *Television Believers*, 1986, 1986176 DCT 1 of 1, PAC, http://dlg.galileo.usg.edu/peabody/id:1986_1986176_dct_1.

22. KABC News, "Justice on Television," July 18–August 18, 1978, 78082 PST 1 of 1, PAC, http://dlg.galileo.usg.edu/peabody/id:1978_78082_pst_1.

23. WTRC, *The Place: Youth News*, no. 88, 1973, 75021 CYT 1 of 1, PAC, http://dlg.galileo.usg.edu/peabody/id:1975_75021_cyt_1.

24. KYW, *Evening Magazine*, "Rock 'n Reality Special II," 1984, 84026 ENT 1 of 1, PAC, http://dlg.galileo.usg.edu/peabody/id:1984_84026_ent_1.

25. Matt Shedd, "Interview with Creator of 'The Sopranos' David Chase," October 29, 2014, www.peabodyawards.com/stories/story/interview-with-creator-of-the-sopranos-david-chase-15-years-after.

DEREK KOMPARE

THE PEABODY AWARDS COLLECTION AND THE PRODUCTION OF AMERICAN LOCAL MEDIA HISTORY

In the 1972 television documentary "Stops in the Circle: A Here It Is Special," reporter Bill Jacocks investigates the state of racial and class mobility in northeast Ohio. Viewers are shown disparate neighborhoods and hear directly from some of the families that live in them. Prompted by Jacocks and interviewed on their front steps, they tell their own histories and the histories of their neighborhoods. An African American family, the McGowans, describes the grim activities ("nuisances") going on in an adjacent abandoned house and their frustrations with government inaction about the worsening condition of their neighborhood. Another, the Sissons, white and originally from Appalachia, describe their frustration with their income and job prospects. Over a sonic backdrop of vehicle traffic and kids playing, Jacocks frames these participants and locations through the expectations of middle-class Americans, documenting the gap between these expectations and the reality of urban decay and poverty. It would have been a novel experience for viewers in the early 1970s to see Jacocks, a black man, presented as an authority. Nevertheless, at the outset, looking directly into the camera, he gets right to the heart of the matter of the "circle" of the title: "Racism and classism in the United States form a vicious circle, and one that perpetuates itself. . . . The ideas are somewhat camouflaged now, but the results are almost the same. There are depths of unbelievable deprivation in the circle, and heights that almost reach the ideal. But the majority of Americans are just above the depths and just below the heights."

This program was originally broadcast by Cleveland commercial station WKYC in July 1972, but it has been preserved and made accessible in the Peabody Awards Collection of the Walter J. Brown Media Archives at the University of Georgia. It is a rare example not only of television of that era that has been retained from the ceaseless normative flow of broadcasting but, more specifically, of *local* television. It documents a particular construction of a particular moment in the life of the community assembled from the presumed audience of WKYC. Every aspect of its presentation—how the topic is addressed, how the reporter frames and relates to the interviewees, who is seen and heard, how the story is shot and edited (e.g., its use of unbroken long takes, a staple of broadcast journalism at that time)—can be analyzed as historic examples of late twentieth-century culture and specifically of local television journalism. However, that it is preserved and accessible online makes it a historic example of twenty-first-century archival practice, whereby discrete physical materials (and their accompanying metadata) are rendered into digital bits, copied onto file servers, and made remotely available to distant researchers. Our ability to find the program through its searchable metadata, view and review it as often as we like, and bookmark it for later recall indicates how primary-source media history has become more fluid and accessible in the internet age. But as with any archive, while it is undoubtedly a rich and pragmatic document of the media past, it is still, understandably, not a comprehensive record of that past.

"Stops in the Circle" documents the gap between the expectations of this family from West Virginia and the reality of poverty in Cleveland.

While most of the chapters in this volume explore particular historic examples like this from the Peabody Awards Collection, this chapter focuses on the collection itself. More specifically, it concerns how the collection structures our historical conception of local broadcasting, and particularly—since the collection is assembled from producers and broadcasters who sought contemporary recognition for their work—how it frames the idea of excellent local broadcasting. Intriguingly, while the Peabody Awards have regularly honored local producers and broadcasters, only rarely have Peabody Award citations been categorized as local or national. As far as Peabody Awards practice is concerned, excellence in broadcast media can be produced and perceived at any level. While media and cultural historians largely focus on nationally broadcast programs, the Peabody Awards Collection also provides a rare opportunity to explore local programming as well, since a substantial portion of the collections consists of programs that were produced and aired in and for relatively specific geographic areas.

With over ninety thousand programs from radio, television, and online sources, covering over seventy years, the Peabody Awards Collection is a unique resource for its scale and range alone. However, as with any archival collection, we should also consider its boundaries: not only what it includes but what it leaves out. This is particularly important in the case of media archives, which have developed over a relatively rapid period of great cultural change and shifting archival practices over the past several decades. As television historian Lauren Bratslavsky writes, "The [social, economic, and technological] dimensions of media further complicate the kinds of materials that archives may seek out as historical material and how such material aligns with prevailing knowledge structures. . . . [What] we tend to think of as media brings in additional levels of representation, contexts of production, and literacies when framing media as historical artifacts or evidence."[1]

In evaluating the Peabody Awards Collection, we need to particularly consider how local broadcasting was constructed in federal radio policy dating back to the 1910s, in Peabody Award practices since the 1940s, and in prevailing conceptions of American media and cultural history. The nature of the collection and the difficulty in preserving local broadcasting in general means that these materials are far from typical broadcast fare. They are, instead, exemplary: programs built on the foundation of quotidian broadcasting but exceeding (or at least *aiming* to exceed) the range of its usual aspirations. This ambition manifests itself in a number of ways, such as through a deeper exploration of an important issue, innovative aesthetic choices, expansive social representation, or any combination of these. Many of the submitted programs, particularly those programs that garnered awards, attempted to reframe the parameters of local broadcast communication by expanding the possibilities of representation and empathy, challenging viewers' perceptions, and, most importantly, regardless of topic or style, presenting an alternative register for the relationship between viewers/listeners and mass communicators. Accordingly, as historians reviewing these materials decades later, we are challenged to account for these programs as both typical and unique. In addition, we must acknowledge what the archive and similar collections have accomplished while recognizing that the bulk of audiovisual media history is forever lost.

Radio broadcasting came into legal purview in the United States with the Radio Act of 1912, which required broadcasters to license their transmitters with the federal government. Later, as the culture and business of broadcast radio developed, technical standards and regulatory oversight—making clear geographic rationales and jurisdictions—extended the role of the federal government in local, licensed broadcasting through major legislation passed in 1927 and 1934. This legal category—the broadcasting license—produced a new kind of locality based around the geographically limited reach of broadcast signals and obligated license holders to serve the "public interest, convenience, and necessity" in their communities.[2] Before the rise of the networks and a national mode of address in the late 1920s, this new medium, by virtue of the immense geographical size of the United States and the way the population was dispersed, took root in very particular places. At the same time, the explosive growth of broadcast advertising prompted the development of audience research firms like CAB, Hooper, and Nielsen in the 1920s and 1930s and made broadcasting localities into "broadcast markets": geographic territories that were derived from models used to assess print publication circulation and that were designed to facilitate advertising transactions, centered in particular cities and towns.

The resulting combination (of media channel, advertising market, and concentrated populations) has generally been taken for granted in media history, but it is one of the most significant achievements in the history of communication. It has financed and fostered synchronous virtual local communities assembled through electronic signals broadcast over the air, along with the people and programming needed to sustain them. The local broadcaster came to represent the local community to itself, with familiar voices and faces (and related sounds and images) securing local bonds. Local radio and TV became and are still channels where the people, places, and issues nearest to people's actual lives are electronically validated and beamed back to the community, confirming their significance. In naming or showing particular streets, buildings, parks, schools, restaurants, sports teams, politicians, preachers, doctors, teachers, and other local places and people, local broadcasting has long constructed particular senses of community. It may not always match up with everyone's version of that place (especially when particular neighborhoods or identities are either not represented or only marginally so), but it still serves as a common connection: an accessible means to connect to your geographical home. Indeed, even today, despite the rapid spread of cable, satellite, and broadband internet service, local over-the-air television news consumption still closely correlates with engaged involvement in the community.[3]

While the primary hub of local media today is news, locally originated programming assumed a wider variety of genres in the first decades of broadcasting. The necessity of filling schedules and fostering opportunities for local connection (in order to attract advertisers or fulfill public service obligations) prompted stations to make their programming diverse so that they could draw different audiences throughout the day and week. Local talent was found and groomed to moderate public affairs discussions, interview passing celebrities, or supervise cooking demonstrations (often on the same show). Others created even more elaborate personas, appearing in makeup and costumes as wacky pirates on weekday afternoon kids' shows or creepy vampires on weekend night horror movies. Along the way, the local community participated, filling out studio audiences, appearing on camera or microphones in vox pops, showcasing their athletic or performance talents, appearing as seated interview subjects, or even getting caught lying on camera in investigative reports. Regardless of the genre or circumstances, these were all programs where one could hear or see, for better and for worse, one's town, one's school, one's business, one's neighbors, one's friends or family, and maybe even oneself.

While the distinction between local and national address was commonly understood by audiences and well entrenched throughout the broadcasting industry by 1940, boosted by advertisers, producers, and policy makers, the founders of the Peabody Awards chose to not formally acknowledge this distinction, opting for a broader remit of recognizing "excellence in broadcasting," much as founders of the Pulitzer Prize created the award to celebrate the best achievements in American journalism.[4] Initially this only included radio; television was added in 1948, cable television in 1981, and online media in 2003. The Peabody Award nomination process has always cast a wide net in seeking excellence, not excluding candidates on account of the scope of the program or where it originated. Aside from a handful of submissions in the 1950s and 1960s that were awarded citations that specifically mentioned local and regional excellence, winners have not been awarded in discrete categories. This has made the process and the prospects highly eclectic, with national and local media effectively competing on the same plane, and has encouraged a wide range of submissions.

EXEMPLARY LOCAL MEDIA

From the very beginning, the Walter J. Brown Media Archives at the University of Georgia has housed the Peabody Awards Collection, which consists of all submitted entries. As a repository of decades of Peabody Award–seeking programs and related materials, representing tens of thousands of broadcasts and other media, the collection uniquely represents American broadcasting history. It is an archive of exemplary media, much of which was originated in local markets for local audiences. Its materials were not found, pursued, or donated but self-nominated and delivered directly to the Peabody program by broadcasters seeking Peabody recognition. Accordingly, these materials represent a *selected excellence* (however variably perceived) rather than the systematically accumulated happenstance of everyday broadcasting. Accordingly, while the collection is certainly singular in its scope and variation, it can still only provide a relatively narrow view of the totality of local U.S. broadcasting. In order to best understand and utilize the collection, we need to be clear-eyed about what it is and what it is not.

Regardless of the motives or aspirations of the broadcasters who pursued Peabody glory and submitted their productions for consideration, their entries all made claim to contemporary significance. That is, they were competing for recognition among the best of their peers, as exemplars of the state of the art of broadcasting at that time. Accordingly, a sharp awareness of the aesthetic, technical, and social possibilities of broadcasting at the time of submission informed the horizon of excellence framed by the foundation's awards criteria, perceived by submitters, and ostensibly recognized and reinforced by Peabody jurors. Regardless of content or approach, all Peabody submissions are programs that its makers recognized as exemplary under the shifting conditions and expectations of American broadcasting. As with any other comparable juried recognition (the National Book Awards, the Academy Awards, the Emmy Awards, etc.), the Peabody Awards shape a normative sense of quality, as recognized by credible peers. In this case, this has meant a vision of broadcast excellence that foregrounds public service. Indeed, while there are no fixed awards categories (as there are in the annual awards in the film, television, and recording industries, for example) much of the language used in the awards citations reinforces the emphasis on civic-mindedness. For example, a 1957 award to Denver station KLZ for its program *Panorama* recognized the program's "intimate glimpses of Americans at work, at play, at prayer—in rural isolation. This is indeed a notable achievement in creative television on the local level."[5] For its 1982 "Oklahoma Shame" exposé of brutal conditions in state-operated facilities for the mentally disabled, Oklahoma City station KOCO was given an award "for undertaking a tough task which resulted in important and tangible results."[6] The 2009 award citation for Greenville, South Carolina, station WYFF for its series on organ donation, "Chronicle: Paul's Gift," celebrated its intimacy and affect: "Rarely have the details of this most intimate of procedures—organ donation—been presented so clearly, so precisely and in such a compassionate manner."[7]

Local broadcasters seeking Peabody recognition must reaffirm and demonstrate that original connection between broadcast station and geographic place; that is, they must represent their particular communities. The Peabody Awards Collection carries the most historical weight at this nexus, or, more specifically, its deliberate production in programming. Most often, given the journalistic focus of most local broadcasting operations, this is material that directly engages the power of the media with the ideals of the community: news stories, public affairs shows, or documentaries that highlight and display the civic potential of shared sounds and/or images. For example, a 1973 compilation episode of Des Moines station KRNT's talk show hosted by Mary Brubaker (*The Mary Brubaker Nite-Time Special*) demonstrates the ability of a charismatic personality to lead her community into discussions of potentially difficult topics; in one segment, for instance, she thoughtfully and objectively interviewed a local prostitute and subsequently countered viewers' rejections of her nonjudgmental approach to the topic. Similarly, another program in the collection, *CPT: Colored People's Time* (1968), from Detroit public TV station WTUS, positively showcases black culture at a pivotal moment of broadening representations.[8]

At a time when public trust in the media and civic institutions in general has ebbed and the civic potential in media is most often found in programs that

CPT: Colored People's Time (1968) showcases black culture at a pivotal moment of broadening representations.

Whether cooking a recipe, interviewing a prostitute, or demonstrating karate, a local TV host like Mary Brubaker provides a "public service" by engaging and entertaining the local community.

critique and mock both, like *The Daily Show*, *Last Week Tonight*, or even, post-2016, *Jimmy Kimmel Live*, it can be difficult to acknowledge the positive social power that local media can still articulate. However, all of the submitted local materials in the collection at least aspire to this public service, and they present broadcast versions of their communities borne out of convention, crisis, or cooperation. Among the collection are programs that are certainly banal—talk shows on forgotten issues, homespun talent shows, earnest investigative reports— but even in banality, there's something significantly civic in the act of connection entailed by broadcasting. Public service normatively and understandably lends itself to higher-minded programming that seriously informs and even challenges audiences. But taken more broadly, even a cooking show, or a teenage dance show, or a forum for farmers, or (in the case of *The Mary Brubaker Nite-Time Special*) a fashion show is a public service in that it successfully engages and entertains the local community.

In addition to the programs themselves, the submitters' entry forms and accompanying materials, housed adjacent to the archive in the Hargrett Rare Book and Manuscript Library, offer us rare glimpses into how this idealized relationship between broadcasting institutions and local communities was perceived and expressed. While most entries are only accompanied by a few lines describing the program, some contain more extensive information. For example, *What's New in the Kitchen?*, a globally themed cooking show from Milwaukee station WTMJ in 1956, submitted a scrapbook filled with testimonials from viewers and local officials about the role of the series in promoting world peace and cultural understanding.

Even when factoring in the inevitable puffery that accompanies any award citation or submission, there is an authentic sincerity in many of these descriptions, a sense that what they're doing is important and that it fulfills a promise of the medium of mass communication. For example, Denver cable system Mile Hi Cablevision submitted a compilation of a 1984 break-dancing competition, touting the special's "value as an entertaining program that shows break dancing as a positive and creative activity" and claiming that for "many of the performers, break dancing became an alternative to street fighting."[9] It would be too cynical to completely disregard such self-description today. Instead, we should see such framing discourses as forming a significant paratext around the programs: rhetorical auras intended to sway Peabody jurists, certainly, but also a means to differentiate *this particular program* from the hundreds or thousands of hours of other material that they produced and aired that they could have submitted.

An important factor visitors to the collection should keep in mind as they examine these materials—the descriptions, testimonials, and the programs themselves—is how broadcasting *with the expectation of recognition* advances the forward (if not always cutting) edge of media expression. That is, even before they submitted their entries, most of those making submissions (and arguably all of the winners) were aware that what they were doing was pushing against the prevailing norms of the medium. Exploring the range of these differences offers an intriguing view into the possibilities of broadcasting at particular moments, including who can be in front of cameras or on microphones; which places, people, and issues can be represented; how media technologies can be utilized; and how audiovisual style can be expressed. In "Stops in the Circle," the piece described in the opening of this chapter, we see a reporter make an effort to talk directly to local residents of various races and backgrounds, in their homes. A more common approach in that era would have been to use a short, edited package of these comments and have the bulk of the program shot back in the studio as a discussion between the reporter and various local authorities, representing city government, the print media, local businesses, and so forth (which would also be the more common approach today). By focusing entirely on the people, rather than the local power structure, reporter Bill Jacocks and WKYC attempted to give them relatively unrestricted voices. Another example of a broadcasting technique from a specific moment in time that the archive brings to light is the use in the 1970s of speculative frames to shift the modern conventions of television broadcast news into the past (seen in programs about the 1976 bicentennial) or future (seen in programs addressing concerns about population growth and pollution). The archive provides endlessly deep veins of research for historians that collectively show us how particular configurations of representational politics, aesthetics, and technologies came to assume significance at particular times. Throughout this volume, contributors explore similar such examples from the archive in greater depth.

THE MISSING BACKGROUND

The Peabody Awards Collection is an exemplary media archive, filled with exemplary media. However, if this is the foreground—the material that broadcasters put on a virtual pedestal—what's missing here, and everywhere, is the background that this material ostensibly exceeds: the banal flow of daily local broadcasting. This material is paradoxically present and absent. It is familiar from our memories of television and radio and still all around us (if changing over time) in our daily consumption today. Because of the nature of archival collection, however, it is unlikely to have lasting historical significance or end up being preserved. As Bratslavsky details, decisions on what materials to include in media archives have often foundered on this very issue of foreground and background. The standards of historical significance have varied considerably over time.[10] In an earlier archival era, at most only a few "sample" episodes or scripts, from a handful of programs, if at all, might have been retained in a local media collection. Most local broadcasts were not preserved by their owners or in archives, and so they are permanently lost.

The primary issue for preservation is the sheer volume of physical audiovisual media generated by full-time radio and television production; this volume necessitates a high, and even ruthless, degree of selectivity. The default environment of local media is, and always has been, the present. This attention to the present is an understandable reality of a news-focused production apparatus and also appropriate given the nature of the relationship of local media to the community. Local media functions most effectively as a chronicler of immediacy: information that the community needs at that moment. History is, understandably, a bonus consideration, and preserving it can be difficult particularly when it is stored in bulky, and often frequently obsolescent, media formats. Films and tapes take up a great deal of space and continue to accumulate, as present productions are shelved. Even the latest digital formats take up physical space on file servers and hard drives, en route to ending up on tape after all in the archive (on LTO cartridges, which hold terabytes of data). Migrating media to newer formats, meanwhile, is time consuming and expensive and usually only undertaken in circumstances of dedicated archival preservation, as in the signature series of American television (e.g., *I Love Lucy, M*A*S*H, Seinfeld, Star Trek*, etc.) or the cultural remit of the BBC Archive Centre in Perivale, which aims to gather archival copies of everything broadcast by the BBC.

In the case of the Peabody Awards Collection and similar archives, materials are beginning to be digitized on both an ad hoc and (resources permitting) systematic basis, allowing researchers access to materials that would otherwise be completely inaccessible due to location and medium. For example, the Boston TV News Digital Library, a joint endeavor of several Massachusetts broadcasters, universities, and libraries, has made thousands of programs available for online viewing.[11] On a smaller scale, the Jones Film and Video Collection at Southern Methodist University is digitizing and posting links to the sixteen-millimeter news film shot practically daily from 1960 to 1978 by Dallas news crews at WFAA television and has invited researchers and artists to use these images and sounds in their work.[12]

The only other repositories of quotidian local broadcast history today aside from the Peabody Awards Collection and these limited collections donated to archives, libraries, historical societies, or universities are private collections of off-air recordings that some owners have migrated online to YouTube or more curated open-access collections like the public-serving Internet Archive. However, what tends to be preserved and recirculated by collectors on YouTube are not, unlike what is collected in the Peabody archive, well-planned and executed programs or even the banal daily flow of broadcasting but notable disruptions to the normative flow of events. These range from innocuous bloopers in newscasts (e.g., distracting background bystanders in remote shots, mispronounced names, and awkward encounters with animals) to more shocking and even tragic events caught on camera or microphone. While such famous moments as Herb Morrison's description of the Hindenburg's destruction in 1937 or the morning news shows' dawning realization of the events of September 11, 2001, are fascinating because they capture real emotion in real time, these "accidents" can make us overlook the power of both the framing mundanity of the normal flow of the day's media events, where everyday reality is produced, and the relatively purposeful reframing of that reality by the exemplary broadcast events available in the Peabody Awards Collection.

But in lieu of more "official" audiovisual archives and in spite of their incompleteness and random availability and quality, these definitively unauthorized and unofficial archives are an important resource for preserving these materials in accessible, future-oriented forms. As Abigail De Kosnik reminds us, the "rogues of digital archiving have effectuated cultural memory's escape from the state; memory will never again be wholly, or even mostly, under the control of the state or state-approved capitalists."[13]

CONCLUSION

In her consideration of digital archiving, historian Abby Smith Rumsey articulates concerns about the fragility of the past in times of upheaval. "In periods of great instability, the past becomes more useful as we increasingly tap into the strategic reserve of humanity's knowledge. Yet it is at moments like this when the past is most easily lost."[14] What's lost without access to local media history is an understanding of how places have told stories about themselves. Granted, across the past several decades of licensed radio and television at least, this history has been a mostly elite, mostly white, mostly heteronormative, mostly upper-middle-class account of community. But, nonetheless, the primary way local places have been represented to their citizens has been via local media, and at its best, local media has always made sincere efforts to engage with citizens by presenting inclusive stories of challenge and change in their communities.

As Rumsey argues, the cultural role of archives of all sorts is particularly important at this moment, when analog materials are becoming digital and political instability is on the rise. History is fragile under the best of circumstances, and our times clearly aren't that. Moreover, archives preserve historical knowledge and artifacts but remain peripheral to culture unless they are actively supported and accessed. Historians should work with archivists, as they have in this Peabody endeavor, to highlight archival materials. Writing about film history specifically, media archivist and historian Caroline Frick points out how access is particularly critical: "In the twenty-first century, equal attention to and support of access and preservation would prove an important, democratizing shift and one that offers almost endless possibilities and opportunities for future research towards the development of a more holistic 'American' film history."[15]

The Peabody Awards Collection is a model of how materials that stations, networks, and other producers were once particularly proud of but which otherwise would almost certainly be lost today can be preserved and made accessible to the public. As the other essays in this volume show, it offers us a limited but nonetheless valuable and illuminating window to the past. It reveals constructions of local communities at particular moments, such as WKYC and Bill Jacocks's "Stops in the Circle," that both situate us in a time and place (and in their representational codes) and remain resonant to this day. Experiences like these are why history is valuable at all, and why archives, of many forms and scopes, remain essential.

NOTES

1. Lauren Bratslavsky, "From Ephemeral to Legitimate: An Inquiry Into Television's Material Traces in Archival Spaces, 1950s–1970s" (PhD diss., University of Oregon, 2013), 62.

2. Radio Act of 1927; see www.americanradiohistory.com/Archive-FCC/Federal Radio Act 1927.pdf.

3. Michael Bartel, Jesse Holcomb, Jessica Mahone, and Amy Mitchell, "Civic Engagement Strongly Tied to Local News Habits," Pew Research Center, November 3, 2016, www.journalism.org/2016/11/03/civic-engagement-strongly-tied-to-local-news-habits.

4. "Origin of the Award," Peabody Awards, www.peabodyawards.com/about#origin awards.

5. "Panorama," Peabody Awards, www.peabodyawards.com/award-profile /panorama.

6. "Oklahoma Shame," Peabody Awards, www.peabodyawards.com/award-profile /oklahoma-shame.

7. "Chronicle: Paul's Gift (WYFF-TV)," Peabody Awards, www.peabodyawards.com /award-profile/chronicle-pauls-gift.

8. See Herman Gray's contribution in this collection.

9. "Center Stage Breakin'," Peabody Award submission description, Mile Hi Cablevision, September 28, 1984, 85010 ENT 1 of 1, Peabody Awards Collection, Walter J. Brown Media Archives and Peabody Awards Collection, University of Georgia, http://dlg.galileo.usg.edu/peabody/id:1985_85010_ent_1.

10. Bratslavsky, "From Ephemeral to Legitimate," 78–95.

11. "About," Boston TV News Digital Library, www.bostonlocaltv.org/blog/about.

12. WFAA Newsfilm Collection, ca. 1960–78, G. William Jones Film and Video Collection, https://sites.smu.edu/cdm/cul/wfaa.

13. Abigail De Kosnik, *Rogue Archives: Digital Cultural Memory and Media Fandom* (Cambridge, MA: MIT Press, 2016), 3.

14. Abby Smith Rumsey, *When We Are No More: How Digital Memory Is Shaping Our Future* (New York: Bloomsbury, 2016), 29.

15. Caroline Frick, *Saving Cinema: The Politics of Preservation* (New York: Oxford University Press, 2011), 180.

ERIC HOYT

AGGREGATING ASPIRATIONS

WHAT PEABODY'S METADATA TELLS US
ABOUT LOCAL TV HISTORY

The Peabody Awards Collection is a rich archive of media productions that, as other scholars in this book point out, challenge our assumptions about television and American cultural history. The collection includes over ninety thousand media artifacts that have been submitted for awards consideration since 1941. In addition to the completed submissions forms, the archive contains radio recordings, TV tapes, books, pamphlets, and other forms of media and supporting documentation—all trying to make the case to the Peabody board that the works really matter, that they are significant, and that they should receive an award. The Peabody archivists created a database to organize all of this information, making conventional queries (e.g., keyword searches) as well as large-scale metadata analysis possible.[1]

What trends in local television can we identify through a large-scale metadata analysis of Peabody submissions that we might miss from the close study of individual television programs? This is the central question that animates the chapter that follows. The benefit of a quantitative approach is that it vastly expands our sample size (the n in statistical terms) and forces us to look beyond the canon, beyond the familiar. In doing so, metadata analysis takes advantage of the Peabody Awards Collection's potential to challenge our assumptions about television and American cultural history. But answering complex historical questions also necessarily leads us back to the archive and the practices of close reading and close viewing that have long been part of the humanities. By combining scales of analysis—toggling between the macro and micro levels—we can formulate computationally contextualized case studies of programs, stations, and media markets.

I have structured this chapter into four sections. The first section discusses the method of metadata analysis, as well as the local TV markets dataset (I use the term "dataset" rather than "metadataset" for the purposes of readability, but to be clear, I am still referring to the metadata of media entries submitted to Peabody). In the second, I explore what changes and trends over time we can observe and how we might draw on these changes and trends to make inferences about the larger history of local American TV stations. The third section adds a spatial dimension to the time-based analysis. In particular, I am interested in which American cities punched above their weight—submitting far more entries for Peabody Awards than we would expect based on their market size. Identifying outlier cities is relatively easy. Answering the more important question of *why* they were outliers is much harder, requiring that we look beyond the spreadsheet and engage with primary and secondary sources. To answer the why question for one particular outlier, I move into the fourth and final section: a computationally contextualized case study of station WHA in Madison, Wisconsin.

One of the goals of this chapter is to advance methodology. I hope to model how media historians can productively utilize quantitative methods and large-scale datasets, learning how to take advantage of their assets while also acknowledging their limitations and the continued importance of close reading and archival research. But this chapter ultimately points beyond merely the numbers, inviting us to consider why stations choose to compete for Peabody Awards and how these decisions are linked to a broader ecosystem of institutions, incentives, and pressures.

METADATA ANALYSIS AND THE LOCAL TV STATION DATASET

As Derek Long has pointed out, media historians have long depended on metadata. We use newspaper databases to run searches, we look at credits to determine authorship, and we examine studio and network affiliations to speculate about programming strategies.[2] Most of these uses of metadata start with a particular text, person, or topic and grow from there (we go on to explore Norman Lear's *Maude*, for example, after investigating *All in the Family*). In other words, the *n* starts small, then grows a bit bigger through curiosity, serendipity, and some smart sleuthing. But what would it mean to start with a very large *n*, then narrow things down and select our examples from there?

The quantitative analysis of metadata offers a simple yet powerful means of casting a wide net to identify large-scale trends and patterns. By counting, filtering, and graphing entries, we can test out long-held assumptions about historical change and potentially identify patterns and outliers that we had previously missed. Franco Moretti and Matthew L. Jockers have productively applied metadata analysis to nineteenth-century literary history, and Derek Long has the done the same for American silent cinema.[3] Peabody's rich dataset allows us to turn the data munging spotlight onto the history of local U.S. television.

Before crunching the numbers, I need to acknowledge up front what is included and what is excluded from the dataset. To be clear, the dataset that I'm working with in this chapter is a subset of the entire Peabody Award submissions. Specifically, the dataset includes 13,422 submissions from the top one hundred local TV markets across ten submission categories, spanning the years from 1948 to 2013. Each of the 13,422 submissions is represented as a table row; the columns track fields such as program title, station, year, and submission category. However, the dataset also leaves out quite a lot. The dataset excludes submissions from national networks, cable channels, syndicators, international broadcasters, and local markets beyond the top one hundred, submissions in all categories other than TV and the ten tracked categories, and submissions that have not yet been catalogued by the archive (cataloguing is a labor-intensive process, and most archives confront backlogs of some sort). However, even with these exclusions, the dataset still contains a tremendous amount of information. And it's here, too, before we get into the analysis, that I would like to acknowledge the people who did the hard work of collecting this data. First and foremost, I would like to thank the archivists who catalogue and preserve Peabody submissions, including Mary Miller and Ruta Abolins, and I'm also grateful to Lucas Hatlen for organizing this dataset in Excel, making it easy to analyze. Far more labor goes into structuring and organizing data than analyzing it. Thanks to the efforts of these individuals, we can now put the data to work.

LOOKING FOR TRENDS ACROSS TIME

So what can you do with 13,422 rows of metadata? One thing you can do—and that computers can do quickly—is count the number of submis-

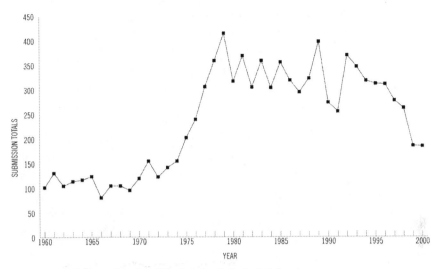

Chart 1. Line graph of annual number of TV submissions to the Peabody Awards from the top one hundred markets, from 1960 to 2000.

sions per year and plot them onto a conventional line graph, which provides a starting point for identifying changes across time.

As chart 1 reveals, Peabody experienced a dramatic upsurge in the number of submissions from local television stations between 1972 and 1980. The number of submissions from stations in the top one hundred markets essentially quadrupled from around one hundred per year in the early 1970s to around four hundred per year for most of the 1980s. What explains this significant growth?

To try to begin to answer this question, I replaced my simple line graph with a stacked graph view (chart 2). Each stack of the graph represents one of the ten submission categories tracked in the dataset: children's, educational, entertainment, news, international understanding, public service, individual (a separate public service category), special, documentary, and bicentennial (a category introduced only for 1976 and that Christine Becker and Lucas Hatlen excavate in their chapter in this collection).

What the stacked graph reveals is that the increase in local TV submissions in the mid- to late 1970s was not evenly distributed across the categories. Instead, two categories account for the vast majority of the growth: documentary and news. The documentary category, which Peabody introduced in 1978, immediately began attracting a high volume of submissions (fifty to one hundred per year) from local TV stations. One

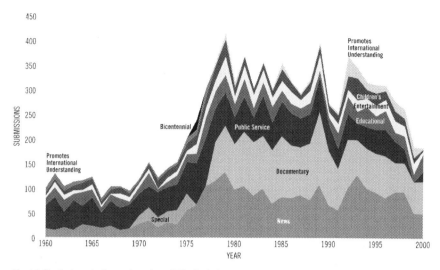

Chart 2. Stacked graph of annual number of TV submissions to the Peabody Awards—segmented by submission category—from the top one hundred markets, from 1960 to 2000.

possible explanation for the success of this newly introduced category is that it attracted submissions that previously went to other categories—especially public service and the phased-out "special" category—while also drawing in documentaries being produced by local television stations that were not being submitted for Peabody consideration at all.

However, it was the news category, even more than documentary, that accounted for the rise in submissions during the 1970s. From 1974 to 1979, local TV news submissions grew at an annual rate of 37.7 percent. This finding is interesting on its own, but it's especially interesting when we see that the local news submissions then dipped again—going from a peak of 134 in 1979 to an average of 89.5 per year across the 1980s (roughly 33 percent less than the peak). What explains this dramatic growth, followed by a leveling off and slight decline? One hypothesis is that the documentary category started attracting more submissions that would have gone to news. Another possible hypothesis is that local TV stations produced fewer hours of news in the 1980s than the late 1970s, but there is no evidence that was the case.

To find a satisfying explanation of the rise and decline in news submissions over this period, we first need to answer a different question: why do TV stations submit their programs to Peabody in the first place? Although the 37.7 percent annual growth rate in the news category from 1974 to 1979 can be partly explained by the increase of local affiliates producing their own news and not just depending on the network news (a historical shift that is documented in the trade press and Craig M. Allen's book *News Is People: The Rise of Local TV News and the Fall of News from New York*), another part of the explanation is that winning a Peabody Award conferred something else media producers covet: prestige.

The prestige of a Peabody may have been especially valuable for a local news station in the mid- to late 1970s as a way to distinguish itself from the competition. Indeed, the competition among local newscasters during this period was stiff. "Where once news was a loss leader at a local station—something the station had to do as a licensee on the public airwaves—news has become one of most stations' profit centers," reported the trade paper *Broadcasting* in 1976.[4] And although *Broadcasting* reported no violent street fights among local news teams like the one in *Anchorman* (2004), the trade paper made it clear that there was fierce competition and that what was driving it was the profitability of local news and the fickleness of viewers.

Critics at the time argued that the profit motive and competition were destroying broadcast news. Ron Powers's 1977 *The Newscasters: The News Business as Show Business* presents a scathing critique of the vacuous "happy talk" of local TV news. Powers directs his most venomous attack at WNBC's News Center 4 team, led by the dapper anchorman Tom Snyder.[5] But what Powers never mentions in *The Newscasters*, and what I can see in my dataset, is that WNBC and News Center 4 submitted work for Peabody consideration nearly every year during the 1970s. News Center 4 was the most watched local news in the New York market. While the prestige of a Peabody might have helped WNBC remain the most watched local news, it would have helped the station even more in answering its critics—in showing that while other local news stations might be guilty of giving too much attention to dunk tank stunts and alleged UFO sightings, News Center 4 was in the business of serious journalism.

The spike in local TV news submissions clearly *correlates* to the era of increased profitability and competition and to a perceived drop in journalism quality. That these were likely all causal factors as well is suggested by which stations and programs were submitting to Peabody.

LOOKING FOR TRENDS IN SPACE

Peabody's metadata reveals trends across *time* in the history of U.S. local television. But can we leverage the metadata to tell us something about trends across *space*? My research collaborators and I had explored spatial trends in our work on Project Arclight: Analytics for the Study of 20th Century Media, a digital humanities initiative sponsored by a Digging into Data Grant from the Institute of Museum and Library Services in the U.S. and Social Sciences and Humanities Research Council in Canada.[6] Using a method called scaled entity search and the Arclight software app, we searched the call letters of 2,002 radio stations within the then 1.5-million-page corpus of the Media History Digital Library, which allowed us to see which stations were especially prominent within the industry's trade press. The results confirmed the significance of flagship big market stations, such as WGN in Chicago and WJZ in New York. But it also pointed us toward outliers, such as Minneapolis's WCCO, which attracted far more attention in the broadcasting trade press than one would expect based on its market size.[7] I became interested in whether the Peabody metadata could point us toward similar sites—local TV markets that punched above their weight, submitting far more entries for Peabody consideration than one would expect based on their size.

To try to identify outlier markets, I employed a crude algorithm. Simply put, I subtracted one ranking from another ranking in order to arrive at a third and final ranking. I started by ranking the top one hundred markets by population size; in this, New York came in first, Los Angeles second, and Chicago third. I then ranked each market by its total volume of TV submissions to the Peabody Awards. From 1951 to 2013, New York's local stations submitted 1,248 TV programs for Peabody consideration, making it first in this second ranking as well. Next, I took the submission volume ranking and subtracted it from the market size ranking, which generated an integer that represented a score. In the case of New York, the algorithm yielded $1 - 1 = 0$. A score of zero means there is nothing surprising—it's not surprising, in other words, that the biggest market in the United States would also submit the most programs. Incidentally, St. Louis and Memphis also ranked exactly the same in market size and number of submissions, and twenty of the top one hundred markets generated scores within +5 or −5. Finally, the algorithm ranked all the positive and negative scores, generating a new list with overperformers at the top, underperformers at the bottom, and the markets that matched expectations (like New York, St. Louis, and Memphis) in the middle.

The top ten stations—the ones that over performed the most, in other words—are, in order from highest to lowest, Baton Rouge, LA, Jackson,

MS, Madison, WI, Columbia, SC, Rochester, NY, Charleston, SC, New Orleans, LA, Honolulu, HI, Louisville, KY, and Davenport, IA–Rock Island, IL–Moline, IL. Before I move into the analysis, it's worth pointing out that the algorithm that generated this list could have been complicated and refined much further. I considered adding some sort of weighting logarithm that would take into account the sheer quantity of submissions from each market and not simply show how the submissions stacked up in terms of ranking. Such a logarithm would have moved the New York stations, which submitted nearly 10 percent of the total programs recorded in the dataset, further toward the top and Baton Rouge's, which submitted eighty-three entries over a sixty-year period in a relatively small market (ninety-fifth in terms of population), down a bit. But then I remembered why I was undertaking this exercise in the first place. I wanted to understand what contextual factors led some stations and markets to be especially ambitious in their television programming. Unlike most big data analysts, I was not interested in making predictions (e.g., who will win the next election?) or maximizing resources (e.g., which pitchers should the Oakland Athletics sign in the off-season?). My algorithm was less like one of those sophisticated computer models than like an old-fashioned divining rod—a stick that I was walking with around the Peabody ranch, hoping it would lead me to a deep well. I was looking for good places to start digging.

In the spirit of digging deep for the well, I focus the rest of my analysis on the market that is ranked third on the list, Madison, Wisconsin. Not coincidentally, Madison is also the media market in which I live. By concentrating on my own town, I realize I am opening myself up to criticism that I've abandoned big data's promise of a larger n in favor of a provincial case study. But I would frame things differently. While metadata spreadsheets can be great for asking historical questions, answering those questions in a satisfying and compelling way requires looking beyond the dataset and consulting primary sources. In Madison, I have access to the archives of WHA and the University of Wisconsin, which together account for the majority of Madison's Peabody submissions. By consulting the archives with the knowledge that Madison was an outlier, I can produce what my Arclight collaborators and I have described elsewhere as a computationally contextualized case study, which blends the breadth of big data analytics with the depth of archival research and the case study.[8]

What made Madison's television producers especially keen to secure the prestige of a Peabody Award? Like Baton Rouge (ranked first) and Columbia (ranked fourth), Madison is home to both the state capitol and a large public university. We can speculate up front that these traits likely contributed to their stations' prolific submissions to the Peabody Awards. After all, universities love the prestige of awards, and public media producers in close proximity to state capitols might connect winning a Peabody with earning the financial support of state government. But what else was going on to make little Madison outperform several mid-size markets, including Kansas City and San Antonio, both on the basis of ranking and sheer quantity of submissions? To try to find the answers, I used the Peabody database to pull up the titles of every WHA program submitted for an award, then consulted the WHA archival papers to learn what I could about the particular programs and, more generally, the station's culture. And, as with any research project, investigating one question led to more questions. Compiling the list of submitted WHA programs revealed that WHA took a twenty-year hiatus from submitting its programs for Peabody consideration. Despite winning one of the first-ever Peabody Awards in 1942 for its radio series *Wisconsin School of the Air*, WHA appears to have submitted nothing for Peabody consideration from 1947 until 1967.[9] Why?

In reading through WHA's internal correspondence and program files from the mid-1960s and early 1970s (as well as Randall Davidson's book about the station), I did not find any explicit discussion of the Peabody Awards. What I did detect is a shift in how the station conceived of itself. WHA had originated in 1917 as the experimental radio station, 9XM, one of the very first licensed broadcasters in the United States. From the time it received the call letters WHA in 1922 through the mid-1960s, the university-owned station was imagined as an extension of the school's teaching mission and the "Wisconsin Idea"—the belief that the university's work should reach beyond the ivory tower and benefit citizens of the state. This philosophy was most clearly manifested in the *Wisconsin School of the Air* radio program that WHA broadcast from 1931 until the mid-1970s.

When WHA expanded into television in 1954, the station's director, Harold McCarty, imagined the new medium as playing a role similar to radio: it would be a way to bridge the gap between classroom and home.

In 1957, WHA (or, more accurately, the University of Wisconsin Board of Regents, which owned the station) received a $37,500 Ford Foundation grant to produce three years of educational television. The grant funded the production of a wide range of televised lectures and programs, including daytime programs, such as *Instruments of the Orchestra*, aimed at in-school children, and an evening-lecture program called *The History of Russian Civilization* (which aired Mondays and Thursdays at 8 p.m. over the course of fourteen weeks—a university semester format applied to prime time).[10] The archival papers indicate that McCarty and others on the WHA staff were proud of these lectures and many of the other educational radio and television programs that the station produced during the 1950s. In its capacity as a leading member of the National Association of Educational Broadcasters, WHA transcribed and kinescoped many programs so that other stations could play them. However, WHA did not submit any of the transcriptions or kinescopes for Peabody consideration. The reason, I suspect, had something to do with the station's old school management (McCarty had assumed leadership of WHA before the Peabody Awards had been created, and he had won one in 1942; what more did he need to prove?), as well as the fact that the station was not experiencing the kind of pressure that would have made a Peabody especially valuable (in other words, a Peabody Award was unlikely to impact the station's funding situation one way or another).

All of this changed in 1967 when a number of internal and external forces converged to make the distinction of a Peabody Award much more valuable. On an internal level, the station's management underwent its most significant change in thirty years. Harold McCarty stepped down as director, and James Robertson, who had previously worked at two big market educational stations, WTTW-Chicago and KCET–Los Angeles, took the helm.[11] Outside of the station, major changes in the funding of nonprofit television were also under way. Although the Ford Foundation had underwritten television programming since the 1950s, it shifted its priorities for broadcasting in 1967, moving away from funding conventional educational television (those prime-time lectures on the history of Russian civilization, for instance) and toward supporting a new form of public television that would address social issues and empower underrepresented groups to create their own programming. As media scholars Devorah Heitner and Laurie Ouellette have chronicled, the Ford Foundation, under the leadership of McGeorge Bundy, spent over $30 million on public television from 1968 to 1974, producing a number of important public affairs and documentary programs in the process.[12] One recipient of a $200,000 Ford grant was WHA. In 1968, WHA, now led by Robertson, developed a program perfectly tailored to Bundy's priorities: *SIX30*, a news program that would be written, performed, and (mostly) produced by Madison's minority residents.[13]

Robertson's WHA also sought and acquired funding from the newly formed Corporation for Public Broadcasting (CPB). Established by Congress in late 1967, the CPB created a network through which stations could share programs with one another as well as a competitive funding program for participating stations. In 1971, WHA received a CPB grant to produce the dramatic radio series *Earplay*, an important if forgotten radio theater program that bridges the imagined gap between the dramas of radio's golden age and contemporary dramatic podcasts like *The Truth* and *Homecoming*.[14] WHA submitted *Earplay* for multiple Peabody Awards, eventually winning in 1977.[15] In the context of the late 1960s and early 1970s, with new management at WHA and new sources of and priorities for external grant funding, the Madison station decided to actively compete for Peabody Awards, submitting at least two programs for awards consideration most years from 1967 to 1977. A Peabody Award connoted quality and prestige—signifiers that could help increase the likelihood of the station's next grant proposal being funded.

One remarkable program that WHA produced and submitted for Peabody consideration during this historical juncture was the three-part series *Portrait of the Police: Drawn by a City*, which was initiated in 1968 and completed in 1969. The most compelling scenes consist of group forums in which Madison citizens talk to—and occasionally shout at—one another about their views of the police. A middle-aged white guy in a plaid jacket explains that "Madison citizens are happy with the Madison police department! I wouldn't be surprised if you took your truck down the streets of the residential areas of this city and the average guy would come out and say, 'They maybe should be a little tougher. They maybe shouldn't be quite as lax as they have been.'" A bearded young man soon interrupts him: "You're really burning me up. . . . What you happen to forget is that there are people who are in here that don't see the Madison police force that way, and they happen to be the people that come into contact with the police force." The discussions and disagreements continue, interspersed with documentary segments that explore recent instances of social conflict and present interviews with Madison residents on the street, at a shopping mall, and other locations. The consensus of the pro-

Madison, Wisconsin, citizens debate police-community relations in public TV
station WHA's *Portrait of the Police: Drawn by a City* (1969).

gram's viewers was that the critics of police practices made their points
more effectively than the defenders and apologists. WHA received several complimentary letters from leftists and university intellectuals, along
with some terse messages from conservatives, including one lamenting
that the program "ended up as a *sounding board* for the *radicals*."[16]

Portrait of the Police was exceptional in the true sense of the word.
It was unlike anything that WHA had previously produced—an outlier
even within the context of this outlier station. The funding came from
the city of Madison, which was reeling from the high-profile violent con-
frontation in October 1967 between police and students protesting Dow
Chemical's campus recruitment efforts and the Vietnam War.[17] And even
before "Dow Day" and other protests against the Vietnam War, the Madison Police Department had a poor record of policing in the city's largely
segregated minority communities. There was not a single African American cop on the force. The city obtained federal funding for a "police-
community relations program" from the newly passed Omnibus Crime
Control and Safe Streets Act of 1968. This enabled Madison to embark
on a series of measures aimed at repairing "the shattering disruption, if
not complete breakdown, in communications between Madison police,
members of the City's minority groups, a sizeable University population,
and other elements in the Madison community."[18]

WHA received $14,300 from the federal grant and had to bring in an
outside producer, Barbara Roos from the University of Michigan Television Center, to achieve the project's goals. The unusual nature of *Portrait
of the Police*, by the standards of WHA, turned into a problem when an
administrator at the University of Wisconsin–Extension grew incensed
that his continuing education division wasn't being consulted for this effort in "law enforcement training." WHA's leaders tried to explain that

this was an unusual program and to diplomatically patch things up.[19] But this was really a foreshadowing of more to come. Although WHA continued producing educational programs into the 1970s and officially remained part of the university, the station became increasingly autonomous. By the end of the 1970s, WHA's relationships with NPR, PBS, and CPB were arguably just as important as its relationship with the university. The station's desire for Peabody recognition only increased during this transitional time.

In the end, WHA did not win a 1969 Peabody for *Portrait of the Police* (the awards went that year to *Sesame Street*, Bing Crosby, and fifteen other programs and individuals). Yet I can watch *Portrait of the Police* today, and I can marvel at its contemporary relevance, because the Peabody Awards Collection has preserved the two-inch quadruplex videotape that WHA submitted (I have not been able to locate a copy of the program anywhere else, including Madison). The archive staff did something else quite valuable too. They entered the program's metadata into a catalogue record, laying the foundation for a future online database, an Excel spreadsheet with 13,422 entries, and the book chapter that you have just read.

CONCLUSION

The dataset of local TV submissions could be analyzed from many more vantage points and utilized to pursue any number of research questions. The histories of 1970s local news and Madison station WHA are just two that I chose to focus on based on what stood out from graphing the submission categories and ranking the stations. I remain especially curious about what was happening—or not happening—in the underperforming markets. The market that the algorithm ranked dead last, in one hundredth place out of one hundred, was the Wilkes Barre–Scranton market in Pennsylvania. Despite being the nation's fifty-fourth largest market, the local stations of Wilkes Barre and Scranton only submitted three television programs for Peabody consideration over a sixty-year period. Did the close proximity to big markets, like New York and Philadelphia, lead TV stations in Scranton and Wilkes Barre to conceive of themselves more as distributors of Peabody-worthy programming and less as producers? Further research into the stations of this region could answer this question and potentially uncover interesting histories.

In this chapter, I have tried to describe and model how metadata analysis can be productively used by media historians. At its best, this method can point us in interesting directions and help us formulate new questions that we otherwise would have never thought to ask. These same assets can turn into liabilities, though, if the method of metadata analysis steers us away from the questions of media history that we care about most. This is the reason it's so important to still answer the *why* and *so what* questions—questions that can only be answered by integrating the methods of archival research and close reading back into metadata analysis.

One similarity between 1970s local news reporters and the educational/public television station WHA was that they both pursued Peabody Awards more actively when there were institutional pressures on them to do so. Earning a Peabody could translate into a way to silence a critic, break away from the competition, or win the next Ford or federal grant. The Peabody Awards incentivized local TV stations to do really good work and simultaneously offered cover from the not-so-good work. Is this still the case in our contemporary landscape? The best place to start investigating that question is the Peabody database and submissions metadata.

NOTES

1. The Peabody Awards database and catalogue at the University of Georgia is publicly accessible at www.libs.uga.edu/media/collections/peabody.

2. Derek Long, "Excavating Film History with Metadata Analysis: Building and Searching the ECHO Early Cinema Credits Database," in *The Arclight Guidebook to Media History and the Digital Humanities*, ed. Charles R. Acland and Eric Hoyt (Falmer: REFRAME Books with Project Arclight, 2016), 145–64.

3. Franco Moretti, "Style, Inc.: Reflections on Seven Thousand Titles," *Critical Inquiry* 36, no. 1 (2009): 134–58; Matthew L. Jockers, *Macroanalysis: Digital Methods and Literary History* (Urbana: University of Illinois Press, 2013), 35–62; Long, "Excavating Film History with Metadata Analysis."

4. "The First Amendment and the Fifth Estate: Local Television's Best Foot Forward," *Broadcasting*, January 5, 1976, 82, www.americanradiohistory.com/Archive -BC/BC-1976/1976-01-05-BC.pdf.

5. Ron Powers, *The Newscasters: The News Business as Show Business* (New York: St. Martin's Press, 1977), 8–14.

6. For more on Project Arclight, see projectarclight.org and *The Arclight Guidebook to Media History and the Digital Humanities*.

7. Kit Hughes, Eric Hoyt, Derek Long, Kevin Ponto, and Anthony Tran, "Hacking Radio History's Data: Station Call Letter, Digitized Magazines, and Scaled Entity

Search," *Media Industries Journal* 2, no. 2 (2015): n.p., www.mediaindustries journal.org/index.php/mij/article/view/128/182.

8. Derek Long, Eric Hoyt, Anthony Tran, Kevin Ponto, and Kit Hughes, "Who's Trending in 1910s American Cinema? Exploring ECHO and MHDL at Scale with Arclight," *Moving Image* 16, no. 1 (2016): 57–81; Hughes, Hoyt, Long, Ponto, and Tran, "Hacking Radio History's Data."

9. WHA, *Wisconsin School of the Air*, "Afield with Ranger Mac," 1942, 42113 PSR 1 of 1, Walter J. Brown Media Archives and Peabody Awards Collection, University of Georgia (hereafter PAC), http://dlg.galileo.usg.edu/peabody/id:1942_42113 _psr_1.

10. University of Wisconsin Division of Radio-Television Education, "Summary Report: Faculty Released Time Project in Educational Television Supported by a Grant from the Ford Foundation," WHA Radio and Television Papers, General Subject: Educational TV—Channel 9, Frequency Assignment, series no. 41/06/02-5, box 9, University of Wisconsin–Madison. The report is undated, but it covers 1957–60.

11. Randall Davidson, *9XM Talking: WHA Radio and the Wisconsin Idea* (Madison: University of Wisconsin Press, 2006), 184.

12. Devorah Heitner, *Black Power TV* (Durham, NC: Duke University Press, 2013), 16; Laurie Ouellette, *Viewers Like You? How Public TV Failed the People* (New York: Columbia University Press, 2003), 49–50.

13. "Revised Budget: WHA-TV Storefront Studio Ford Foundation Grant Project," circa 1970, WHA Radio and Television Papers, General Subject: Personnel-Programs, Series no. 41/06/02-5, box 15, University of Wisconsin–Madison.

14. Davidson, *9XM Talking*, 187. For more on *Earplay*, see Eleanor Patterson, "Reconfiguring Radio Drama after Television: the Historical Significance of *Theater 5*, *Earplay*, and *CBS Radio Mystery Theater* as Post-Network Radio Drama," *Historical Journal Of Film, Radio And Television* 36, no. 4 (2016): 649–67.

15. *Earplay*, "The Temptation Game," November 20, 1977, 77044 ENR 1-2 of 2, PAC, http://dlg.galileo.usg.edu/peabody/id:1977_77040_enr_1-2.

16. Unsigned letter, circa 1969, WHA Radio and Television Papers, "Portrait of the Police (1969)," General Subject: Personnel-Programs, series no. 41/06/02-5, box 15, University of Wisconsin–Madison.

17. For a detailed, narrative history of "Dow Day," see David Maraniss, *They Marched into Sunlight: War and Peace, Vietnam and America, October 1967* (New York: Simon and Schuster, 2004).

18. Governor's Commission on Law Enforcement and Crime, memorandum, August 23, 1968, WHA Radio and Television Papers, "Portrait of the Police (1969)," General Subject: Personnel-Programs, series no. 41/06/02-5, box 15, University of Wisconsin–Madison.

19. Jim Robertson to Dick Lutz, November 18, 1968, WHA Radio and Television Papers, "Portrait of the Police (1969)," General Subject: Personnel-Programs, series no. 41/06/02-5, box 15, University of Wisconsin–Madison.

JONATHAN GRAY

OFF-SCREEN EDUCATIONAL TELEVISION AND THE SOCIAL VALUE OF CHILDREN'S PARATEXTS

Ranging from promos to licensed toys and merchandise, spinoff video games to billboard ads, paratexts are all those elements that surround a television program yet are not seen to be "the thing itself."[1] Paratexts are also regularly derided and serve as touchpoints for criticism simply by existing. Shoring up Adorno and Horkheimer's postulation of a culture industry in which art and commerce have joined in an unholy alliance, the latter corrupting the former in the process, paratexts can be seen as nasty, conspicuous reminders of a text's industrial, commodity shackles.[2] With some notable exceptions—a Criterion DVD with austere commentary from the revered director and scholars of note, a rare interview with the auteur, a stylized Saul Bass movie poster—many paratexts wear commerce and not art on their sleeves, thereby inconveniently standing in the way of any attempt to elevate their text to a sublime level that is removed from "all that." And particular opprobrium is often reserved for paratexts of kids' media, as the merchandise and extras that surround almost every children's franchise are seen as forcing parents to dig ever deeper into their wallets and compromising the supposed precapitalist innocence of childhood. The licensing of children's media has a long history, but the 1980s strategy of selling toys via cheaply made kids' shows and the subsequent overpopulation of the world by Transformer, GI Joe, Care Bear, and My Little Pony toys overlapped with the rise of video games and their own look to (and often overreliance on) Hollywood for licensed material.[3] On top of the global army of four-inch Star Wars figures deployed in the late 1970s, this produced a new era of paratextual proliferation for children, epitomized perhaps in *The Simpsons'* Krusty the Clown, who exists largely to satirize the excess of child licensing and merchandising, with his prerecorded announcements saying "I heartily endorse this event or product" and the inevitable shoddiness of product, like the Krusty Home Pregnancy Test, which "may cause birth defects."

I do not seek wholly to reverse this criticism, nor to suggest that all is right in toyland. However, since it is easiest to roll one's critical eyes at these paratexts, their impact outside of their contribution to the overcommercialization of the planet has regularly been ignored and their noncommercial variants have often been overshadowed and forgotten. Scholars, activists, and tweeters alike, though, have recently realized the particular potency of paratexts to frame the identity politics of franchises. Suzanne Scott, for instance, has discussed the #wheresrey campaign that accompanied the 2015 theatrical release of *Star Wars Episode VII: The Force Awakens*, when many fans noted a conspicuous absence of the film's lead, Rey, in much of the merchandise (as with the *Force Awakens* Monopoly set, which failed to include a Rey token).[4] These fans realized that it was not enough for Disney to center the movie on a strong woman; her strength would also have to be represented in toys, stationery, party supplies, books, and clothing if the would-be feminist was to truly impact the Star Wars franchise and its dominant meanings. Of course, paratexts can damage or negate a text's would-be politics, and Disney has often stumbled here, as when Merida, the young heroine of *Brave* who rejects dresses and behaving "like a girl" in the film, was turned into just another fancy-dressed princess in toyification. But I am interested not only in rethinking how the objects, toys, exercise books, merchandise, and general "stuff" that accompany many children's texts can—as the #wheresrey campaigners believed Rey merchandise could—meaningfully serve the public and amplify the social value, importance, and reach of texts but also in reclaiming a past in which objects, toys, exercise books, merchandise, and general stuff has often done so. Certainly, since kids' paratexts are regularly despised, their value, independent of how much they cost, is also often forgotten and written out of the stories of high-quality shows.

The Peabody Awards Collection allows us a rare opportunity to probe into paratextual histories. When nominators now submit media for consideration, they do so digitally, but for much of the award's long history, the submission process required mailing first reels and then tapes in boxes. Additional materials were welcome, and thus many nominators over the years slipped a few extra items in the box. *The Simpsons*, for instance, regularly sent a barrage of paratexts with each year's submission, including magazines, children's books, Homer Etch-a-Sketch toys, comics, t-shirts, calendars, and more. Nominators often sent scrapbooks too, and though these may include letters of support, scripts, and press kit materials, they also at times tell us more about the world in which the show aired, revealing both contexts and paratexts. Children's and educational programming in particular are richly represented in the archive by paratexts. In this chapter I make an argument for the forgotten potential social value of kids' and educational paratexts by delving into these materials.

In doing so, I introduce the language of paratextuality into educational and public service television. I make this move in part to defamiliarize paratexts by removing them from their more usual contextual bedding as hype, promotion, and hypercommercialization to characterize them instead as potential additional resources, learning materials, and vital contributors to educative purpose. Educational television has regularly struggled to assuage critics' concerns that television is a passively consumed medium, and within this context its additional resources and learning materials—its paratexts—have served important roles both in ensuring certain levels of activity and continued and/or applied learning and in reassuring would-be critics that such activity is indeed occurring. Paratexts have thus at times contributed significantly to creating the social value—both real and perceived—of educational television, and this chapter represents an attempt to chart several instances of this construction of social value.

A recent example, and the launch point for this article, comes from *Doc McStuffins*, winner of a 2015 Peabody Award in my first year on the board of jurors. The Peabody commendation notes: "While teaching children not to be scared of a trip to the doctor and encouraging them not to hide inner pains, but instead to talk things through with others, the series refreshingly centers its action on a young African-American girl who is a skilled doctor and engineer. What is more, her expertise at fixing toys is acknowledged and respected by those around her: everyone knows that Doc, like her mother, a 'real' physician, is the best at what she does."[5] Accompanying episodes of the show was a digital nomination package that included three PDFs prepared by *Doc* creator, writer, and producer Chris Nee herself (so she told me) that offered not just episode summaries but information on a wealth of paratextual extensions of the show; this was followed by a large toy doctor's clinic sent in the mail. These additional materials remind us that the show's work by no means ends at the limits of the screen; rather, its toys, books, and other licensed materials invite girls

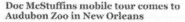

Doc McStuffins mobile tour comes to
Audubon Zoo in New Orleans

Ava McStuffins-Starks, 3, checks the heartbeat of a doll during the Doc Mobile tour of the Audubon Zoo on Tuesday, September 10, 2013. The 17-foot Airstream trailer is women-designed to teach kids ages 2-7 about health and nutrition. (Photo by Dinah Granger Morris Lann | The Times-Picayune)

Excerpt from nomination
materials for *Doc McStuffins*,
detailing the Doc Mobile Tour and
the Artemis Medical Society's use
of toys to encourage children to
be healthier and consider careers
in the medical profession.

to play as this smart, self-assured curer of "boo-boos" and to trade in their princess dresses for doctor's coats, stethoscopes, and otoscopes. The submission materials contain little direct address; instead, they largely take the form of press clippings and statistics, and alongside complimentary reviews of the television show are, for instance, a cover page *New York Times* article that expresses considerable excitement at the success of *Doc* merchandise among white children, an *Independent* article that is more declarative in its headline, "Doc McStuffins: The Toy Breaking Down Gender and Race Stereotypes," and two *Time* articles whose headlines respectively praise the *Doc* toy line as the "Perfect Answer to Barbie" and one of "The 13 Most Influential Toys of All Time."[6] The submission materials also include a thirty-one-page description of the Artemis Medical Society, a group that supports women going into the medical profession, and details its use of Doc toys in its outreach via the Doc Mobile Tour. President Myiesha Taylor offers a letter of support that, in addition to praising the show effusively, notes that due to the success of its toys, "There are millions of children pretending to be Doc and dreaming of becoming the physicians our nation so desperately needs," thereby directly applauding the toys for their social impact too.[7] The materials recognize, in short, that the paratexts work toward moving the message of the show into children's everyday lives through their play worlds, art time, story time, choices of what to wear, and more.

Where else might we find such educational paratexts?

MORE THAN MEETS THE EYE: PARATEXTS FOR THE CLASSROOM

Critically hailed and much adored Peabody Award–winner *Sesame Street* offers a similar tale. Surely, *Sesame Street* needs no introduction, representing as it does educational television par excellence, but some of the submitted materials suggest that its creators mean for it to be more than "just" something to watch. The Peabody Awards Collection holds binders made available to teachers, for instance, that pivot off lessons from the given season's curriculum, offering greater detail, exercises, and learning resources. When the show was focused on teaching children to recognize and name their own and others' emotions, it made "flash cards" for various emotions that described them. The deck also includes valuable information for teachers and parents, listing other resources that cover similar material. Admittedly, as with every piece of *Doc* merchandise, it could be argued that they compel children to implore parents to buy ever more products, but one binder of teacher activities introduces and centers around a Muppet who is local to that binder and for whom there is no purchasable toy counterpart. Thus, while *Sesame Street* is sometimes envisioned as an alternative, precursor, or complement to the classroom, these

Flash cards developed in conjunction with Northern Ireland's *Sesame Tree*.

paratextual materials remind us that it regularly works in the classroom itself, binding its own curriculum to other national curricula (the materials submitted to Peabody include those from Northern Ireland's *Sesame Tree*, too), and they challenge us to consider *Sesame Street* working as much, if not perhaps more (via apps, toys, exercise books, and the like), at its paratextual outposts as on its televisual homes of PBS and HBO.[8]

To explore further back in the archive, and especially to explore children's television and paratexts before the supposed explosion of kids' paratexts in the 1980s, I hired Lucas Hatlen to dive deep into the extra materials in the archive. Hatlen found an abundance of material, and thus here I only note a few examples. My purpose is to survey in order to bring these materials to light, and thus I skip rather quickly from one to the other. Undoubtedly, though, further analysis that situates each within its moment in history and within prevailing understandings of what relationship television had to its audiences at the time would be valuable.

Sesame Street stands out as the most successful children's television show in global history, but it was by no means exceptional in attending to education off screen as well as on. *Operation Alphabet* (1963), for instance, one of several shows in the archive that aimed to help children (and some adults) learn to read, is accompanied by a wealth of paratextual aids.[9] The program itself was broadcast on WFIL in Philadelphia, but through collaboration with the Annenberg School of Communication at the University of Pennsylvania and the Philadelphia public schools' Division of School Extension, "Operation Alphabet Kits" were made available to teachers, parents, and schools. Each of these included one hundred lesson plans, practice sheets, a pencil, and a plastic practice writing sheet.[10] Study books could also be purchased for $2. Ambitiously, moreover, the show was made available at no cost to other channels, and the nomination materials included tools these other channels could use to promote the program, such as advertising posters, news releases, church bulletin covers and sermon folders, car cards, radio spots, newspaper ads, and bill stuffers. Certain of these tools accompa-

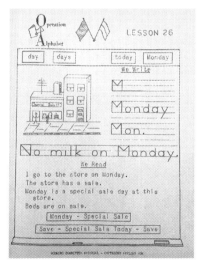

Practice sheet from an *Operation Alphabet* kit, 1963.

nied the show, such as news releases and radio spots, while others could be purchased for a marginal extra cost (for example, fifty church bulletin covers could be purchased for $1 and one hundred bill stuffers for $1).

The 1950s and 1960s were a heyday for experiments in educational television broadcasting in the United States. As Allison Perlman notes, these experiments came not just in response to a medium in the process of defining itself but in response to prevalent concerns over a "crisis" in the state of American schooling:

> At the core of the crisis were three interlocking concerns: the lack of material resources and staff to accommodate swelling enrollments, the ability of the American educational system to compete with that of the Soviet Union, and the content of school curricula and the degree to which reigning pedagogical theories fostered or hindered educational goals. Enthusiasts of educational television trumpeted the expanded reach of excellent teachers afforded by television, the test results which indicated that the students in televised classrooms do as well as students in conventional learning environments, and the ability of televised instruction to improve upon and supplement curricula.[11]

But in cases such as *Operation Alphabet*, we see that the move to television wasn't *only* to television, as it was accompanied and facilitated by paratextual materials that broadcasters, in conjunction at times with interested outside parties, circulated and that were as central to the educational experiment and mission as the programs themselves.

Experiments came not only from local public service initiatives but from the networks and their affiliates themselves, as with the *More Than Meets the Eye* program conducted by five CBS-owned stations in the early 1960s. Nomination materials note a "concentrated campaign of community-minded, *off-air* activities, designed to widen the interest and heighten the practical effectiveness of [the stations'] public affairs programs."[12] Launched in St. Louis by KMOX in 1961, then expanded on in 1962 by WCBS in New York, WBBM in Chicago, KNXT in Los Angeles, and WCAU in Philadelphia, the project specialized in offering reading lists and further resources to teachers, eventually reaching a million and a half students in over two thousand schools in the five markets that participated in the project. An informational booklet offers a rallying cry for paratextual work in a short epigraph on the opening page: "To the responsible television station, there is more—far more—to community service than what viewers see on the home screen." Though the nominating pitch to the Peabody judges was that the reading lists were curated and shared with educators in these five communities, the lists were only offered in connection with certain public affairs programs, and so they would also have served as handy guides for which upcoming television shows CBS and its affiliates saw as relevant and appropriate to the interests and needs of elementary and secondary school students. Thus, for teachers interested in getting their students to engage with educational material via television in ways that might further the goals of classroom education and for parents seeking guidance on especially "worthy" programs to screen for their children, the guides offered ways to bridge television programming, additional reading, and classroom time.

Another similar paratextual educational experiment was carried out by the *CBS Reading Projects*, a program that began in 1977. Its 1982 nomination materials, some from a document titled "Television and the Classroom: A Special Relationship," explain how the network would broadcast films drawn from literature and theater or based on American history, including *Oliver Twist, All Quiet on the Western Front*, and *The Blue and the Gray* and at the same time circulate scripts and teacher's guides to schools.[13] The nomination materials boast of having circulated over twenty million scripts to date, largely to schools but also to prisons and homes for the elderly. "We hope," the program administrators note in a preface for educators, "you will find that the television script motivates your students to read. We also hope that this Teacher's Guide will provide you with adequate material for studying the story, for discussing the television play as an art form and for involving your students in a variety of related uses of the language arts. . . . Feedback from teachers indicated that the most popular use of the script is reading it aloud in class for one or two weeks prior to the broadcast, which students take turns volunteering to read various parts."[14]

The guides (prepared, they state, by teachers) also included vocabulary, language, and comprehension tests that teachers could use, along with suggested activities, crossword puzzles, and word search games based on the scripts, "pre-reading information," and maps when relevant. Far from being quickly knocked off, the exercises address their given subject in depth and are educationally sound.[15] Several pages of *The Blue and the Gray*'s guide, for instance, are devoted to an exercise on understanding and then locating instances of literary devices such as irony, foreshadowing, alliteration, simile, and metaphor. The bibliography for further information is similarly impressive and surely a helpful resource for pursuing further examination of the Civil War. Especially noteworthy, too, is a suggestion in the preface that "students not necessarily be assigned to watch the broadcast."[16] While this suggestion may have been motivated in part by concern that CBS's broadcasts would be perceived by students as "homework" and so they would not want to watch them, it also acknowledges that for some, the social value of the project would lie entirely in the circulated scripts, and not at all in the program, which might not even be watched.[17] Part of the project, titled "Read More about It," then suggested ways to obtain further information about central topics explored in the script or show in question, curated by the Library of Congress in partnership with CBS. These were presented in on-air announcements from a variety of celebrities, including Christopher Reeve, Mikhail Baryshnikov, Cicely Tyson, and Charlie Brown, who parlayed their celebrity status to direct children, parents, and teachers outward to the paratexts.

One could of course be cynical and see the networks' reading projects as public relations stunts. Each of these projects would have cost relatively little, especially in comparison to the high costs of producing television and purchasing advertising. One might also note critically how they help to associate CBS with austere literature in the case of literary adaptations and with the historical record with programming such as *The Blue and the Gray*. At a time when television was regularly derided as "an idiot box" and regarded as low culture devoid of depth, CBS conveniently and strategically aligned itself with education, history, and literature via its reading projects that proposed "the television play as an art form."[18] But while I do not wish to be naïve in proposing that these paratexts had social value in addition to a branding role, I also do not see the branding role as necessarily discounting the social value entirely. I take the view that while social services are often compromised in some way and donors often have ulterior motives, that does not necessarily and automatically obviate the value of the services in question. In each case here, if the nominating documents are to be believed, significant numbers of students benefited in various ways from the materials that accompanied television programs, the work of those "programs" being conducted as much and at times more at the paratextual outskirts than at the supposed textual core.

TRAIL MAPS FOR AT-HOME EXPLORATION

Paratexts for children's programs in the archive address not only children in classrooms but also the child at home. *The Children's Corner*, produced by WQED in Pittsburgh and developed by Josie Carey and Fred Rogers, offers one such example. The nomination materials include a booklet called *Our Small World* produced for child viewers in 1955 that extends the imaginative play of the television show, offering an early instance of "transmedia" in its presenting itself as written on behalf of the fictional characters from *The Children's Corner*, including the now iconic Daniel Tiger, Grandpere, Lady Elaine, and King Friday XIII.[19] A recipe for Daniel's hamburger liver pudding fruit cake—calling for a fruit cake to be mixed with seventeen pounds of medium grind hamburger and two pounds of liver pudding—is playfully proposed as the centerpiece for a day-before Daniel's birthday party. The introduction tips off young readers and their parents to the joke: "We don't advise trying all of Daniel's recipes . . . but, we do want you to know that we have presented the writings of all these characters just as they, *themselves* have written them. We know you will like what they have had to say, and we hope you will have fun with the Attic play. Maybe you will want to act it out with some of your friends."[20] This play is included, as are some songs, such as sheet music for *The Children's Corner*'s theme song. In this way, Daniel Tiger and friends are offered passage into children's play worlds, and not just rendered as characters to be watched on a television show.

Another children's program submitted in 1956, *The Finder*, similarly moves beyond the boundaries of the screen through circulated trail maps. Produced for KETC in St. Louis, *The Finder* describes itself as intended for children between the ages of nine and thirteen, who, its submission materials declare, "are in the period of dreams of adventure and discovery, of exploring the real world, of collecting things. This is precisely what the Finder does—he travels, explores, finds and collects. And he ranges as widely as the curiosity of the children to whom he is trying to appeal. The things, people and facts the Finder finds, he brings back to the studio for children to see and hear. He does this in an endless variety of ways. He may use still pictures, movies, and tape recordings. When he can, he brings his people and things into the studio and presents them 'live.'"[21] And yet, we're told, "The Finder demands that his viewers do more than just watch."[22] The on-screen audience was actively engaged when, for example, an episode on dog training culminated with a dog show. But another key offering of the Finder for his off-screen audience was trail maps that children and their parents could use to continue exploring. Some of these maps were included with the submission package, such as a 140-mile driving trail map, prepared by the Automobile Club of Missouri from Columbia, Missouri, south to Chester. Nomination materials

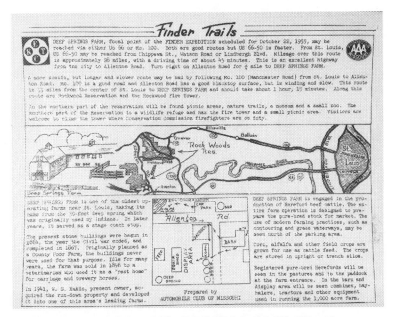

A trail map produced in conjunction with *The Finder* by the Automobile Club of Missouri.

also describe periodic organized expeditions led by the Finder for fellow "Finders and their families," and details are provided of several of these, including a tour of a farm and exploration of a local cave.[23] The program's mission to get kids out and interested in their surroundings is not, then, only ironically carried out by relaying a message to children sitting attentive in their living rooms but is supported by its encouraging actual outings and also by hosting outings that are at times led by the lead character of the program. Nomination materials also include a map of the northern sky intended to accompany a program about stargazing, thereby once more extending the Finder's reach beyond the show alone.

NBC's partnership in 1958 with the Girl Scouts of the USA produced another interesting experiment in educational television with broad, paratextual reach. *Adventuring in the Hand Arts* was a ten-week program examining, nomination materials announce, "the hand crafts of primitive cultural orbits existing in the midst of the Nuclear Age—Mexican, Peruvian, Polynesian, Melanesian and Alaskan among them."[24] Episodes featured guest experts and a group of Girl Scouts learning more about the meanings and artistry of pottery, weaving, puppetry, woodcarving, and more. Materials quote Mrs. Charles U. Culmer, president of the Girls Scouts of the USA, as expressing hope that the "series will be a milestone for us and for other public service organizations who, like us, are looking for new and better ways to bring program resource material to their membership," and she further notes that she is confident that all three million Girl Scout members will interact with the series in some fashion.[25] Clearly, the program was intended to circulate material and information to an ever-growing organization while providing access for others outside the organization, and certainly a broad collection of affiliates aired the show. But alongside the program were printed materials listing further reading, places in local communities where one could acquire materials for engaging in the handcraft of the week, suggested activities to accompany the show, and more. The submission materials offer evidence that the Girl Scouts saw the program as raw material that would be fashioned, directed, and curated by troop leaders armed with its paratextual materials. *Adventuring in the Hand Crafts* serves as an interesting forerunner of today's "freemium" strategy for digital delivery of all sorts of services, offering the basic program to all but supplying the paratexts to Girl Scout leaders as a form of value added.

Yet another example that more profoundly challenges the vocabulary of text and paratext, show and project, is WBBM in Chicago's *The Friendship Show*, submitted in 1958. Submission materials describe the program as "experimental, . . . based on the belief that brotherhood is partly a matter of practice," and the experiment saw host Lee Phillip work with a racially and economically diverse group of fifteen children each week to foster "brotherhood."[26] Phillip led the children in numerous televised activities including storytelling, performances, dances, and games, and the program even featured—materials boast—"a pony ride!" in the studio.[27] Many of these activities drew from various world cultures, teaching children, for example, a Chinese song and then a Slovakian dance. Interestingly, though, Phillip continued her work outside the program, visiting children's homes with her staff and holding meetings without the cameras present—and not just before the show to prepare them for the camera but also afterward. There is no paratext on offer in the tangible form of a *Children's Corner* booklet or a *Finder* trail map, but we nevertheless see a *paratextualization*, as the work of the show continues beyond its televisual frame. Indeed, the program offered Peabody several letters of support from educators and parents who had seen children's lives affected in positive ways by their involvement in the greater project, and their letters are telling for praising not just the program but the entire project.

The archive, then, offers numerous instances of programs venturing into classrooms and also into everyday life itself via paratexts. I have discussed a range here, from toys, educational flash cards, teacher's guides, and practice sheets to sheet music, trail maps, recipes, and transmedia booklets and even visits and events with hosts. Few of these paratexts are anomalous, though, and together they are representative of an equally diverse, eclectic, and voluminous assortment of paratexts in the archive that indicate a healthy, vibrant participation of paratexts in their accompanying shows' educative work throughout television history. Though the archive does not contain much documentation regarding audience response beyond the occasional carefully selected letter of support included in a package or beyond Nielsen data, we might speculate that paratexts may have played an important role in convincing parents that their children weren't "just" watching television and that these shows weren't "just" shows. Even now, in 2017, the rhetoric surrounding children's viewing habits deplores the ills of "screen time," yet many of the programs I have discussed here arguably faced even stronger headwinds at the time of airing, operating when television was more roundly criticized as low and when concerns about television included fears not just of its messages but of its supposed radiation.[28] A largely untold part of children's television history is the story of the various roles that paratexts played, intentionally and by design or not, in legitimating the genre of children's television and in furthering the educative and imaginative missions of its producers.

CONCLUSION

We should be unsurprised to hear complaints about the corrupting effect of paratexts for children's shows when our history of children's television regularly overlooks the plethora of paratexts and when it often forgets the integral role they played in many prominent shows' lives. Parents object to Daniel Tiger toys and books, seeing these paratexts as the crass commercialization of their beloved *Mr. Rogers's Neighborhood* and of their children's beloved *Daniel Tiger's Neighborhood,* but what they don't know is that the Peabody Awards Collection shows us that Daniel was starring in "spinoff" booklets long before many of these concerned parents were born. However, my purpose in this chapter is ultimately not to argue that children's paratexts have been unfairly maligned. As much as I believe they have at times been misunderstood—just as the complex meanings and uses of toys in general have not been fully appreciated in society and even within media and cultural studies—my purpose is to suggest that we may have let our concerns about commercialization limit our expectations for children's television.[29] As I noted at the outset of this chapter, hashtag activism surrounding the merchandise of several prominent franchises has acknowledged that merchandise and other paratexts matter: they are an important site for the construction of meaning and social value. These activists have thus called for and demanded that merchandise follow its text's lead and continue its political work. So too, I propose, should we demand that children's paratexts expand on, amplify, and otherwise positively transform the work of their shows. Granted, the Peabody archive is self-selected, and thus my dive into its texts is by nature a dive into better examples. But that is good, as I want us to think about what paratexts for social value should look like. Although parents may gripe about children being "glued to" television, children will often spend as much if not considerably more time with the paratexts of favorite shows. Rather than ruing their existence and simply wishing these paratexts would disappear, we might instead (or at least in addition) challenge producers to be more thoughtful, purposive, and innovative in creating paratexts that matter.

NOTES

1. For more, see Jonathan Gray, *Show Sold Separately: Promos, Spoilers, and Other Media Paratexts* (New York: New York University Press, 2010).

2. Theodor Adorno and Max Horkheimer, *Dialectic of Enlightenment* (New York: Herder and Herder, 1972 [1944]).

3. See Avi Santo, *Selling the Silver Bullet: The Lone Ranger and Transmedia Brand Licensing* (Austin: University of Texas Press, 2015).

4. Suzanne Scott, "#wheresrey? Toys, Spoilers, and the Gender Politics of Franchise Paratexts," *Critical Studies in Media Communication* 34, no. 2 (2017): 138–47.

5. Citation for 2015 award, http://www.peabodyawards.com/award-profile/doc -mcstuffins.

6. Karen Attwood, "Doc McStuffins: The Toy Breaking Down Gender and Race Stereotypes," *Independent*, November 30, 2014; Eliana Dockterman, "Disney's Perfect Answer to Barbie is Doc McStuffins," *Time*, August 4, 2014; Olivia B. Waxman, "The 13 Most Influential Toys of All Time," *Time*, October 29, 2014.

7. *Doc McStuffins*, supplemental PDFs, pts. 1, 2, and 3, 2014145715 CYT 25, 26, and 27 of 27, Peabody Awards Collection, Walter J. Brown Media Archives and Peabody Awards Collection, University of Georgia, http://dlg.galileo.usg.edu/peabody/id: 2014_2014145715_cyt_25, http://dlg.galileo.usg.edu/peabody/id:2014_ 2014145715_cyt_26, http://dlg.galileo.usg.edu/peabody/id:2014_2014145715 _cyt_27.

8. BBC2, *Sesame Tree* brochure, publicity report and *Out and About with Hilda* educational resource, and *Let's Play and Learn Together* activity kit, 2008, television entry exhibits, 1949–2011, carton 886, folder 08003 CYT, George Foster Peabody Awards Records, ms3000, Hargrett Rare Book and Manuscript Library, University of Georgia (hereafter HAR).

9. WFIL, *Operation Alphabet* scrapbook, 1962, OS box 110, folder 62031 EDT, George Foster Peabody Awards Collection, Series 2: Television Entries, Peabody Awards Collection, ms3000_2a, HAR.

10. Ibid.

11. Allison Perlman, "Television Up in the Air: The Midwest Program on Airborne Television Instruction, 1959–1971," *Critical Studies in Media Communication* 27, no. 5 (2010): 480. Perlman cites L. C. Fletcher, "State of the Questions: The Growth of Educational TV," *America*, October 31, 1959, 130, John C. Schwarzalder, "The Promise of Teaching by Educational Television," *College English* 20, no. 4 (1959): 180, and Edward Stasheff, "Can Television Help Solve the Teacher Crisis? Yes!," *Senior Scholastic*, February 20, 1959, 13–14.

12. KMOX, *More Than Meets the Eye* scrapbook, 1962, OS box 110, folder 62012 PST, Peabody Awards Collection, Series 2: Television Entries, Peabody Awards Collection, ms3000_2a, HAR.

13. CBS, "Read More about It," *CBS Reading Projects* entry form, 1982, *CBS Reading Projects* scrapbook and teacher guides, television entry exhibits, 1949–2011, box 125, folder 82022 PST, George Foster Peabody Awards Records, ms3000, HAR.

14. Ibid.

15. Ibid.

16. Ibid.

17. Ibid.

18. Ibid.

19. Henry Jenkins, *Convergence Culture: Where Old and New Media Collide* (New York: New York University Press, 2006).

20. WQED, *The Children's Corner* entry form, scrapbook, and program guide, 1955, box 10, folder 55018 CYT, George Foster Peabody Awards Collection, Series 2: Television Entries, ms3000_2a, HAR.

21. KETC, *The Finder* entry letter and scrapbook, 1955, box 10, folder 55003 CYT, George Foster Peabody Awards Collection, Series 2: Television Entries, ms3000_2a, HAR.

22. Ibid.

23. Ibid.

24. NBC, *Adventuring in the Hand Arts* entry form, *The NBC-ETRC Educational Television Project* boxed set, 1958, OS box 90, folder 58036 EDT, George Foster Peabody Awards Collection, Series 2: Television Entries, ms3000_2a, HAR.

25. Ibid.

26. WBBM, *The Friendship Show* bound volume, 1957, OS box 84, folder 57007 CYT, George Foster Peabody Awards Collection, Series 2: Television Entries, ms3000_2a, HAR.

27. Ibid.

28. See, for instance, Jerry Mander, *Four Arguments for the Elimination of Television* (New York: William Morrow, 1978).

29. Dan Fleming, *Powerplay: Toys as Popular Culture* (Manchester, UK: Manchester University Press, 1996).

PART 2

LOOKING FOR MEDIA CITIZENRY AND SUBJECTIVITY

READING PEABODY

TRANSPARENCY, OPACITY, AND THE BLACK SUBJECT(ION) OF TWENTIETH-CENTURY AMERICAN TELEVISION

> To the real question, "How does it feel to be a problem?" I answer seldom a word. —W. E. B. DU BOIS

> Errant, he challenges and discards the universal—this generalizing edict that summarized the world as something obvious and transparent, claiming for it one presupposed sense and one destiny. —ÉDOUARD GLISSANT

> You can come in and you can sit, and you can tell me what you think, and I'm glad you are here, but you should know that this house isn't built for you or by you. —TONI MORRISON

One approach to critically assessing the black image in media is through the politics of representation. In the politics of representation, the truth of the image, its resonance, and meaning are measured by the proximity to the experiences of black people and black life. The authority and relevance of the image reside in the circumstances of reception and the conditions of production that structure and ensure its legibility.

This politics of representation is committed to visibility, legibility, and recognition by the market, the state, and civil society. Dedicating the image to visibility and recognition is one way to use it in the struggle for cultural and social justice. This commitment, by the way, accompanied the very formation of technological mediation of the image and its entanglement with race and representation.[1] The desire for recognition in the mediated cultures of U.S. civil society, which representation makes possible, also engenders a commitment to the right to know the rights-bearing citizen subject of liberal democracy. This commitment to liberal citizenship is particularly vexed, as Saidiya Hartman and Fred Moten have shown, for the former enslaved subjects of racial slavery.[2] Indeed, for the formerly enslaved in the United States the lack of bodily possession was a precondition of their condition as socially dead and as property.[3]

So, I begin this chapter with the hunch that it is possible to detect in the Peabody Awards Collection the traces of a politics of representation that is a site of cultural dispute, where the desire for the transparency of the black subject is a condition of its media representation, of its legibility, which grounds citizenship and national belonging. I am also betting that the Peabody archive offers researchers and scholars clues about ways of seeing blackness by its refusal to be known. That is, seeing blackness need not depend on fulfilling the desire for recognition; it can instead depend on acknowledging the desire for what Édouard Glissant calls the right to opacity. Starting with the assumption that the Peabody holdings of twentieth-century television's representations of blackness and race relations are conditioned by the guidelines of the submission process, rules of classification and access, and the genre of the archive, I explore the nature of subjectivity of black people presented in public service, documentary, news, and entertainment television submissions from the 1950s through the late 1970s.[4] That is, looking closely at a selection of materials from the collection, I ask which discourses produce black television subjects as legible, knowable, recognizable, and representable and for whom these subjects are produced. These examples from Peabody's holdings prompt my theoretical speculations about the conditions of possibility for television representations of blackness in the twentieth century. The examples I selected seem to suggest the alignment of local television and the discourse of race relations in race-making projects. Other examples convey, as Devorah Heitner shows in another context, black subjects of race relations and television negotiating the confusing terms of visibility and citizenship and media representation and power in mid-twentieth-century United States.[5] So, the examples that I work with are theoretically resonant and analytically rich, enabling me to see and think about questions of citizenship, representation, race, and blackness.

In my analysis of the examples from the Peabody archive, I draw on the concepts of transparency and opacity methodologically and conceptually, using them as points of engagement with the politics of representation and race as a twentieth-century technology of power. The liberal desire to know the subject of democracy depends on the transparency of the individual liberal subject; the disclosure of this subject forms the basis of trust in and sets the terms of belonging to liberal democracy. Avery Gordon argues that appeals to law, culture, and civic recognition represent conditions of impossibility for civically and socially dead members of society, since these discourses are literally incapable of culturally recognizing or civically acknowledging members of such groups as people whose histories, socialities, intimacies, and needs are legible in the first place.[6] That is to say, from the vantage point of rights discourse and juridical sovereign power, this discursive incapacity or condition of impossibility produces the desire for social transparency, social transparency being seen as a way for subjects to meet the threshold of citizenship and civic reliability. From the vantage point of those putative subjects who are constituted as a problem, this condition of impossibility produces relations, traditions, histories, and intimacies that exceed the limits of rights discourse and social science indexes of social problems and that defy the demand of a cultural politics of representation to know them as something other than transparent subjects of sovereign power and authority.

Since it is a condition of social relations, transparency sets the terms for recognition by the state and civil society as well as defines what counts as an acceptable subject of liberal democracy.[7] Normative whiteness and more recently postracial race are the default here, so that to achieve recognition and visibility one must measure up to them. Television is central to the production and circulation of these forms of social knowledge based on racial difference.

Within the racial order that power-knowledge secures there is also slippage, a refusal on the part of "the other" to be known. Refusing power-knowledge's desire to know the other, to be known by the knowledge of a discourse of race relations as a problem, is to refuse to participate in the desire for legibility. I take the social production of blackness and its thick nexus of meanings constructed within the logics of race and its discourse of race relations as an instance of this refusal of opacity. But this refusal of legibility is not just the inverse of legibility; rather different modalities—the transparency of race relations and the opacity of black refusal—of knowledge and power operate together within the mediated spaces of 1950s and 1960s U.S. television accounts of the meanings and effects of race.

I propose seeing mid-twentieth-century U.S. television as a scene where race operates as a form of power through the field of race relations, a discourse that uses social science research techniques to solicit, gather, and mobilize expert knowledge about racial attitudes, experience, and meanings as a way of addressing the problems of race. This knowledge orders the terms of social relations in U.S. liberal democracy. At the same time, the operation of power-knowledge sets the terms for the production of black opacity or excess.

Accordingly, there are two potential interpretations of the material I have selected from the archive: one, which I would say is the most common in media studies, is to see selected materials from the archive (and perhaps even the archive itself) as performing a conception of liberal democracy and its ideal subject whose desires for inclusion are set by a politics of representation committed to state recognition, rights, and cultural visibility; the second, and the one I am more interested in, is to see the materials as creating a space in mid-twentieth-century U.S. television that operates as a site of refusal that might challenge our understanding of television history and the presumed legibility and meaning of the blackness produced there.

I proceed first with a brief elaboration of race as a technology of power where knowledge and the desire for transparency come together in the discourse of race and intergroup relations. My elaboration links Foucault's disciplinary and biopolitical account of power-knowledge to Édouard Glissant's critique of transparency as a condition of (post)colonial subjection. I suggest that the commitment to transparency as an effect of power-knowledge is on display in two examples from the Peabody archive, WDTV's 1953 program *The Case against Communism* and WBBM's 1963 program, *Feedback*. I then consider black refusal of the terms of legibility established by the field of race relations in press coverage of the civil rights movement and according to television conventions required for representability. I look to several locally produced programs, including *Harambee* and *Tell It Like It Is*, from the late 1960s for clues about what conditions both the discursive commitment to recognition and the refusal of this recognition and then consider what these clues might mean for media studies, social movements, and media histories.[8] I conclude with some remarks about the implications of Glissant's work for the conceptualization of media histories and television studies of twentieth-century race making and cultural politics.

In *The Citizen Machine*, Anna McCarthy suggests that in the mid-twentieth century, civic clubs, labor unions, business organizations, and local media outlets organized focus group discussions and engaged in role-play, drawing on social science (especially social psychology), to address issues of racial conflict and interpersonal misunderstanding.[9] Local commercial and educational television outlets often aired shows that focused on race relations in order to meet the public interest requirements of broadcasters, thus fortifying the alliance between intergroup focused social psychology, race relations as a social problem, and television.

The idea that broadcasters were neutral players who were meeting their civic responsibility and public service obligations did not go unchallenged. As Allison Perlman shows in *Public Interests*, civil rights organizations applied direct legal pressure on broadcast licensees to get local station owners to expand their conception of their audience as well as their reach and make more of an effort to serve the public.[10] Local stations were relatively independent, which meant that broadcasters could (without scrutiny or challenge) treat "public" as synonymous with "white," ignoring racial, gender, cultural, or religious difference. In short for local broadcasters, the ideal public whose interest was being served with their programming was always and already assumed to be white, middle class, and homogeneous.

The voluminous body of historical literature and media research on the history of television and especially its relationship to the civil rights movement tells the story of black civil rights struggles in the South for civil recognition, equal protection, and full participation in the public life of the nation. Television and its capacity to *show* (with transparency) black people was central to each of these projects. The role of television news and the press in these struggles was especially important.[11]

These attempts to use broadcasting, social science, and the law to address race relations turn on the importance of social recognition and visibility in civil society and the role of media like television in producing a visibility underwritten by the commitment to transparency. The social science discourse of race relations is productive—that is to say, it produces a "subject" that, as Glissant might put it, is transparent or knowable by the empirical measures and evidence of race relations research. This transparency is a condition of subjection to the discourse and the metrics of power-knowledge that produce and vouch for recognizable, visible, accessible, verifiable citizen-subjects of American liberal democracy. To know and to see black Americans as citizens is to know them through the expert knowledge produced and authorized by social science and the conventions of television journalism.

In his discussion of disciplinary power and biopower Foucault identifies different sites and practices of power that variously take hold of the body, norms, and ethics. In studies of prisons, the clinic, sexuality, madness, and government Foucault repeatedly shows that the subjects of discipline and regulation are produced through the exercise of power-knowledge—his expression for the power that priests, clinicians, scientists, and administrators implement via various techniques, practices, and knowledge. Focusing on the body, morality, desire, and norms, this expertise seeks to produce knowable, that is, transparent subjects.[12] While the disciplinary order is trained on the body, especially the other as a nonnormative body, biopolitics regulates populations by targeting norms, rules, and desire. The hinge between Foucault and Glissant through which I think about blackness, television, race relations, and transparency and the production of race as a technology of power in the post–World War II American social order is this desire to know the rights-bearing subject, to target its desire for state recognition and cultural visibility, which itself is, I am suggesting, an exercise of power.[13]

Writing in the context of a Caribbean postcolonial condition, Glissant uses the concept of transparency to describe the relations of domination and subordination between colonial powers and formerly colonial subjects. Through the presumed universalization of language of colonial power, a defining condition of this relationship is the colonizer's need to know those whom it subjects. Such a desire to know the subordinated subject was apparent under Jim Crow and in de jure and de facto segregation, mass incarceration—what Saidiya Hartman calls the afterlife of slavery.[14] Whether in the form of body measurements, market value, census data, fugitive slave laws, or birth and death rates, as an exercise of disciplinary and biopolitical power, human sciences and related administrative technologies designed to surveil and regulate have been used to make legible and enable the state to know the enslaved, immigrant, the sharecropper, the deviant, the incarcerated, the dispossessed, and the culturally different. Academic disciplines like sociology, social psychology, anthropology, and associated social science fields have focused on unraveling the mystery of the other by making them more transparent.[15]

Indeed, by the mid-twentieth century the discourse of race relations in sociology set its sights on the production of empirical knowledge to address the question of who is the other. These empirical studies and the conceptual accounts they offered gave rise to the fields of social relations and race relations. In the areas of social persuasion, communication studies, and advertising, researchers investigated forms of civic participation and consumer attitudes about social problems. The administrative/technocratic and social science methods used to produce a transparent understanding of immigrants, migrants, so-called deviants, the mentally ill, homosexuals, and others were predicated on the idea that accurate, reliable knowledge about them and their interior lifeworlds could be generated empirically. Data was generated through surveys, confessions, testimonials, participant observation, and focus groups and assessed in studies of public opinion, attitudes, and interpersonal dynamics. Furthermore, this data provided researchers with evidence of levels of civic participation, habits of media consumption, and extent of political engagement.

The use of these techniques aimed at generating knowledge about the other in the mid-twentieth century is evident in two examples from the Peabody archive, *The Case against Communism* and *Feedback*. These programs illustrate the complex relationship between empirical research, disciplinary expertise, local television news, and the problem of race relations. Both programs were produced locally and aired in the 1950s. On display are techniques like confession and testimonial that social science and legal experts used to make judgments about the extent of a person's national loyalty and civic participation. According to Glissant, the colonial power assumes uniformity and homogeneity among the colony (or former colony) on the part of those who live in the space of the colony; this assumption makes possible the exercise of control over the colony,

The mock trial of *The Case against Communism* aligns racial transparency with civic loyalty.

the nation, and public opinion. *The Case against Communism* is a multipart series presented in the form of a mock trial, wherein communism personified (by a shadowy silhouetted figure quoting passages from Lenin and Stalin) is the defendant.[16] Individuals who have either renounced communism or suffered at the hands of communist regimes give evidence to a panel of judges; the aim is to present the viewing audience with an indictment of communist ideology and to caution against the dangers of leaving communism unchecked. When a purported black former communist party operative is asked to reveal personal information as a way for him to establish his loyalty and trustworthiness as a rights-bearing citizen, it becomes clear that the discourse of anticommunism, the civil rights movement, and the petition for recognition of cultural differences have set the terms of confession and testimony. In short, we need to know him to trust and vouch for him. Testimony and confession are key in the attempt to render blackness transparent and in ensuring the loyalty and commitment of African Americans to American anticommunism.

Part role-play and part reenactment, *The Case against Communism* sets the terms for what counts as racial transparency and civic loyalty. This framework and the civic and racial performance of citizenship and loyalty that it enables is also a form of social management. The expert judge panel suggests that William Patterson, a black former communist sympathizer, is to be believed because of his status as a former party organizer, because he is black, and partly because he has turned against communism. In other words, as a witness against communism, Patterson's primary task in the piece is to disavow his prior loyalty to communism and not only to confess to his error in judgment but to explain how awful communism is compared to American democracy. At the level of production as part of a locally generated public affairs television program, Patterson's disavowal and renunciation is made more compelling through the visual alignment of his race, the legal authority of his interlocutors/interrogators (signified by their professional work as actual judges), his personal confession, his status as a (partial) rights-bearing subject, and his testimony.

In the questions and responses, the admission, and conversion, we literally see disciplinary power target Patterson's body and affective state (loyalty, betrayal) to produce a subject and citizen of liberal democracy and racial capitalism. This exercise of power establishes a discursive truth: the superiority of democracy as a social order and Patterson as an example. Through his disavowal of communism and his commitment to democracy, Patterson becomes transparent and knowable, trustworthy and loyal. His blackness is made to vouch for an exploitive racial capitalism and racist liberal democracy without the least bit of irony, apprehension, or critique of racism and its impact on the conditions of black life in the United States and the partial citizenship that it confers.

Where *The Case against Communism* vouches for Patterson in an at-

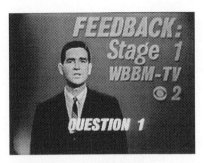

Feedback attempts to achieve racial understanding through the combination of interviews with community members and confessions solicited from surveys.

tempt to establish the superiority of democracy, *Feedback: The Race Dialogue* illustrates the workings of power-knowledge through the social science field of race relations. *Feedback* is a public service program that utilizes a race relations expert and a combination of interviews with community members and surveys distributed through various area newspapers to gauge public opinion on race relations.[17] The program is split into two parts. The first features individual interviews that provide viewers with the range of opinion related to topics like civil rights demonstrations, school integration, housing segregation, and civil rights legislation. The second focuses on interpreting and communicating the results of viewer surveys. *Feedback* illustrates the material and discursive effect of identifying (and framing) race as a problem of the relations between races. It is an instance of power-knowledge where professional expertise, social science methods of data collection and analysis, media consumption, and public interests intersect to make knowledge about race.

Feedback (along with archival footage of the civil rights movement protest) produces a form of knowledge that assumes that it is possible to know race as a condition of social life (not just as a category describing individual subjects but a socio-psychological and political category), to access purported differences among racial subjects through confession and testimony generated by social science surveys. In each segment, opinions regarding race relations are solicited from viewers using the language of ballots, voting, civic duty, and feedback. Television viewing and newspaper reading constitute forms of civic activity and engagement. Race and community are framed throughout the program in homogeneous terms both by blacks and whites, experts and lay. *Feedback* displays its commitment to transparency in the form of expert knowledge, social science research, and civic participation for purposes of achieving racial understanding among blacks and whites in Chicago, manifesting a will to understand that Glissant sees as the desire of power to illuminate and explain everything, especially blacks and the purported threat they pose to the normative racial order.

In *Poetics of Relation*, Glissant elaborates on his thinking about opacity and transparency and embraces the refusal of those Caribbean populations subjected to colonialist desire to make themselves known.[18] In exploring the critical nature of difference and the complex social relations the entanglements of difference produce, including the destruction of any referent or scale that measures difference against a universal norm, Glissant concludes that difference can "still contrive to reduce things to the Transparent."[19]

Glissant insists "not merely to the right to difference but . . . to the right to opacity that is not enclosure within an impenetrable autarchy but subsistence within an irreducible singularity. . . . Thought of the self and thought of other here become obsolete in their duality. Every Other is a citizen and no longer a barbarian."[20] This recognition of the critical importance of difference as a basis of tradition, history, culture, and life beyond the gaze and authority of the colonizer challenges the scale of measurement and its enforcement within the Western hierarchy of value that underwrites colonialism. For Glissant "the opaque is not obscure, though it is possible for it to be so and be accepted as such. It is that which cannot be reduced, which is the most perennial guarantee of participation and confluence."[21] On the question of opacity and identity, his own as well as the other, Glissant notes, "I . . . am able to conceive of the opacity of the other for me without reproach for my opacity for him. To feel in solidarity with him or to build with him or to like what he does, it is not necessary for me to grasp him. It is not necessary to try to become the other (to become other) not to 'make' him in my image. These projects of transmutation . . . have resulted from the worst pretensions and the greatest magnanimities on the part of the West."[22]

As I have noted, Glissant's refusal is not a simple binary that can be reduced to an oppositional cultural politics of resistance, since often in the same text and historical space of encounter, as in the television programs from the archive that I have been considering, the logic of transparency is fully operational and in full effect at the same time that a desire for (black) opacity is apparent. So I want to be careful to avoid positing a binary opposition between transparency and opacity while proposing that there are twentieth-century television shows that stand as momentary cultural sites and expressions of a fugitive blackness, one defined and organized through a willful opacity (despite the logic of transparency embedded in the forms of power-knowledge) that still remain an enigma to this day even with the proliferation of black television platforms and representation.[23] The politics of representation that produced black television and media reform movements is informed not just by access to and control of the image but by refusal of transparency.

BLACK SUBJECTS

Harambee from the Washington Post-Newsweek Television Stations and *Tell It Like It Is* from KNBC are examples of media texts motivated by a politics of representation. On the one hand, they enlist viewers in a commitment to see, and on the other, they offer performances of wandering, multiplicity, and entanglements across black differences, reflecting Glissant's concept of opacity.

The 1968 program *Tell It Like It Is*, for instance, hosted by Godfrey Cambridge, features a selection of audiovisual presentations and interpretations of work by poets, writers, and artists of the Douglass House Foundation/Watts Writers Workshop that demonstrates a black self-representation and self-crafting.[24] Art and expressive culture is the means through which young black artists tell it like it is and tell their audiences who they are. Despite its use of direct address and of its airing of readings of radical black prose and poetry (certainly for its time), as a media text the piece establishes a desire to know these writers and their work. This desire is on display from the very beginning, when Godfrey Cambridge says, "Many of you know me but you don't know my heroes. . . . You are going to have to learn to know my heroes. . . . Look and listen because you are gonna learn a lotta new things. . . . Look and listen."

This segment's address is directed to a viewing subject presumed to need educating. The introduction thus appears to construct a (white) viewer to whom the show will reveal things about this creative community (which is a proxy for black worlds). The segment then cuts to exterior shots of Douglass House, home of the writer's workshop, to introduce the program host who in turn introduces the nine segments of prose, poetry, and visuals featured.

Probably the most productively opaque segments of the episode are Ojenkie's "The Promise" and Lillian Tarry's "Black like Me" during which the narrator describes the search for pride and respect among black Amer-

In the segment "Black like Me," the frame is saturated with candid shots of the everyday life of black people, images seldom seen on television at the time.

"The Promise" refuses the desire for transparency, opting for opacity, with images of graves, headstones, and shadows during a conversation about black loss and grief in black communities.

icans while onscreen shots show women, children, and the elderly immersed in the everyday life of black people. The television frame is literally saturated with the joyous faces of members of this community. Familiar yet strange to KNBC's audience (and to normative whiteness), such images were certainly seldom seen on television at the time, and yet the activities they depicted were commonplace in black communities across the country. We seem to know these folks, but do *we* really?

Of all the segments in the program, "The Promise" most steadfastly refuses the desire for transparency that underwrites race relations discourse, opting instead for an opacity rooted in cultural difference and social history. That is, the explicit point of the segment and the poem does not seem to be to provide the viewer with insight or to help the viewer appreciate the encounter with social and cultural difference that appears on the screen and in the poetry. The segment stages a conversation about black loss and grief in black communities and those communities' worries over the Vietnam War and the incarceration of black Americans. These concerns are powerfully conveyed in the form of letters, prose, and visuals of everyday life, including a funeral procession (a graveyard and burial site signify the grief and trauma of black loss) and street scenes. There are references to black nationalism and the global struggle for liberation in Vietnam and Africa. There is something urgent in "The Promise" and its representation in this segment, an urgency that relates both to its own time and to the now of its archival life.

Similarly, the powerful excerpt of David Henderson's performance of "Die Nigga" on the Post-Newsweek program *Harambee* questions the hegemony and racial order of things, including black complicities in that

Poet David Henderson's appearance and performance on the Post-Newsweek program *Harambee* suggests the possibility of seeing television in terms of black itineraries, space, and place.

racial order.[25] *Harambee* was a morning show created by and for members of the black community in the Washington, DC, area.[26] The program featured interviews with prominent politicians and activists and showcased local productions as well as interviews with artists and producers. One program segment of *Harambee* highlights the film *Right On* and features a performance by poet and writer David Henderson.

Thinking about television performances like "Die Nigga" and "The Promise" through Glissant's poetic of relations makes it possible to see television and black programming from the late 1960s and early 1970s from the Peabody archive not in terms of social problems and race relations but in terms of black itineraries and black space and place. In other words, by approaching the archive's entries through the prism of opacity, we can see black difference and multiplicity in art, politics, civil rights, economic justice, and everyday life despite public discourses describing black people as socially and culturally monolithic and politically one-dimensional and race relations as a black problem. The presumed multiplicity of blackness also potentially disrupts and even challenges the hegemony of the national as the natural and appropriate space of television, culture, and politics.

Yet another way to think about these instantiations of black self-representation and self-crafting through regional networks like the Post-Newsweek Network is as affirmations of and testaments to the cultural links among blacks across differences of geographical and social location. Opacity in this context is a useful critical optic through which to view the presumed alliance of the network as a discourse of legal, technical, and cultural relations, the national as a geographical and political category, and the drive for transparency in media historiography. Such an appreciation of black difference and multiplicity as a critical analytic for rethinking media studies' often uncritical reliance on the alliance of the national and the local network is evident in Perlman's and Classen's accounts of the impact of local efforts to push stations to create new publics and develop more complex conceptions of the local.[27]

These concerns about geography, space, and scale, on the one hand, and difference, multiplicity, and representation, on the other, bear on questions of method. Does reading an archive like the Peabody enable and perhaps even encourage theorizing the role of television as an apparatus of representation for producing transparency and opacity? Given the quite dramatic and quickly changing nature of television in the twenty-first century perhaps the archive is the best point of entry for addressing how these twentieth-century issues bear on contemporary concerns regarding race and difference. Television archives like the Peabody help illuminate the conjuncture of the civil rights struggle for social justice, the formation of textual and production conventions, and shifting international alliances and perspectives on governance.

One can draw on the materials related to race relations, civil rights, and black power movements collected in the Peabody archive, as well as other television archives, to understand the relationship between transparency and opacity, especially the overlapping and uneven distribution of conventions and practices through which they are actualized as discursive truth. Even as certain programs emphasize the capacity and the desire of black people to refuse to be known as a social problem in the press, television news, and social science research as a condition of full citizenship and inclusion, they also reveal the lure of transparency and expose the entanglement between a politics of representation and transparency. As certain other programs from the Peabody show, the refusal of such transparency is a condition of possibility for the production of a different kind of story of and about blackness. Put differently, the very commitment to recognition and visibility with a politics of representation carries with it an investment in transparency and legibility. The theoretical and analytic usefulness of opacity for television studies (including especially television histories of race and blackness) is that it provides a tool with which to challenge canonical readings of television shows. What our media and television histories offer as radical examples of black self-making may also be saturated with the logic of transparency, an effect of power expressed as the will on the part of the dominant racial order to see, know, and manage blackness as a problem. To begin with a commitment to visibility and recognition, as most histories and accounts of race and media do, is to accept a commitment to a politics of transparency as a condition of recognition. Given the complexity and reach of the relationships between the state, the media, the market, and mid-twentieth-century civil rights movements, the desire for opacity of the other, in this case blackness, bears a critical relationship to the politics of representation based on visibility and recognition. This critical relationship follows from Glissant's idea spelled out in *Poetics of Relation* that relationality based on difference does not dissolve into either the evasion or elision of difference. By the same token, the measure of difference in relation to other is not based on a singular or normative subject with a hegemonic will to know. Insofar as the Peabody archive is concerned, this formulation prompts the question: does the politics of the archive manifest a relationship between transparency and opacity? Is it possible to discern a poetics of the kind urged by Glissant in the archive in general, and not just in the examples I selected?

The pressing challenge of this brief engagement with Glissant and the Peabody archive is how to see black multiplicity and difference within the ecology of the archive and the spatial optics of television as a technology of race committed to homogeneity, singularity, and unities as a condition of recognition and inclusion. Reading the Peabody from the angle of black opacity can produce evidence of black refusal of transparency and sensitize us to see blackness not as an "other" measured against a normative whiteness but in terms of a poetics of relation that neither rejects difference nor attempts to reduce it to sameness. Opacity enables a different reckoning with the archive; it offers another way of engaging blackness. It makes possible the very question that the commitment to transparency forecloses—where are we and who are we on television when the gaze of whiteness and the desire of whiteness to know is no longer the point.

NOTES

1. Cedric J. Robinson, *Forgeries of Memory and Meaning: Blacks and the Regimes of Race in American Theater and Film before World War II* (Chapel Hill: University of North Carolina Press, 2007; Shawn M. Smith, *Photography on the Color Line: W. E. B. Du Bois, Race, and Visual Culture* (Durham, NC: Duke University Press, 2004).

2. Saidiya Hartman, *Scenes of Subjection: Terror, Slavery, and Self-Making in Nineteenth-Century America* (Oxford: Oxford University Press, 1997); Fred Moten, *In the Break: The Aesthetics of the Black Radical Tradition* (Minneapolis: University of Minnesota Press, 2003).

3. Herman Gray, "Subject(ed) to Recognition," *American Quarterly* 64, no. 4 (2013): 771–98; Sylvia Wynter, "Unsettling the Colonality of Being/Power/Truth/Freedom: Towards the Human, After Man, Its Over Representation: An Argument." *New Centennial Review* 3, no. 3, (2003): 257–337.

4. Submissions to the Peabody Awards Collection that I consulted for the period 1949–75 are organized according to year, state, media platform (radio or television), and genre (news, public service, youth and children, entertainment, education, promotion of international understanding). In the early years (1949–62), race is often framed as a social problem of race relations and is treated in programs in public service and news categories. In other words, the archival categories (and popular common sense about race of the time) used to sort and classify the submissions govern how ethnicity, race, and difference appear in the collection.

5. Devorah Heitner, *Black Power TV* (Durham, NC: Duke University Press, 2013). See also Tommy Lee Lott, "Documenting Social Issues: *Black Journal*, 1968–1970," in *Struggles for Representation: African American Documentary Film and Video*, ed. Phyllis R. Klotman and Janet K. Cutler (Bloomington: Indiana University Press, 1999), 71–98, and Lori Kido Lopez, *Asian American Media Activism: Fighting for Cultural Citizenship* (New York: New York University Press, 2016).

6. Avery Gordon, *The Hawthorn Archive: Letters from the Utopian Margins* (New York: Fordham University Press, 2017).

7. Western Europe, Australia, and the United States have seen vexed debates over immigration, national borders, and mass displacement in recent years.

8. Peabody submissions that I viewed and considered but do not discuss here include *Black Dignity* (1968, KGO, San Francisco), an episode of *Community Profile* that features an interview with James Brown (1971, WJCL, Savannah, GA), and *CPT, Colored People's Time* (1968, WTUS, Southfield, MI).

9. Anna McCarthy, *The Citizen Machine* (New York: New Press, 2010).

10. Allison Perlman, *Public Interests: Media Advocacy and Struggles Over U.S. Television* (New Brunswick, NJ: Rutgers University Press, 2016).

11. According to the media conventions of the time the commitment to transparency was synonymous with and ensured by the commitment to realism, representing the point of view of different parties, and journalist impartiality.

12. Michel Foucault, *Discipline and Punish: The Birth of the Prison*, trans. Alan Sheridan (New York: Vintage, 1995); Michel Foucault, *Society Must Be Defended: Lectures at the Collège de France, 1975–76*, ed. Alessandro Fontana and Mauro Bertani, trans. David Macey (London: Penguin, 2008).

13. On the one hand, the transparency the state desires is produced and guaranteed by the scholarly field of race relations. On the other, the commitment to transparency on the part of the other is expressed in the commitment to be seen that accompanies the investment in a politics of representation.

14. Hartman, *Scenes of Subjection.*

15. Roderick A. Ferguson, *The Reorder of Things: The University and Its Pedagogies of Minority Difference* (Minneapolis: University of Minnesota Press, 2012).

16. WDTV, *The Case against Communism*, November 29, 1953, 53023 ENT 1 of 1, Peabody Awards Collection, Walter J. Brown Media Archives and Peabody Awards Collection, University of Georgia (hereafter PAC), http://dlg.galileo.usg.edu/peabody/id:1953_53023_ent_1.

17. WBBM, *Feedback: The Race Dialogue*, November 18, 1963, 63036 PST 1 of 1, PAC, http://dlg.galileo.usg.edu/peabody/id:1963_63036_pst_1.

18. Édouard Glissant, *Poetics of Relation*, trans. Betsy Wing (Ann Arbor: University of Michigan Press, 1997).

19. Ibid., 189.

20. Ibid., 190.

21. Ibid., 191.

22. Ibid., 193. Teju Cole summarizes Glissant's insistence on the right to "say no" this way: "One of Glissant's main projects was an exploration of the word 'opacity.' Glissant defined it as a right not to have to be understood on other's terms, a right to be misunderstood if need be. The argument was rooted in linguistic considerations: it was a stance against certain expectations of transparency embedded in the French language. Glissant sought to defend the opacity, obscurity and inscrutability of Caribbean blacks and other marginalized peoples. External pressures insisted on everything being illuminated, simplified and explained. Glissant's response: No." Teju Cole, *Known and Strange Things: Essays* (New York: Random House, 2016), 148.

23. See Moten, *In the Break.*

24. KNBC, *Tell It Like It Is*, 1968, 68001 PST 1 of 1, PAC, http://dlg.galileo.usg.edu /peabody/id:1968_68001_pst_1.

25. Glissant, *Poetics of Relation*, 28–29.

26. WTOP, *Harambee*, "For My People," November 1, 1975, 75002 PST 1 of 1, PAC, http://dlg.galileo.usg.edu/peabody/id:1975_75002_pst_1.

27. Perlman, *Public Interests*; Steven D. Classen, *Watching Jim Crow: The Struggles over Mississippi TV, 1955–1969* (Durham, NC: Duke University Press, 2004).

CHRISTINE BECKER AND LUCAS HATLEN

BROADCASTING THE BICENTENNIAL

The year 1976 did not seem like the best time for a national birthday party. Two years prior, Richard Nixon had vacated the presidency amid the Watergate scandal, while 1975 saw the fall of Saigon and the withdrawal of U.S. troops from Vietnam. Following the social upheavals of the 1960s, the country was heavily fractured along generational, gender, class, and racial lines, and there was rising distrust in American institutions and declining faith in American exceptionalism, with fears of an economic crisis and concerns about the Cold War pervasive throughout the country. President Gerald Ford even admitted in his 1975 State of the Union Address that "the state of our Union is not good."[1] So what could have been a delightfully ostentatious nationalist celebration of patriotic unity instead became a challenge that raised questions about what exactly should be celebrated and how, but it also provided an opportunity to interrogate what America's values were at this point in the country's history and how they compared to the founding fathers' vision.

Television was there to showcase all of these values and visions and to broadcast them to national and local audiences via documentaries, historical dramas, dramatic reenactments, regional reflections, news specials, panel discussions, and live celebrations of the founding of the United States. The bicentennial commemoration overall was a decentralized and dispersed affair, but television provided a central space for the American citizenry to experience its varied representations and meanings. A 1977 government report looking back on bicentennial events praised the medium for what it delivered to viewers on July 4, 1976, specifically, "a great exposition that some felt would be missing during the historic period—

an exposition of the nation itself."[2] And in many ways, that exposition was as wide ranging as the nation itself, with flag-waving patriotism appearing alongside subversive dissent on the station scheduling grid. This chapter analyzes the bicentennial through the television schedule, screen, and archive in an effort to identify how the medium brought this commemoration into the nation's living rooms. After first surveying the general organization and parameters of the bicentennial celebration and offering a theoretical understanding of how American political and cultural traditions are typically framed, we explain what types and tropes of bicentennial-related television programming appeared on national networks and local stations in the mid-1970s, finishing with a case study of Atlanta. A considerable amount of nationalism and patriotism was exhibited on the small screen, but a complex array of national critique and questioning, as well as, inevitably, corporatism, also accompanied the jingoism.

OVERVIEW OF THE BICENTENNIAL CELEBRATION

Symbolic of the fractured state of the United States at the time, planning for the bicentennial celebration was chaotic. Formed by order of President Lyndon B. Johnson on July 4, 1966, the American Revolution Bicentennial Commission (ARBC) expected to spend the next decade planning a proper national celebration, but it floundered right away due to disagreements over direction and mandate, as well as a lack of funding.[3] The commission then became politicized under the Nixon administration, as the president made numerous partisan appointments to it with the alleged intent to ensure that not just the country but Richard Nixon himself would be celebrated. Additional accusations of misappropriation of funds followed, which prompted congressional hearings. The end result was the dissolution of the ARBC in 1973.[4]

In its wake, the American Revolution Bicentennial Administration (ARBA) was formed, but the change from the ARBC was much deeper than one word in its name. The ARBC had been run by a fifty-member team. The ARBA was led by only eleven people, with Secretary of the Navy John Warner in charge. The ARBC's grandiose hopes for the celebration had at one point included a $1.5 billion World's Fair–type event in Philadelphia. The ARBA instead pushed for a decentralized organization that would foster a wide range of small-scale events and that would inspire local participation across the country. The ARBA's final report on the bicentennial states that the commemoration ended up being "a hometown affair," and when giving speeches about ARBA activities, John Warner frequently reiterated that the bicentennial celebration would belong to the people rather than the ARBA.[5] Given the level of distrust of the federal government at the time, this was prudent. It also offered the financial benefit of placing the burden of funding events on state and local entities.

While the celebrations would be heavily localized, the ARBA did suggest a trio of themes around which events could be oriented. Heritage '76 ("Let Us Remember") was intended to honor the country's founding documents, politicians, and values; Festival USA ("Let Us Celebrate") encouraged explorations of the country's diversity and cultural traditions; and Horizons '76 ("Let Us Shape a Better Tomorrow") called for a focus on the future of America.[6] These themes offered guidance for state and city bicentennial commissions and helped to foster a common framework that could allow bicentennial events across the United States to seem unified.

Of course, there was an unspoken fourth theme: commerce. With the ARBA offering minimal federal funding, corporate America stepped in to subsidize events.[7] According to the ARBA's final report, 241 companies contributed $38.9 million to officially sponsored programs across the country, and businesses spent millions more on independent activities.[8] Corporations also took advantage of advertising and merchandise opportunities tied to the patriotic groundswell, which ultimately generated a backlash. A leftist activist group called the People's Bicentennial Commission coined the term "buy-centennial" to mock the commercialization of the event, which saw everything from ice cream sandwiches to toilet seats sold in bicentennial-themed versions.[9]

While some had concerns about overcommercialization, more profound schisms emerged due to the social fracturing of the country and the challenge of incorporating the perspectives of marginalized communities like African Americans and Native Americans. ARBA organizers were well aware that the country would be divided over how to celebrate America's past and its values, and they pushed for respect of cultural and ethnic differences.[10] In the wake of the civil rights movement and ethnic and social identity pride movements of the 1960s, as historian Christopher Capozzola writes, "it had become increasingly clear that one historical narrative could not tell the whole nation's story."[11] However, one historical moment did come to dominate the bicentennial: the American Revolution itself. Historian Lyn Spillman argues that there was "semiotic flexibility" in the concepts of revolution, liberty, freedom, the right to happiness, and other notions tied to the founding moment, allowing both groups that wanted to celebrate the event and those that were critical of it to shape their rhetoric through them.[12] This also offered space for critiques to be framed not as unpatriotic but as yearning for a restoration of foundational American ideals. As Capozzola writes, "The Bicentennial offered a means for the politically disconnected to articulate a critique of the status quo by showing how far the nation had supposedly fallen from its original, noble principles, an approach accessible to people across the political spectrum."[13]

The combination of ARBA's push for decentralization and regionalism, corporate underwriting of the bicentennial, and the variability of perspectives that revisiting revolutionary principles made possible helped to push television to the forefront of the period's discourse. While the national networks offered programming one might expect during any era of historical reflection—miniseries, biopics, news reports, live coverage of celebrations—American broadcasting's local station infrastructure offered ample opportunity not only to cover local events but also to provide a platform for community leaders, academics, and activists to discuss re-

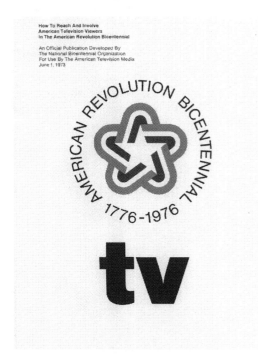

Cover art from *How to Reach and Involve American Television Viewers in the American Revolution Bicentennial*, published in 1973 to encourage television productions by local stations.

gionally and nationally relevant issues. Television's economic base also invited considerable corporate interest, driven by intertwined commercial and civic motivations. From the national to the local level, then, television became a vital outlet for bicentennial expressions.

The ARBC recognized this potential, which led the commission in its final year to distribute a pamphlet to local stations titled *How to Reach and Involve American Television Viewers in the American Revolution Bicentennial*. The pamphlet offered inspiration to station owners to not just cover history but make it: "You are the channel through which America can achieve total citizen involvement, in the Bicentennial Commemoration and in the continuing effort to Improve the Quality of American Life in the years beyond."[14] The publication highlights the theme of citizen involvement throughout the publication, explicitly so in a list of three functions that the ARBC foresaw for television: providing a forum for discussion and debate, helping to transform citizens' ideas into civic actions, and initiating projects and activities that involve viewers. There is also a list of suggested programming ideas, including documentaries on topics and sites of historic interest in the community, talk shows featuring community leaders and activists, comprehensive coverage of local bicentennial efforts, contests and quizzes about historical topics, and public

Illustration of performers and media workers from *How to Reach and Involve American Television Viewers in the American Revolution Bicentennial.*

service spots. All of these types of programming did air on stations across the country during the period. But the pamphlet closes by stressing that station owners should feel free to modify any of these ideas or add new ones that would be more relevant to their individual communities: "Apply the themes and pursue the subjects that you think are warranted in your Community. Use that special 'feel' only you have for your own viewers. In other words, use the limitless ingenuity and initiative the American Television Media has always demonstrated to gain the highest possible levels of citizen involvement and to assure the success of the Bicentennial Commemoration."[15] The publication also issues a patriotic call: "What is critical is to have every American thinking and feeling and acting 'America' in his day-to-day life."[16] The theoretical concept of civil religion helps to illuminate what it might have meant for bicentennial television to foster the conditions of "feeling America."

CIVIL RELIGION AND THE BICENTENNIAL

Robert Bellah first articulated the concept of American civil religion in a 1967 scholarly publication, right as bicentennial planning was beginning. Bellah's "Civil Religion in America" explores what he saw as "an elaborate and well-institutionalized civil religion" unique to America that existed alongside of but was "obviously distinct from the churches of the Republic.[17] The term "American civil religion" was no mere linguistic flourish, according to Bellah, but referred to a mindset that had a history and depth and that "require[d] the same care in understanding that any other religion does." Biblical symbols have a storied history in American political thought. The Declaration of Independence locates "Nature's God" as the source of its authority, and presidents from Washington to Kennedy took care to acknowledge the role that the "Almighty Being" and the "hand of God" played in American society. While Bellah concedes that many of the symbols of the American civil religion are "derived from Christianity," he argues it is "not itself Christianity." The founding fathers and the documents they authored paid deference to a higher power but conspicuously avoid reference to Christ. This omission is offered as evidence that "from the earliest years of the Republic," there was present a unique system of "beliefs, symbols, and rituals with respect to sacred things," separate from the Christian faith.[18]

For Bellah, American civil religion was not static and unchanging but incorporated events and individuals into its system of symbols and myths over time. The Constitution and Declaration of Independence as "sacred scripture," Washington as the "divinely appointed Moses," delivering his people out of bondage, the American state as a "City upon a Hill," a "New Israel" that would shine as a beacon to the rest of the world—these were the foundational myths and symbols of the nation's civil religion. Arlington National Cemetery, "the most hallowed monument of civil religion," demonstrates the manner in which American civil religion incorporates history into its system of symbols and myth. From World War I came the Tomb of the Unknown Soldier, and each successive U.S. conflict provides the cemetery with additional patriots to memorialize. John F. Kennedy, another martyr, is interred under the eternal flame. Memorial Day, Independence Day, Thanksgiving, and other national holidays provide the nation with "an annual ritual calendar for the civil religion." Public schools, in giving children time off to celebrate many of these holidays and in institutionalizing the daily loyalty pledge offered to the enduring symbol of the flag, serve as a "particularly important context for the cultic celebration of the civil rituals." Ultimately, American civil religion, as Bellah interprets it, is a source of cohesion and national understanding, functioning to unite Americans of all religious traditions in an inclusive expression of common faith.[19]

Bellah did not conceptualize American civil religion as purely laudatory or celebratory, however. John Winthrop, the first governor of the Massachusetts Bay Colony, characterized the American colonies as a city upon a hill, and this characterization has endured to the modern day. Although more recent invocations of the city upon a hill, such as that by President Ronald Reagan, have pushed the symbol toward the utopian, Winthrop's original reference seems more contractual in nature. He stated: "For we must consider that we shall be as a City upon a hill. The eyes of all people are upon us. So that if we shall deal falsely with our God in this work we have undertaken, and so cause him to withdraw his present help from us, we shall be made a story and a byword throughout the world."[20] For all of Winthrop's apparent ambition for his new colony, an anxiety pervades proclamation. Continued divine blessing hardly appears guaranteed; indeed, future success appears to depend on the maintenance of virtue in the city upon a hill. In a similar manner, the bicentennial moment provided an opportunity for citizens to reflect on the nation's past, present, and future and to ask if the nation was failing to uphold its end of the deal.

More recent scholars have challenged the assumed "integrative function" and neutrality of civil religion.[21] Marcela Cristi argues that those in power have a vested interest in shaping the direction of civil religion, given that a perceived sanctified authority serves to legitimize the domination of the social and cultural groups from which the symbolism is derived. The use of a specific set of religious symbols can then be understood not as a unifying practice but instead as one that elevates certain faith traditions and cultures at the expense of others. Civil religion represents the dissemination of "the values of the dominant group in America" rather than the "religious self-definition of the American people as a whole."[22] Rhys H. Williams complicates matters, arguing that civil religious discourse fosters an "uncivil" impulse to "heighten boundaries" by representing these boundaries as "natural and even sacred" as well as gives rise to "ennobling" impulses that encourage citizens to "critique society" and "to be better than we are."[23] The latter impulse is represented in several bicentennial programs.

NATIONAL AND LOCAL BICENTENNIAL PROGRAMMING

In line with Robert Bellah's conception of civil religion, bicentennial-era television was filled with symbols and myths that explored the nature of America's founding fathers, documents, and ideals. Even the sacred ritual of network television advertising was reworked to embrace this mission. For instance, every night from July 4, 1974, through December 31, 1976, CBS devoted sixty seconds of a prime-time ad break to a segment titled *Bicentennial Minutes*, sponsored by Shell Oil. The minutes were hosted by well-known public figures, from movie stars to politicians, who described key events from two hundred years ago on that day that helped to shape the Revolution and subsequently America. Whether the commemorated event was as famous as Paul Revere's ride or as incidental as a corn-husking bee in New England, the stories were wholly patriotic and reiterated common revolutionary tropes of liberty, pride, and loyalty. The *New York Times* estimated that about thirty-two million Americans saw *Bicentennial Minutes* each night, and the series was even praised in the *Congressional Record*: "The Senate commends the CBS television network for so commemorating the birth of our Nation, and for providing a focus for Americans to foster a sense of deepened pride in their heritage."[24]

Similar praise in the form of a Peabody Award was bestowed on CBS for a single day's presentation, *In Celebration of U.S.*, which was the official title for CBS's "14-hour day-long and night-long TV birthday party" on July 4, 1976.[25] The program hopscotched across the nation, anchored by Walter Cronkite, who described the coverage as particularly local in orientation in his opening monologue:

> Our correspondents and crews, hundreds of people altogether, will report the events in big cities, from Boston to San Francisco, in small towns from New Hampshire to Iowa. We'll see the president of the United States, and watch thousands of aliens become citizens. We'll see events at sacred national shrines. We'll go to an Indian pow wow and visit ethnic neighborhoods. We'll see the greatest parade of sailing ships assembled in our lifetime. Symphony orchestras, Dixieland bands, the Mormon Tabernacle Choir, they're all part of this day, all part of our coverage.

The Peabody Awards' Winner Citation praised *In Celebration of U.S.* for presenting "pure USA," which sounds reminiscent of the ARBA's call for television to leave viewers thinking and feeling America.[26]

The two other bicentennial-related Peabody Awards for 1976 were given to programs that added to the understanding of foundational American history. *The Adams Chronicles*, a thirteen-episode miniseries about the Adams political family that was produced by WNET for PBS as a bicentennial commemoration, was a fairly traditional biopic in form, but its scope with respect to the influence of one family dynasty on the evolution of the country was epic.[27] More formally innovative was *Suddenly an Eagle*, which aired on ABC on January 7, 1976.[28] This hour-long documentary featured American actor Lee J. Cobb and British actor Kenneth Griffith in contemporary dress standing in historic locations and detailing events leading up to the first shot of the Revolutionary War that took place in those places. The documentary alternately becomes performative, as Cobb acts out key moments undertaken by American patriots, such as Patrick Henry's "Give me liberty, or give me death" speech, while Griffith enacts critical points in British colonialism, such as the Crown ordering import duties to be collected on tea. The result is a striking display of ritualistically told stories of America's revolutionary myths underscored by images of legendary historical spaces in their current state, making for a particularly Bellahian reiteration of American ideals.

Local TV stations also provided numerous forms of history lessons, many of which were oriented around fostering pride in the attainment of knowledge about America's founding moments. An example was WCBS's *Great American History Test*, a one-hour quiz program aired on June 30,

1975, which pitted members of a studio audience against New York–area schoolchildren to see who could correctly answer the most questions about American heritage and New York regional history.[29] (The students won.) The program's host closed the show with the words of historian Arthur Schlesinger Jr.: "The present emerges from the past, and a sense of history is one of the means by which a people achieve purpose and strength for the future," adding that "it is important to know where we have been, in order to know where we are, who we are, and where we are going." Some local programming also seemed calculated to encourage tourists to go to historic places in order to learn who they were as Americans, such as 1975's *The New England Experience*. These were half-minute segments produced by WNAC in Boston that presented reenactments at key historical spots and that were followed with a snapshot of those locations in their modern state, highlighting "the history that still lives in twenty-one New England communities, to show how much history you can see right down your street."[30]

While those segments aligned with the ARBA's Heritage '76 theme, the Festival USA theme was captured by programs that surveyed the diverse ethnic populations of their regions, frequently underscoring immigration and the American "melting pot" ideal as essential to the country's core principles. An exemplary example of this was WCVB's *Boston Legacy*, a nine-episode series of one-hour specials that showcased seventeen different ethnic groups in the Boston area. The series was capped off by a live ninety-minute special titled "The Whole World Celebration," a multiethnic festival hosted by the International Institute of Boston. WCVB was awarded a Peabody Award in the institutional category for this and other 1976 programs, which "demonstrated a deep and sincere interest in community affairs and people."[31] Another program in this vein was the twelve-part "American Rock" series, one of which was *Schoolhouse Rock*'s "The Great American Melting Pot," the lyrics to which any child of the 1970s can probably still recite: "Lovely Lady Liberty, with her book of recipes. And the finest one she's got is the great American melting pot. What good ingredients, Liberty and immigrants." Each of these twelve specials is bursting with symbols of civil religion.[32]

Although several bicentennial programs utilized the myths and symbols of civil religion to celebratory ends, other programs used these symbols to highlight a tension that has been present in civil religious discourse from before the nation's founding. This tension pervades several bicentennial programs such as *Life*, the first part of a trilogy of NBC documentaries covering two hundred years of the American experience (the other two are *Liberty* and *The Pursuit of Happiness*). *Life* exhibits a delicate balance between aspiration and apprehension throughout, but it is the ending that best encapsulates the tension. As images of U.S. flags being sewn by a diverse group of immigrant workers pass before the camera, host David Brinkley makes an impassioned argument that the bicentennial provides an opportunity to reflect on what the nation and its sacred symbols mean:

> In some areas of American society in recent years the flag has come to be a symbol of the far right. A political minority offering super patriotism, so called, as a denial of the democratic values that have held this country together and kept it going for two hundred years. And without them it will not go another two hundred years. They are, of course, entitled to say and think whatever they like, but they are not entitled to monopolize the flag. Why let them have it? It is beautiful, it symbolizes some of the greatest ideas that mankind has ever had, and it belongs to all of us. All of us is 214 million individuals. Much the same, even though much different. With backgrounds as varied and diverse as our origins, as the geography of our continent and the accents of our language.[33]

Life recognizes the potential power and pitfalls of American civil religion. Philip Gorski has recently argued that civil religion can be understood as a midpoint between what he calls "liberal secularism" and "religious nationalism."[34] This idea has been expanded on by Rhys H. Williams and Todd Nicholas Fuist, who contend that "liberal secularism is highly inclusive as a political cultural principle, treating people as individuals, all with equal access to the public sphere. However . . . there may not be significant cultural resources to foster social solidarity in such a principle. On the other hand, religious nationalism fosters intense group solidarity, but is non-inclusive for both religious minorities and political dissidents."[35] Brinkley, it seems, recognized a similar tension in the bicentennial moment. *Life* attempts to bring together these two aspects of American culture by reclaiming American sacred symbols for those who celebrate the

A recent immigrant working in a factory manufactures flags in preparation for the bicentennial in the David Brinkley documentary *Life*.

ideals of diversity and inclusion. Unfortunately, Brinkley's warning reveals that the struggle over these symbols was not resolved by the bicentennial celebration.

At times, American civil religious discourse has moved beyond the voicing of a tension and into condemnation. The tradition of the jeremiad, named after the biblical prophet Jeremiah, is a "prolonged lamentation" or indictment of societal failures. If John Winthrop's primary concern was the maintenance of the covenant between America and God, civil theologians like Frederick Douglass represent the prophets in the wilderness warning their fellow citizens that the covenant was not signed in good faith. Although the jeremiad tradition may at first seem to be little more than an unmitigated denunciation and rebuke of society, the purpose of a jeremiad is not to cause despair but to startle individuals into action. Several bicentennial programs followed in this tradition, including *A Man Named Douglass*, an episode of *Bicentennial: A Black Perspective* that was produced by WNBC in New York for airing on July 4, 1976, and featured excerpts from Frederick Douglass's speech "The Meaning of the Fourth of July for a Negro" read by actor Moses Gunn. These excerpts are interspersed with scholarly discussion of Douglass's legacy as well as the legacy of slavery, which "influences all of our institutions today" through structural racism.[36] Rather than Gunn representing Douglass in period-appropriate clothing, Gunn's Douglass was dressed as a contemporary politician. This sartorial decision allowed for a sense of temporal slippage in the presentation of slavery's contemporary legacy. Gunn as Douglass states, "Fellow-citizens, I will not enlarge further on your national inconsistencies. The existence of slavery in this country brands your republicanism as a sham, your humanity as a base pretense, and your Christianity as a lie. It destroys your moral power abroad: it corrupts your politicians at home. It saps the foundation of religion; it makes your name a hissing and a *byword* to a mocking earth," a powerful rebuke from 1852 that serves as a rebuke of the continued racial injustice in America in 1976. As Winthrop had warned so long ago, the eyes of the world were on America, and it was found wanting.[37]

While *A Man Named Douglass* confronted viewers with the nation's failure to live up to the promises of liberty and justice for all, "Freedom of Speech," an episode of *A New Birth of Freedom*, questioned one of the nation's most sacred myths: the absolute primacy of free speech. The program, which aired January 7, 1976, on KING in Seattle, argues that although we give free speech "plenty of lip service," in actuality we offer it little support both at a national and a local level.[38] Complete freedom of speech, the program suggests, is a myth, and KING uses its own station to make this point. The program shows the viewer the process of editing films for broadcast on KING to demonstrate how television is "both officially censored and self-censored." In this portion of the program, the merits of an intimate film scene between lovers is debated by two staff members, a discussion that descends into the comic when they edit out a scene with "implied" nudity because even though the actress in the scene is wearing a sweater, "you know that is all that she has on." One of the editors defends this decision on the grounds that the station has a "responsibility" to its audience, but the editor also notes a desire to avoid any potential paperwork that might result from a complaint to the FCC. The narrator argues that this whole "routine . . . becomes even funnier" when you consider that not just the scene in question "but every broadcast across the country has been pre-censored because of government regulation" and that "it becomes downright silly when you remind yourself that this all happens in a country which prides itself on a history of free expression." Less comic is the program's interrogation of the Condweld Committee, which "hunt[ed] down communists" in Washington State, creating a "local version of the national witch hunt which made Joe McCarthy one of our best-known senators, and started a period which proved just how fragile the right of free speech can be." "Freedom of Speech" uses these examples and others to highlight that it is *acceptable* speech, rather than free speech, that America truly celebrates.[39]

THE BICENTENNIAL IN ATLANTA

A close look at the way Atlanta's media approached the bicentennial offers an instructive example of the combined civic and corporate apparatus of television's bicentennial commemorations, the prevalence of locally oriented discourse on the event, the centrality of identity discourses, and the complex combination of celebratory and critical rhetoric evident in much of the TV programming. Atlanta's WSB, the "Voice of the South," initiated an impressive media production campaign to highlight the historical significance of the bicentennial and to publicize the many celebrations occurring across the city and state. These programs and promotions, which aired on both WSB TV and radio, took a variety of forms and often were cosponsored by local business interests. While the programs were not uniform in their tone or content, the overall body of work produced by WSB for the bicentennial was both proconsumption and progressive.

The flagship example of probusiness, progressive programming is the WSB *Salute to America Parade*, which was recognized as "one of the top twenty Bicentennial events in the nation by Washington's Bicentennial Commission."[40] "An International Salute to America" was the theme chosen "to recognize our actual heritage," and the program featured "many of Atlanta's consular corps highlighted by a Chinese Dragon, the International Polka Society, the Columbian Horse Group, the Hibernian Society, global type floats, Japanese/Americans and many others." Notably, stars were all identified by a dual ethnic heritage: "Italian/American, French/Canadian/American, Norwegian/American, Afro/American, Irish/American" and others. The grand marshal was Uncle Sam, a figure that "represent[ed] all Americans." The station argued that more than a parade, the event was "a television program to foster an understanding of and appreciation for our American Heritage." In promotional materials, the program was said to salute "America's diverse heritage and Atlanta's international role." Interestingly, in some internal documents the event was referred to as "the 'Salute to America' Parade to Promote Patriotism," which was the most explicitly nationalist expression in WSB's original programming. Per the march orders, participants were primarily a mix of municipal groups (Atlanta Police Department, high school bands), social groups (Knights of Columbus, Boy Scouts of America), military groups (navy, national guard), local businesses (Prado Mall, Atlanta State Farmer's Market), and corporate floats and balloons (Delta, Steak n' Shake). In addition to the live telecast on WSB TV, both NBC and CBS devoted portions of their Fourth of July coverage to the parade. WSB claimed that the program was "probably" the "most ambitious effort of any single station in the nation." The parade was a flashy celebration of both commerce and diversity at the local and the national level.[41]

Although much of WSB's programming emphasized both consumption and inclusion, some of the programming produced was quite challenging. Perhaps the most fascinating and forward-thinking program produced for the bicentennial by WSB was the series *Blacks and the American Revolution*. A collection of twenty-five thirty-second television spots, the program aimed to represent the "contributions of blacks during the Revolutionary era," including "the rugged spirit and commitment of such noted individuals as Phillis Wheatley, Crispus Attucks, and Jean Baptiste Point DuSable" as well as that of less noted "but equally important" individuals of the time. The program was "unique in substance and presentation" in offering "a significant glance at the less heralded side of the American struggle—a side without which America would not have grown into the nation she is today."[42] The distinctive slogan "Lest We Forget," which concluded each segment, acted as the program's signature. "Lest We Forget" seemingly served a double purpose by highlighting the contributions of African Americans during the revolutionary period and at the same time condemning, or at least drawing attention to, the occasions when the actions of the founders fell short of their ideals. Notably, the program was conceived of, researched, and funded by persons of color. The commercial sponsor was the Atlanta branch of the Interracial Council for Business Opportunity (an organization designed to help minority businesses), primary research for the series was conducted by Alton Mornsby of Morehouse College, and the series was conceived of and directed by Lester Strong, the community affairs director of WSB TV. Despite these credentials, however, Strong seemed to feel that it was important to emphasize that the "Lest We Forget" logo was created by WSB artist Virginia Staples, who could "trace her family tree back to the Revolution." The program's reach was not limited to the Atlanta area. It was also shown in several other media markets, including "Pittsburgh, Columbus, Fort Wayne, Memphis, Winston Salem, Dayton, San Francisco, Charlotte, and St. Thomas, VI."[43] The program was also distributed to the American Forces Radio and Television Service, which provided media access to service members across the globe.

"Lest We Forget" also had a life outside of *Blacks and the American Revolution*, serving as the logo and "general theme" of the bicentennial task force of the Georgia Black Legislative Caucus. Representative David Scott of Atlanta was the chairman of the task force, which was created in 1975. In an interview, Scott described black participation in the bicentennial as a "national dilemma," adding that "it is right and proper to question whether we [blacks] should celebrate the bicentennial. We were subjected to the most debase treatment, brought here to build a land of freedom, enslaved by another people."[44] The goal of the Black Caucus was to mark the bicentennial not as a "celebration" but instead as an "emancipation." Representative Scott felt that the logo and motto spoke to "every Georgian and every American of every race and religion about the deep and abiding belief, faith and struggle of black people in America, past, present and ... future."[45] The task force asked "area black historians, artists, writers—and community workers" to help design and coordinate activities and programs for the bicentennial, including WSB's Lester Strong. Strong thought that among the black community the "initial impression" of the caucus's outreach would be "outrage" due to the brutal legacy of slavery and segregation, but he was hopeful that African Americans would "see through that outrage and say 'that's the way it is, but we have made some sizable gains in America.'"

As transgressive as some of the broadcasts on WSB may have been, it is important to remember that financial concerns always remained. In the aftermath of a J. C. Penney cosponsored "Speak Up for America" slogan contest, a memo was sent to WSB staff members chiding them to better promote J. C. Penney in the future. The memo, which opens with the phrase "lest we forget," emphasized that the purpose of the slogan contest was to convince the department store of WSB's advertising potential.[46] Redeploying the motto to remind employees of the importance of proper marketing reveals a disconnect between the more reflective and nuanced public face of WSB's programming and the financial realities of the bicentennial in Atlanta. Socially progressive programming and events could occur when business elites saw them as beneficial. In celebrating America, Atlanta elites could celebrate and elevate themselves, and the bicentennial moment in Atlanta saw the local government, business, and media work together to promote the interests of all three.

CONCLUSION

The case of Atlanta illustrates on a small scale that the large-scale bicentennial commemoration was as multifaceted as the country had always been and as steeped in cultural complexities as the medium of television invariably is. In fact, contrary to this chapter's introductory assumption, there was perhaps no better time for the bicentennial to fall than in a period when the fabric of the nation seemed to be torn asunder. Indeed, no one-dimensional nationalist celebration of patriotic unity could have accurately captured what "feeling America" truly meant in 1976.

The event also coincided with the final years of the classic network era, just prior to the period in which local station ownership was consolidated. The medium's infrastructure was such that it was able to mesh the commanding voice of network news authority, embodied by figures such as Walter Cronkite and David Brinkley, with the grassroots activism enabled on the local level by variably autonomous TV stations, as evident in *The Man Named Douglass* and *A New Birth of Freedom*, making the bicentennial's incendiary fireworks as rhetorical as they were literal.

This analysis also prompts reflection on contemporary events. During the 2016 presidential election, Gold Star parent Khizr Kahn delivered a speech at the Democratic National Convention in which he excoriated the exclusionary rhetoric of the Trump campaign. Kahn's status as a Gold Star parent granted him virtually unparalleled moral authority. Kahn challenged then-candidate Trump's proposed Muslim ban by pulling a copy of the Constitution out of his pocket, holding it aloft, and addressing him in absentia: "In this document, look for the words 'liberty' and 'equal protection of law'. Have you ever been to Arlington Cemetery? Go look at the graves of brave patriots who died defending the United States of America. You will see all faiths, genders, and ethnicities."[47] Kahn did not cite the Constitution as part of some legalistic repudiation of Donald Trump's proposed policies. Rather, his referencing of the document served to brand Trump as un-American and his policies as anathema to the spirit of the nation. Months later, Donald Trump addressed a joint session of Congress for the first time as president. He too drew on American myths and symbols in the course of his speech as he looked forward to another national anniversary: "In nine years, the United States will celebrate the 250th anniversary of our founding—250 years since the day we declared our independence. It will be one of the great milestones in the history of the world. But what will America look like as we reach our 250th year? What kind of country will we leave for our children? . . . We are one people, with one destiny. We all bleed the same blood. We all salute the same great American flag. And we all are made by the same God. . . . I am asking all citizens to embrace this renewal of the American spirit. . . . Believe in yourselves, believe in your future, and believe, once more, in America."[48]

Through these speeches, made by two men who could not be more different, we see that the tension present during the bicentennial moment has yet to dissipate. Throughout the course of the nation's history, American myths and symbols have been used to justify both enslavement and emancipation, xenophobia and cosmopolitanism, isolationism and empire. Our reverence for the nation and the desire to elevate and emulate our national heroes, continues to inspire us to heed what Lincoln called the better angels of our nature. It may also lead us to put "America first" at great expense to our neighbors, ourselves, and the world. As during the bicentennial moment, our nation now suffers divisions that seemingly threaten to tear us asunder, but unlike in 1976, we no longer have a Cronkite or a Brinkley to speak to the nation in its entirety. As advancing technologies blur the distinctions of place, like-minded communities threaten to supersede local communities as a primary locus of understanding what it means to "feel America" at the small scale. As we approach the 250th anniversary of the country, the bicentennial celebration, which Walter Cronkite described as both "corny . . . but also undoubtedly moving," provides a useful roadmap for how a nation can reflect on its past, present, and future in a manner that is both commemorative and complex.[49]

NOTES

1. Gerald Ford, State of the Union Address, January 19, 1976, Miller Center, millercenter.org/president/ford/speeches/speech-5599.

2. American Revolution Bicentennial Administration (ARBA), *The Bicentennial of the United States of America: A Final Report to the People*, vol 1. (Washington, DC: U.S. Government Printing Office), 14.

3. Steven Bellavia, "Fanning the Flames of Patriotism: The American Bicentennial Celebration" (MA thesis, Emporia State University), 7–10, https://esirc.emporia.edu/bitstream/handle/123456789/3293/bellavia%20thesis.pdf.

4. Ibid., 10–12.

5. Ibid., 13–14; ARBA, *The Bicentennial of the United States of America*, 9.

6. Laura Barraclough, "The Western Spirit of '76: The American Bicentennial and the Making of Conservative Multiculturalism in the Mountain West," *Western Historical Quarterly* 47, no. 2 (2016): 161–81; ARBA, *The Bicentennial of the United States of America*, 251.

7. Christopher Capozzola, "'It Makes You Want to Believe in the Country:' Celebrating the Bicentennial in an Age of Limits," in *America in the 70s*, ed. Beth Bailey and David Farber (Lawrence: University Press of Kansas, 2004), 32.

8. ARBA, *The Bicentennial of the United States of America*, 253.

9. Bellavia, "Fanning the Flames of Patriotism," 21–27; ARBA, *The Bicentennial of the United States of America*, 263.

10. Lyn Spillman, "When Do Collective Memories Last? Founding Moments in the United States and Australia," *Social Science History* 22, no. 4 (1998): 466.

11. Capozzola, "'It Makes You Want to Believe in the Country,'" 38.

12. Spillman, "When Do Collective Memories Last?," 466–67.

13. Capozzola, "'It Makes You Want to Believe in the Country,'" 37.

14. National Bicentennial Organization, *How To Reach and Involve American Television Viewers in the American Revolution Bicentennial* (Washington, DC: ARBA, 1976), 3.

15. Ibid., 5

16. Ibid., 4.

17. Robert Bellah, "Civil Religion in America," in *American Civil Religion*, ed. Russell E. Richey and Donald G. Jones (New York: Harper and Row, 1974), 21.

18. Ibid., 21, 28–29.

19. Ibid., 30, 33.

20. John Winthrop, "A Model of Christian Charity," https://www.winthropsociety.com/doc_charity.php.

21. Marcela Cristi, *From Civil to Political Religion: The Intersection of Culture, Religion, and Politics* (Waterloo, Ont.: Wilfrid Laurier University Press, 2001), 8.

22. Ibid., 241.

23. Rhys H. Williams, "Civil Religion and the Cultural Politics of National Identity in Obama's America," *Journal for the Scientific Study of Religion* 52, no. 2 (2013): 257.

24. Bellavia, "Fanning the Flames of Patriotism," 76; Senate Resolution 353, June 27, 1974, www.govtrack.us/congress/bills/93/sres353?utm_campaign=govtrack/popup.

25. CBS, *In Celebration of U.S.*, entry form and presentation, box 97, folder 76028 BCT, George Foster Peabody Awards Collection, Series 2: Television Entries, ms3000_2b, Hargrett Rare Book and Manuscript Library, University of Georgia (hereafter HAR).

26. CBS, *In Celebration of U.S.* compilation, July 4, 1976, 76028 BCT 1 of 1, Peabody Awards Collection, Walter J. Brown Media Archives and Peabody Awards Collection, University of Georgia (hereafter PAC), http://dlg.galileo.usg.edu/peabody/id:1976_76028_bct_1.

27. WNET, *The Adams Chronicles: John Quincy Adams, President (1825–1829)*, March 16, 1976, 76037 BCT 1 of 1, PAC, http://dlg.galileo.usg.edu/peabody/id:1976_76037_bct_1.

28. ABC, *Suddenly an Eagle*, 1976, 76024 BCT 1 of 1, PAC, http://dlg.galileo.usg.edu/peabody/id:1976_76024_bct_1.

29. WCBS, *The Great American History Test*, 1975, 75041 SLT 1 of 1, PAC, http://dlg.galileo.usg.edu/peabody/id:1975_75041_slt_1.

30. WNAC, *The New England Experience* entry forms, box 97, folder 75063 SLT, George Foster Peabody Awards Collection, Series 2: Television Entries, ms3000_2b, HAR.

31. WCVB, *Bi-centennial*, July 5, 1976, 76041 NWT 1 of 1, PAC, http://dlg.galileo.usg.edu/peabody/id:1976_76041_nwt_1.

32. Bellavia, "Fanning the Flames of Patriotism," 67–74.

33. NBC, *Life*, no. 1, October 28, 1975, 75026 EDT 1–2 of 2, PAC, http://dlg.galileo.usg.edu/peabody/id:1975_75026_edt_1-2.

34. Philip S. Gorski, "Barack Obama and Civil Religion," in *Rethinking Obama*, ed. Julian Go (Bingley, UK: Emerald Group Publishing, 2011), 184–85.

35. Rhys H. Williams and Todd Nicholas Fuist, "Civil Religion and National Politics in a Neoliberal Era," *Sociology Compass* 8, no. 7 (2014): 932–33.

36. WNBC, *Bicentennial: A Black Perspective*, "A Man Named Douglas," July 4, 1976, 76032 BCT 1 of 1, PAC, http://dlg.galileo.usg.edu/peabody/id:1976_76032 _bct_1.

37. Ibid.

38. KING, *A New Birth of Freedom*, "Freedom of Speech," January 7, 1976, 76007 BCT 1 of 1, PAC, http://dlg.galileo.usg.edu/peabody/id:1976_76007_bct_1.

39. Ibid.

40. WSB, *Salute to America Parade* scrapbook, 1976, OS box 143, folder 76012 BCT, George Foster Peabody Awards Collection, Series 2: Television Entries, ms3000_2b, HAR.

41. Ibid.

42. WSB, *Blacks and the American Revolution*, entry form and transcripts, 1976, box 97, folder 76004 BCT, George Foster Peabody Awards Collection, Series 2: Television Entries, ms3000_2b, HAR.

43. Ibid.

44. Edward Smith, "Atlanta Celebrates the Bicentennial," *Carolina Times*, December 20, 1975.

45. Ibid.

46. Bicentennial Slogan Contest, box 21, WSB-TV and WSB Radio Records, Series 5, Promotional/Public Relations, HAR.

47. Khizr Khan, speech to the 2016 Democratic National Convention, abcnews.go .com/Politics/full-text-khizr-khans-speech-2016-democratic-national/story?id= 41043609.

48. Donald Trump, remarks in a joint address to Congress, www.whitehouse.gov/the -press-office/2017/02/28/remarks-president-trump-joint-address-congress.

49. CBS, *In Celebration of U.S.* compilation, July 4, 1976, Peabody Awards Collection, 76028 BCT 1 of 1, PAC, http://dlg.galileo.usg.edu/peabody/id:1976_76028 _bct_1.

SUSAN J. DOUGLAS

LOCAL TELEVISION NEWS
IN THE 1970S AND THE
EMERGENCE OF GAY VISIBILITY

Our common understanding of the representation of gays and lesbians in the media is either that they were relatively invisible until the 1990s, except for coverage of the AIDS epidemic, or that they were not explicitly identified as gay but given dialogue or mannerisms that coded them as gay. As the 1995 documentary *The Celluloid Closet* notes, gay people are "pathetically starved for images" of themselves. Additionally, gays and lesbians were typically cast, whether in films, plays, or news accounts, as tragic, sick, deviant, and troubled. In the news media in the 1960s, the typical news frame featured psychiatrists and other "experts" talking about homosexuality as a mental illness or "perversion" without featuring any interviews with or profiles of gays or lesbians. As Larry Gross points out, "Gay people were the least important sources of information and opinion about their own lives."[1] This is our understanding of LGBT representations prior to the 1990s and the rise of "gay visibility."[2]

However, the archives of the Peabody collection reveal another history in which various local television stations in the 1970s, in contradistinction to the three broadcast networks that were dominant at the time, did cover and contribute to gay visibility in their communities and thus may have played a more pioneering role in the politics of representation than previously acknowledged.

This chapter documents which television stations in the collection covered LGBT issues in the early 1970s and analyzes the nature of the coverage. Of course, the collection only contains programs from stations that submitted entries about this topic to the Peabody Awards, and there are admittedly only a few—my sample is eleven broadcasts—so it is an incomplete archive, and we do not know how representative it is. The entries primarily come from stations in New York, Los Angeles, San Francisco, and Minneapolis–St. Paul—progressive urban centers with more awareness of the gay liberation movement. I restricted my search to the period between 1969, the year of the Stonewall riots, and 1983, when coverage of the AIDS crisis began to take off and dominate coverage of the LGBT community.

I argue that the interaction between the social and media activism of the time, a new awareness of and sympathy for marginalized groups, the ongoing sexual revolution and its shucking off of 1950s sexual mores, journalists' desire for more cutting-edge stories, and, quite importantly, the FCC's local programming and ascertainment requirements worked together by the early and mid-1970s to bring about coverage on local television and radio stations not matched by that of the networks. In addition, there was a major change of frame in these stories; unlike in the 1960s, gays and lesbians got to speak for themselves, as subjects of their own lives, marking a dramatic and significant development in reportorial styles and representation.

By the late 1970s, however, with Anita Bryant's highly public and successful 1977 campaign to overturn antidiscrimination laws in Dade County, Florida, and elsewhere, an antigay backlash emerged, stoked by some local stations and challenged by others. Thus, this retrieved prehistory in the Peabody collection reveals that homosexuality was made visible and framed in different, often contradictory ways by local stations, often even in the same story. Some stories were progressive, others regressive, yet many of these stations did a much better job than the networks in giving voice to this emerging and transformative social movement.

THE REGULATORY ENVIRONMENT AND MEDIA ACTIVISM

It is crucial to remember that the regulatory environment was much different in the 1970s from the one that was effected by Mark Fowler and Ronald Reagan in the 1980s when they deregulated the FCC. The FCC's 1946 "Blue Book" on the public service responsibilities of broadcast licensees dictated that local radio stations had to include "discussions of public issues, programs covering religious, educational and civic matters," and local news in its programming. No quantity of time was specified, except that it had to be "adequate" and had to air during "the good listening hours." The FCC reiterated these principles in 1960, which now of course applied to television as well, emphasizing that broadcast stations had to meet the "public interests, needs, and desires of the community in which the station is located."[3]

Then, in 1971, the commission issued its *Primer on Ascertainment of Community Problems by Broadcast Applicants*, which gave detailed instructions on how to determine community needs. Stations had to develop an ascertainment procedure that would document the demographics of the station's market, identify "significant community groups," and hold meetings with them to "discuss community needs" and propose programming that would meet those needs. Documentation showing that this ascertainment process had been undertaken had to be filed with license renewals.[4] In 1973 the FCC stipulated that at least 10 percent of a station's programming had to be "nonentertainment," and in 1976 it further specified that 5 percent of programming had to be local programming and 5 percent news and public affairs.[5]

Thus, there was a unique pressure on local stations (unlike the networks) to determine what local needs and issues were and to show that they were meeting them or face possible FCC challenges to their licenses. Many stations found the ascertainment requirement onerous and pushed back against it until it was eventually abolished. But Steve Schwaid, a director of news and digital content at WGCL-TV in Atlanta, notes that ascertainment lunches (where they met with community leaders) were valuable: "You listened to what people were talking about and hearing, what they wanted to discuss. That gave you an idea of what the stories were. . . . The ascertainment requirement forced local stations to be in touch with their communities."[6]

In addition, a three-judge panel of the U.S. Court of Appeals for the District of Columbia in 1966 overturned an FCC ruling that had refused to let citizen groups participate in license renewal cases, holding that the public was entitled to have standing in such hearings. Thus, the court "expanded public access to the decision-making process," and as Allison Perlman documents in her book *Public Interests*, African American and feminist groups took advantage of the decision and filed petitions to deny license renewals on the grounds that certain stations underrepresented or discriminated against them.[7]

This regulatory environment enabled the robust media activism of the early 1970s led by firebrands in various social movements who charged that the media, and television in particular, were stereotyping and underrepresenting women and minorities and failing to live up to the FCC mandate that they serve the public interest. Feminists in cities began sticking labels on ads in public places like subway stations that read, "This ad is sexist." They took on National Airlines' whorehouse-inspired "Fly Me" campaign in which stewardesses in the ads cooed "I'm Cheryl, fly me" and "We make you feel good all over."[8] Peggy Charren, founder of Action for Children's Television in 1968, took on television's ceaseless hawking of sugar, crappy toys, and violence to America's kids. She successfully persuaded the National Association of Broadcasters to reduce the number of commercials on children's programming.[9] Maggie Kuhn and the Gray Panthers launched the Media Watch Task Force that monitored how older people were depicted—if they appeared at all—on the three networks.

In August 1977, the United States Commission on Equal Rights, prompted by much of this activism, released a damning report titled *Window Dressing on the Set: Women and Minorities on Television*, an indictment of the ongoing underrepresentation and stereotyping of women and minorities in the industry. All of these campaigns rested on the conviction that there was a direct relationship between media representations, government and corporate policies, and how people were treated in their everyday lives. In addition, many in the press, themselves prodded by movements for social justice and at a time when news coverage of these movements had an enormous political impact, came to see their mission as exposing the gap between the country's vaunted democratic principles and the reality of discrimination and inequality.

The Stonewall "riots," which we commonly consider to mark the birth of the modern gay rights movement, was surprisingly not a major news story. An account of the incident in June 1969 was buried on page 33 of the *New York Times* and was reported from the perspective of the police. A follow-up story on page 22 referred to the protesters as "youths," although the story did note that the boarded-up windows had graffiti that read "Support Gay Power" and "Legalize Gay Bars."[10] The *Daily News* coverage, a week after the event, appeared under one of the paper's typically snarky headlines, "Homo Nest Raided, Queen Bees Are Stinging Mad."[11]

Stonewall inspired the formation of the Gay Liberation Front and then the Gay Activists Alliance, and one of their main targets was the media, especially news coverage of homosexuality. They demonstrated against the *Village Voice* and staged a sit-in at *Harper's* in opposition to negative depictions and began to target the networks headquartered in New York City. The alliance also organized what it called "zaps"—small but loud demonstrations protesting antigay oppression at public events the press was likely to be covering. The goal was to get media coverage, which it did. According to Larry Gross, there were seven major protests between 1973 and 1978 against the networks and their portrayals, especially in entertainment programming, of homosexuality. Local news outlets were targeted as well, especially in cities like New York, Boston, and Philadelphia, and in 1979 activists formed the Lesbian and Gay Media Advocates, which set up a system of local media monitoring and in 1982 published a book *Talk Back! The Gay Person's Guide to Media Action*.[12]

It was within this context of increased media activism, the emergence of gay pride movements, and regulatory pressure that at least a few local stations began covering homosexuality and gay rights. Other scattered cultural and political events helped break the silence. Groups began to hold gay pride marches in a few cities like New York and Chicago in 1970. ABC in 1972 featured a movie of the week titled *That Certain Summer* starring Hal Holbrook and Martin Sheen as a committed gay couple. The critically acclaimed hit film *Cabaret* (1972) featured a gay male relationship, not to mention its sexually indeterminate master of ceremonies. By 1976, New York's public television station, WNET (channel 13), aired a live three-hour special called "Outreach: Lesbians and Gay Men" (not in the Peabody collection), which emphasized the "tearing down of lies" about the gay community.[13]

NEWS COVERAGE IN THE EARLY 1970S

A search of the Vanderbilt Television News Archive, whose collection of network news begins in 1968, produces no results for Stonewall.[14] I used the online search tool for the period 1968 through 1970 using the search words "Stonewall," "homosexuality," "gays," "gay rights," "LGBT," and "transgender." During this period the archives only collected the network news, and the first result one gets for the search word "homosexuality" is a fifty-second report from CBS in October 1969 about a government panel recommendation that laws forbidding "homosexual acts between consenting adults" be abolished. Aside from a four-minute piece on NBC in the spring of 1973 about a gay student group at the University of Iowa, the Vanderbilt collection indicates that there was no network reporting about homosexuality until April 1974, when, in a twenty-second story on both ABC and CBS, the anchors announced that the American Psychiatric Association had voted to remove homosexuality from its list of mental disorders. The other few reports between 1974 and 1977, most of them also quick stories, covered job and housing discrimination. Until Anita Bryant's antigay campaign, the story receiving the most network coverage was Sergeant Leonard Matlovich's unsuccessful effort to challenge his discharge from the U.S. Air Force because he was gay. It wasn't until Bryant's activism and the backlash it began to evoke in 1977 that the networks began covering gay rights and profiling a few gay men and lesbians and allowing them to speak for themselves. Thus, this sampling of the network news confirms the dominant narrative of general invisibility for the LGBT community in the nearly ten years after Stonewall and its linkage to deviance.

Yet a sampling of local television and radio news stories in the Peabody collection—a forgotten history—tells another more complicated story and reveals that some local stations began covering their LGBT communities in the early and mid-1970s, and not always critically or sensationally. (Because of space constraints, I focus only on television.)[15] Indeed, what is very surprising about the submissions in the collection is how deeply sympathetic much of this coverage was. But it wasn't always positive either, especially after Bryant's campaign gained traction. Conceptions of sexual fluidity and the language used to refer to people of varying gender identities has evolved enormously since the 1970s, but here I use the language of the times from the broadcasts to maintain historical accuracy.

Despite differences, of course, in emphasis, style, and approach, certain elements were common to many of the stories. Most assumed widespread ignorance about, fear of, and hostility toward homosexuality and often opened their pieces by asking what a homosexual is and how a person becomes one. The stories featured the standard journalistic routine of reporters enacting "objectivity" by interviewing those on "both sides," even though one side was typically represented by uninformed lay people or rank bigots. Some featured old-school psychiatrists who still maintained that it was a mental disorder (or ministers or cops who insisted it was a perversion and immoral), but many included psychiatrists who insisted there was no evidence that homosexuality was an illness or, in fact, abnormal. Because the stations interviewed gays and lesbians and let them speak for themselves, viewers heard about the difficulty, even trauma, of coming out, especially to parents. They also heard about bullying and harassment and outright discrimination yet also about people happy in their skin and satisfied in their work and relationships, which offered a stark contrast to the notorious *Boys in the Band* representation of gay men as self-loathing, miserable, and tragic people. Over and over, gay and lesbian informants insisted that they were just like everyone else, with the same hopes, fears, and desire for respect and love, a stance that was more homonormative than queer but that sought to blunt hostility in a still overwhelmingly homophobic society. There was more coverage of gay men than lesbians, virtually nothing on bisexuality, and one story about a trans woman. Most of the informants were white and middle or upper-middle class.

Most of the reporters positioned themselves and their stories as providing a vehicle for bringing together expert knowledge, the experiences of a marginalized group, and reportorial integrity to expose injustice. Ideologically, then, many advanced the then prevailing news value that the country (and the government) must uphold its democratic ideals and that it is problematic when it fails to do so by denying certain citizens equal protection under the law.[16]

An early local story notable for its efforts to combat negative stereotypes—and not from New York or Los Angeles—was *Coming Out* on WLAC, Nashville (a CBS affiliate, now WTVF).[17] In 1971, a man named Jerry Peck opened Nashville's first gay dance and show bar, Watch Your Hat & Coat Saloon. Peck then decided to establish the first national contest for the best female impersonators and held the competition at his bar in 1972.[18] WLAC documented the event and used it as a platform to explore homosexuality. As a saxophone—that signifier of sexuality—plays, and we see red neon bar signs and city night scenes, the reporter Denise Schreiner says "there is a segment of our society that is almost universally distrusted, criticized, and viewed with disgust. It is also a segment of our society about which the public has little knowledge and many misconceptions. It's the community of homosexuals; gay people." This opening introduces the oscillations between two standards of newsworthiness, sensationalism and education of the public, that runs throughout the piece.

The segment then cuts to the Miss Gay America Pageant, which Schreiner describes as a "manifestation of gay liberation" as we see men parading in drag. Schreiner then goes on to provide a brief history of attitudes toward homosexuality, from its acceptance in ancient Greece through the "dark ages," a period of "religious fanaticism" when homosexuals were thought to be cursed, up to Freud, who "frowned sternly on the condition."

Schreiner notes that in the past three years the gay rights movement has grown "nonviolently" and "is just beginning to touch Nashville." She then asks a doctor, who appears dressed in a white jacket, what exactly a homosexual is, and he explains simply that it's someone who "engages in emotional activity" with members of the same sex that ranges from kissing to "actual genital contact." One psychologist states that there's no evidence that any physical or mental "problem" causes homosexuality and that it is rooted in "early learning." Another doctor cites hereditary or metabolic "defects" as the cause and adds that there may be an inherited predisposition to homosexuality. The first doctor then asserts that there is no evidence that genetics or hormonal imbalance causes "this sort of problem." Although these experts use what would now be considered derogatory terms, their tone is surprisingly not condemnatory, and they even seem to be trying to naturalize homosexuality as something that just is.

The story then cuts to a series of interviews. A divinity student and counselor maintain that homosexuals are "people like everybody else; if you met them on the street you wouldn't know if they are gay or straight." This "normal, average" discourse is reiterated by other informants throughout the piece and is juxtaposed with that of a Baptist minister who asserts that homosexuals have "deviated from [what] God intends" and that "this kind of livelihood will ultimately destroy, it just takes them a lifetime to realize that." Although a cop who is interviewed says he believes these people are sick and charges them with violating the law and being "a nuisance to the public," the more normalizing discourse prevails, with the psychologist stating no homosexual he's ever treated has ever wanted to change, just as none of his heterosexual patients want to change.

In her interview with Miss Gay America 1972, reporter Denise Schreiner teeters between the iconography of sensationalism and the journalistic effort to promote understanding.

Schreiner then cuts to the pageant, noting that the event is not representative of "the entire gay culture" but that the growth of the movement is never as evident as it is there. The camera pans the truly gorgeous twenty-two contestants from sixteen states, showing them in evening gowns, singing, dancing and, yes, twirling fire-lit batons. When the winner, Norman Jones, identified by her stage name "Norma Kristie," is announced, she cries just like Miss America would, to the applause of others. When interviewed, she reiterates that most gay people are "just like you or anyone else." "Do people consider you a freak?" "I hope not, I try not to act as such." Here Schreiner is tipping on that seesaw between the iconography of sensationalism and the rhetorical, journalistic effort to promote understanding.

What for many viewers at the time would have been provocative imagery of gay men as cross-dressing "others" sits uneasily with the counterstereotypical and normalizing discourse Schreiner also evokes, especially as the story closes. She features one expert debunking people's fears about having homosexuals around their children, noting that heterosexuals molest children at a higher rate than homosexuals. Even the cop admits that they are "harmless." Despite this, one of the gay men points out that gay men constantly have to combat the stereotype that they "molest little boys." "You've met three people," Schreiner concludes, "who have talked candidly about their way of life; they all feel what is needed from society is understanding." Kristie insists that "we're just people, have to accept them as people, not what they do in bed, just accept people as people."

The log of praise and complaints the station submitted as part of its entry reflects the story's mixed reception, which included "waist [*sic*] of time," "trash," "ugh," and "bad show," but also "best damn program," "best news show," "very open show," and "needs to be shown again." Two of the experts, including the doctor, who submitted follow-up letters to the station, were concerned that while the show was sympathetic the focus on the drag queens was overly sensational and would reinforce the stereotype that gay men were "real weirdos." But the most moving response came from one of the men interviewed on the show who reported that a "mixed bar" of gay and straight people held a party to watch the program and that "it was packed and there were frequent cheers. Gay people were unanimously pleased," but they too questioned the focus on Miss Gay America as possibly trivializing.

But at the end of his letter the man revealed that the night after the show aired he got a phone call from a woman who had seen the show and said that she "needed to talk with me, tonight if possible." So he met with her, a middle-aged wife and mother who had come to realize that she was a lesbian and really needed help and support. He was able to put her in touch with a therapist and "some gay women who could give her some community." Because of the show "she was able to begin to identify herself." So even though the program did not feature any lesbians, it nonetheless deeply affected a woman desperate to come out.

This broadcast shows both how important it is to let gay men speak for themselves as well as the pitfalls. The emphasis on gays and lesbians being "just like everyone else" was crucial in countering stereotypes and fears, but it also undercut the often transgressive and revolutionary aspect of LGBT politics and lifestyles. Giving full voice to the queer persona of Norma Kristie did provide representation of the pleasures and iconoclasm of sexual fluidity, but also at the cost of reinforcing the very stereotypes—especially in 1972—that the LGBT community was seeking to overturn. Whether consciously or not, the piece did lay out the dilemmas, not just for TV news but for LGBT activists themselves, about which subjectivities should be salient in media representations, assimilationist or defiantly queer.

"The Gay Experience," an episode of *It Takes All Kinds*, a weekly thirty-minute television show from KNXT Hollywood (CBS owned and operated) in 1973, introduces viewers to "six very different people" who are "saddled with stereotypes" that may fit categories "but not people."[19] The men include an attorney, a self-employed landscape artist, a photographer, a psychiatrist, a third-year law student, and an artist, all gay, all professionals. There are no outside experts, doctors, ministers, or cops.

This is a deeply sympathetic and informative portrait about men being closeted and feeling scared and confused by their feelings when they were young. One man says he had his first feelings about other men when he was twelve: "It was something I didn't understand and didn't know why it was there." Another, who also discovered his sexuality in his teens and had a brief adolescent relationship, points out that it alienated him from his friends and left him feeling very guilty. Yet another explains that "it was a nightmare for me" because "I was carrying around this enormous secret about myself. . . . I felt like a freak." One notes the "cruelty" of feeling love arise in oneself yet knowing that that feeling puts one in serious danger.

They talk revealingly about how they coped: one says he assumed a tough guy pose to prove he wasn't gay because "it's the next thing to death, people knowing you're a homosexual." Various of the men describe how they struggled against being gay; they went to therapists (often at great expense) thinking they could be cured, but of course they couldn't. As one puts it, "I tried every single thing I could to try to get over being gay." The piece moves on to their struggles to finally accept who they were and then to come out, especially to family members. One man pointedly notes that when people ask him what makes him gay, he responds by asking them what makes them straight, adding that such a question is dangerous because "it's premised on the belief that there's something wrong with us." The men then itemize how they are oppressed: by religions that call them sinners, by the psychiatric profession that diagnoses them as sick, and by the criminal justice system that criminalizes their behavior. They then celebrate the diversity of the gay male community. As one explains, "The revolutionary thing is that it is quite possible being happy being gay." We have no data on the reaction to the program, but it is striking just in its simply letting the men speak for themselves. Audiences heard about their dilemmas and they powerfully contradicted the notion that being gay was "a choice."

In an episode from another show from 1974, *Moore on Sunday*, a "locally produced, weekly prime-time public affairs documentary magazine" that aired on WCCO Minneapolis (CBS owned and operated), the host, David Moore, acknowledges that his show generated a great deal of controversy, especially about social and moral issues. He explains that an episode that "explored some of the facts and myths around homosexuality" produced the "most violent viewer response" of any of the episodes that

had so far aired.[20] He describes the episode, which is titled "Karen and Cindy and Jack and Jim," as a "different kind of love story." Like *Coming Out* and "The Gay Experience," "Karen and Cindy and Jack and Jim" is a sympathetic account in which gays and lesbians speak for themselves. Moore shows footage of a gay marriage, highly unusual at the time, intoning that now the couple can live "happily ever after, unchallenged except by the Internal Revenue Service." Moore emphasizes that gays "are always discriminated against, threatened and called names." One man reports how he was sitting with his boyfriend when men at the table next to them began discussing whether they should shoot the men or just beat them up. The story shows the male couple having dinner, just like most couples, talking about coming out, and then, shockingly, walking through a park and stopping to kiss, where the segment ends. This is a stunning feature of the program, as one hardly ever saw a gay couple kissing on television then.

A 1974 episode of *Moore on Sunday* from WCCO in Minneapolis includes footage of a gay marriage.

The local NBC station in New York City in 1973 aired a documentary report hosted by Edwin Newman as part of its *New York Illustrated* documentary series titled "Homosexuals: Out of the Closet."[21] The collection does not have a copy of the program, but the print materials indicate that the show features "various leaders from the Gay Liberation movement who articulated their goals and beliefs." The report includes footage of a gay dance, a meeting of the Gay Activist Alliance, and a discussion session between local police and representatives of various gay groups. While I can't quote from the program, the fact that it headlines two gay activists and the editor of *Ms.* magazine suggests that it follows what by this time had become the new playbook of having gay people speak for and represent themselves.

THE POST–ANITA BRYANT TURN

Of course, not all stories were so enlightened, and after June 1977, when Anita Bryant succeeded in getting Dade County's antidiscrimination law overturned, coverage took the backlash against her activism into account, and some programs even promoted it. "Gay Rights, Who's Right," an episode of *Impact* from WBZ-TV (then an NBC affiliate) that aired in July 1977, opens with its host Paul Benzaquin explaining how homosexuality was once seen as "a dread disease, a loathsome perversion," whereas now it's "a condition, a choice."[22] Now, he adds, gay people want to "be accepted, known for this choice that they have made; they are demanding rights that they believe are theirs. Would granting them these rights threaten you . . . or your children?"

Benzaquin, in his efforts to air "both sides," traffics in provocative antigay stereotypes. He asks a panel of four psychiatrists whether homosexuality should be regarded as a "disease, an affliction, a disorder, or merely an alternate condition." One psychiatrist notes that the profession has gone on record saying that homosexuality is not a mental disorder, but another counters that it is an affliction that needs a cure. Benzaquin asks if it can be cured, to which one responds that it cannot and should not, while another argues that if the patient wants to be cured the doctor should try, adding that he has cured many. Yet all agree that homosexuals have been heavily stigmatized. Then Benzaquin moves on to the question of whether homosexuality is "a contaminant" on society, a suggestion that is roundly condemned.

Benzaquin then interviews a lesbian and a gay man, asking when they knew they were gay and whether they were "seduced into a homosexual condition," a question that horrifies the male respondent. Benzaquin admits "I'm right down to where Anita Bryant is right now, I'm worried about children, I'm worried about young people being so persuaded and swept off their feet," to which the lesbian replies that she doesn't know anyone who would try to seduce someone they thought did not want to be seduced. Benzaquin brings up "recruiting" and notes that "this is where most people find it difficult to find an accommodation with homosexuality." Because you don't "birth kids" who are gay (that is, he means homosexuals aren't born but made), gay people have to "seduce them" to "keep their numbers up." He then asks, "Are you diseased?," to which the gay man replies, "Of course I'm not diseased, . . . and to call it a disease is incredibly insulting and demeaning."

The question guiding the next segment is "should we allow people who are teachers to be gay in that kind of context with our children?" The panel addressing this issue includes a Catholic mother of six with a "strong feeling about homosexuality," a gay teacher, a lesbian mother, and a psychiatrist who rejects the notion that homosexuality is a "mental disorder." That the uninformed and bigoted Catholic mother is, in the interest of "objectivity," placed on an equal footing with the others illustrates the problematic false equivalencies of the "two sides" approach. When the gay teacher points out that he's no longer teaching high school, Benzaquin quips, "Well, then you're not a threat." Despite allowing gay people to speak for themselves and featuring psychiatrists contradicting stereotypes about homosexuals, Benzaquin privileges the Bryant-inspired homophobia that reasserted its hegemony in the late 1970s.

In May 1978, not quite a year after Bryant's success, WCKT in Miami (an NBC affiliate) aired a lurid ten-part investigative report titled *The Chicken and the Hawk* about young male prostitutes in Dade and Broward counties that reinforces the notion of gay men as sexual predators; they are the "chickenhawks."[23] Here two teenage boys, both runaways, talk about being picked up by men for sex in exchange for money or temporary shelter. The interviewer presses them, observing that "once they've used you [for their own pleasure] that's it." One boy says he really doesn't like having sex with men, but he needs the money, adding that his first homosexual encounter was with a married schoolteacher who gave him good grades and money in exchange for sexual favors. The other describes an older man who bought him a soda and then took him to the man's apartment and forced himself on the boy.

While there is no reason to doubt the veracity of these accounts, they once again buttressed the stereotype of most gay men as pedophiles who prey on unwilling boys and young men. The series goes on to describe Boy Scouts being made available to "out of state chickenhawks" and an account of boys at a private school who, instead of learning academic subjects, were allegedly taught "sodomy, fellatio, and pornography," which was accompanied by nude pictures of the boys with their faces and private parts blacked out. The next segment offers further exposés of child pornography (featuring more nude pictures of boys) and of sexual activity at a local bus station restroom where men have been arrested for "unnatural sexual activity between men and boys." The segment then turns to child pornography again, showing numerous images of nude boys that had been "seized by police."

These confiscated pictures and others like them are used again and again in the other segments of the series, making the program appallingly sensationalistic. The report then notes that some of the boys end up dead, as the Dade County medical examiner asserts that "20 percent of our homicides involve homosexual males" even though only 5 percent of the population is homosexual. The reporter fleetingly interviews a gay rights activist who warns that the series is going to provoke "a blanket condemnation" of homosexuals on the grounds that "we're all child molesters," even though "that's not true," but to no avail. At the close of the series, the white male on-air commentator returns to "the kinky world of male childhood prostitution" in which boys "take money from strangers to indulge their perversion."

In 1978, as part of the antigay backlash, California state senator John Briggs sponsored a ballot initiative that would have banned gays and lesbians and even those who supported gay rights from working in California's public schools. As the campaign heated up, Los Angeles station KCET (PBS) aired four programs examining Proposition 6 that featured Briggs, a profile of a gay high school biology teacher, and person-on-the-street interviews, including one with Cher.[24] While Briggs and an antigay radio preacher vehemently vilify gays as psychopaths and "sexually disoriented" predators in the program, the profile of the obviously dedicated, well-spoken biology teacher is so sympathetic as to make them seem hysterical. This is a series in which the "two sides" approach exposes the homophobes as bordering on berserk. Various prominent politicians, including Governor Ronald Reagan, opposed Proposition 6, and thanks especially to energized gay activism, it went down in flames.

Local PBS stations in particular seem to have resisted the post-Bryant backlash. St. Paul, Minnesota, was one of the cities that took up the Bryant campaign and voted in April 1978 to repeal its antidiscrimination ordinance. On its newsmagazine show *Electronicle* in October 1979, KTCA (PBS) in St. Paul examines this "sensitive and explosive topic" and the effects of the repeal.[25] In its profiles of gays and lesbians—a comedienne, a naturalist who taught biology to children, various gay rights activists, a singer—there is an enormous emphasis on their just-like-us normality. This is the only program I viewed from the collection that highlights the double discrimination that lesbians face as women and as lesbians, especially in the workplace. The program notes that since the repeal, harassment and violence against gay men in particular had increased (three gay men were killed in the city). Nonetheless, the gay activists interviewed vow to continue fighting the ordinance and note that since its passage misunderstandings between the gay and straight communities had decreased. At the end of the program, host Michael Boyle asks, "How many of our rights could survive a vote of the people?" In 1990, St. Paul's city council passed an ordinance making it illegal to discriminate based on sexual orientation.

A search for the period 1968 through 1970 in the Vanderbilt archives for the word "transgender" reveals no results; there were nine for "transsexual," seven of them being stories about the trans tennis star Renee Richards. But WCCO in Minneapolis, in 1983—decades before transgender

WCCO profiles Susan Kimberly, formerly Bob Sylvester, in 1983—decades before transgender people gained visibility.

visibility—profiled Susan Kimberly, formerly Bob Sylvester, identified as a transsexual woman.[26] This highly sensitive two-part series was way ahead of its time, especially as transgender identity was, particularly in movies, pathologized as deranged.[27] Kimberly was going through a transsexual medical program that required her to live openly as a woman for a year prior to surgery. When Susan started telling people about the sex change she expected the worst; she feared that "almost no one would understand," that she would "lose all [her] friends," and that she "would be the subject of ridicule."

But then we see friends and colleagues hugging her, including the former mayor who admits his "jaw dropped" when he got the news but adds that "Susan is a much more interesting person" and that she retains the strong qualities of "character, honesty and integrity" that she had when she was Bob Sylvester. The reporter notes the many adjustments Susan has had to make, including getting used to the fact that as a woman, she doesn't feel as important because people don't listen as much to her as they did to Bob: "It's much easier to get ahead as a man, to be listened to, to be taken seriously," Susan observes. She admits that she questioned whether she should go through with the transition but explains that it was "such a relief to stop lying." In the second installment we see her socializing with a group of friends; she confesses that she is "amazed" that people are still willing to remain friends with her and work with her. The former mayor says that Bob had gone through phases when he was lonely and depressed; "Bob was in a hellish kind of search," whereas "Susan knows who she is." Since childhood Bob had "felt like a little girl" and spent the next thirty years trying to deny his feelings, and hoped marriage would cure him but it didn't work; she describes movingly how hard it was to end her marriage because the relationship was so good. "After years of agonizing," the sex change was the only option that made sense. One friend says Susan is happier than Bob ever was, adding "I can't imagine a tougher decision anyone would make. . . . I've seen a sense of freedom in Susan."

It is hardly surprising that some local stations used the Bryant backlash to produce homophobic pieces that could serve as ratings' bait; what is surprising is that in this climate others doubled down in defying bigotry and continued to give voice to their LGBT communities.

In contrast to the programs produced by local stations that sympathetically cover homosexuality, "Gay Power, Gay Politics," which aired on CBS in April 1980, represents the rise of gay power in threatening terms even as it seems to let gay men speak for themselves.[28] The story opens with a gay man proclaiming, "Look out, . . . here we come!" Harry Reasoner, who anchors the show, was known for his disdainful coverage of the women's movement and sexist treatment of his coanchor Barbara Walters at ABC, and he brings a similarly derisive tone to this hour-long show.

Doing a stand-up in front of the Washington Monument, Reasoner announces that "for someone of my generation it sounds a bit preposterous, political power for homosexuals?" He states that the report will look at how the gays of San Francisco were using the political process "to further their own special interests." What we'll see, he explains, is the "birth of a political movement and the troubling issues it raises for the '80s, not only for San Francisco, but for other cities around the country." The report then cuts to a gay man on stage twirling a baton in a Superman costume as Reasoner intones that the message of the gay liberation movement is "come out of the closet"; homosexuals, he claims, also encourage other homosexuals to come to San Francisco where they can be "proud and powerful." Reporter George Crile asserts that the homosexual community in San Francisco had by that time "achieved full civil rights," which was no doubt news to many in the LGBT community, adding that now that they had so much power they were "moving provocatively into the political arena." When representations are rare, they carry extra burdens, and this one—on the eve of the AIDS crisis—is a shameful example of casting a movement for social justice as simultaneously trivial and dangerous.

CONCLUSION

In 1984, under the Reagan-Fowler FCC, license renewal guidelines that included ascertainment requirements were lifted for local television stations.[29] In addition, the requirement to offer a certain percentage of non-entertainment programming—locally produced documentaries, talk and public affairs programs—was eliminated, although stations were still expected to "provide programming responsive to community issues."[30] Also in the 1980s, stations' and networks' entertainment divisions no longer were tasked with "carrying" the news divisions; now news divisions were expected to generate their own profits. At many local stations, as we know, this led to more sensationalism—"news you can use" and "if it bleeds, it leads" journalism—instead of in-depth reporting about their communities.

Although the sample from the Peabody archive is small, it does nonetheless complicate the history of gay representations in the news media, especially on local stations. We see how the ingrained journalistic routine of showing "both sides" resulted in inclusion of cringe-worthy, bigoted commentary from interview subjects and even from the on-air talent. Nonetheless, in stark contrast to the network news, these stations covered the rising gay rights movement with considerable empathy and respected the subject positions of LGBT people, most of whom bore no resemblance to preexisting media stereotypes. Uninformed or prejudiced viewers of these broadcasts—whether their minds were changed or not—got to hear about gay people's own initial confusion about their sexuality and their struggles to come to terms with it and learned that homosexuality was not a choice. With the exception of the WBZ and WCKT reports, these stories truly sought to promote understanding and to expose the wages of ignorance and bigotry. That these stations did so is testimony to the power of media activism, especially as it interacted with the more self-conscious, entrepreneurial journalism that emerged in the age of Watergate. And these stories attest to the impact that prosocial regulation—the ascertainment process—however onerous and no doubt flawed, had on promoting greater community service among television stations that, in turn, gave voice to marginalized people who played a key role in the prehistory of gay visibility in the media.

NOTES

1. Larry Gross, *Up from Invisibility: Lesbians, Gay Men, and the Media in America* (New York: Columbia University Press, 2001), 31.
2. On the rise of gay visibility, see Suzanna Danuta Walters, *All the Rage: The Story of Gay Visibility in America* (Chicago: University of Chicago Press, 2001).
3. Heidi R. Young, "The Deregulation of Commercial Television", *Fordham Urban Law Journal* 12, no. 3 (1983): 378–81.
4. Ibid.
5. *Charting the Digital Broadcasting Future* (Washington, DC: Advisory Committee on Public Interest Obligations of Digital Television Broadcasters, 1998), 35, https://www.ntia.doc.gov/files/ntia/publications/piacreport-orig.pdf.
6. Steve Waldman, *The Information Needs of Communities: The Changing Media Landscape in a Broadcast Age* (Washington, DC: Federal Communications Commission, 2011), 281–82, https://www.fcc.gov/sites/default/files/the-information -needs-of-communities-report-july-2011.pdf.
7. Christopher H. Sterling and John M. Kittross, *Stay Tuned: A Concise History of American Broadcasting* (Belmont, CA: Wadsworth, 1990), 424–25; Allison Perlman, *Public Interests: Media Advocacy and Struggles over U.S. Television* (New Brunswick, NJ: Rutgers University Press, 2016), 65–73.
8. "Feminism, Impact of," *Ad Age*, September 15, 2003, adage.com/article/adage -encyclopedia/feminism-impact/98471.
9. Bruce Weber, "Peggy Charren, Children's Television Crusader, Dies at 86," *New York Times*, January 22, 2015.
10. "Four Policemen Hurt in 'Village' Raid, *New York Times*, June 29, 1969, 33; "Police again Rout 'Village' Youths, *New York Times*, June 30, 1969, 22.
11. Gross, *Up from Invisibility*, 41.
12. Ibid., 49–50.

13. Rebecca J. Rosen, "A Glimpse into 1970s Gay Activism," *Atlantic*, February 28, 2014, www.theatlantic.com/politics/archive/2014/02/a-glimpse-into-1970s-gay-activism/284077.

14. Although this has not been my experience, and it is impossible to know what is not in an archive, some researchers have found the Vanderbilt Television News Archive to be somewhat spotty or incomplete during this era.

15. I do not discuss the radio entries on this topic, but it is important to note that local radio also covered gay and lesbian issues. In October 1973, KDKA aired ten minidocumentaries over a two-week period during its evening news program titled *Ready or Not, Here's Gay Lib*, featuring interviews with gays and lesbians and gay acitivists. *Out of the Closet* on KNX in Los Angeles in 1974 focused on "the changing views of the 'gay' community" both by the general public and by law enforcement. In 1976 KFRC, a top forty station boasting 1.5 million listeners a week in San Francisco ran a thirty-minute documentary titled *The Gay Way* designed to "explain what gay means and what it's like to be gay." Given that the station estimated that "one-fifth of the population in San Francisco is gay," it's hardly surprising that it reported "listener response in favor of the program was overwhelming." KMOX in St. Louis aired a forty-two-minute documentary in 1978 titled *Homosexuality Means You're Different* that emphasized the fear and hostility many in the gay community experienced in St. Louis, a city they note did little to "help them adjust to their homosexual lifestyle." In 1982, WCCO radio in Minneapolis aired an hour-long documentary *More Than Just Friends* showcasing interviews with gays and lesbians and the "unique problems and discrimination faced by gay-identified Americans." ABC radio in New York broadcast a twenty-minute documentary in 1983 titled *Kids in the Closet: Gay Youth in America* examining what it's like to grow up gay. And KYW in Philadelphia in 1983 aired a twenty-part series titled *Gay in the 80's: The Pride and the Prejudice* in response to the increased attention being brought to the gay community by the AIDS epidemic.

16. Herbert J. Gans, *Deciding What's News: A Study of "CBS Evening News," "NBC Nightly News," "Newsweek," and "Time"* (New York: Vintage, 1980), 43–45.

17. WLAC, *Coming Out*, August 11, 1972, 72076 PST 1 of 1 Peabody Awards Collection, Walter J. Brown Media Archives and Peabody Awards Collection, University of Georgia (hereafter PAC), http://dlg.galileo.usg.edu/peabody/id:1972_72076_pst_1.

18. "Miss Gay America," Wikipedia, en.wikipedia.org/wiki/Miss_Gay_America.

19. KNXT, *It Takes All Kinds*, no. 4, "The Gay Experience," November 25, 1973, 73035 PST 2 of 3, PAC, http://dlg.galileo.usg.edu/peabody/id:1973_73035_pst_2.

20. WCCO, *Moore on Sunday* sampler, 1974, 74159 SLT 1 of 1, PAC, http://dlg.galileo.usg.edu/peabody/id:1974_74159_slt_1.

21. WNBC, *New York Illustrated*, "Homosexuals: Out of the Closet," February 11, 1973, 73053 NWT 1 of 1, PAC, http://dlg.galileo.usg.edu/peabody/id:1973_73053_nwt_1.

22. WBZ, *Impact*, "Gay Rights, Who's Right," July 26, 1977, 77057 PST 1–3 of 1, PAC, *http://dlg.galileo.usg.edu/peabody/id:1977_77057_pst_1-3*.

23. WCKT, *The Chicken and the Hawk*, May 1–12, 1978, 78008 NWT 1–2 of 2, PAC, http://dlg.galileo.usg.edu/peabody/id:1978_78008_nwt_1-2.

24. KCET, *28 Tonight*, Proposition 6 composite, October 22, 1978, 78033 PST 1 of 1, PAC, http://dlg.galileo.usg.edu/peabody/id:1978_78033_pst_1.

25. KTCA, *Electronicle*, no. 1, "Gay Rights," Ocotber 9, 1979, 79089 DCT 1 of 2, PAC, http://dlg.galileo.usg.edu/peabody/id:1979_79089_dct_1.

26. WCCO, Susan Kimberly profile, April 28–29, 1983, 83134 NWT 1 of 1, PAC, http://dlg.galileo.usg.edu/peabody/id:1983_83134_nwt_1.

27. See Andre Cavalcante, *Struggling for Ordinary: Media and Transgender Belonging in Everyday Life* (New York: New York University Press, 2018).

28. CBS, *CBS Reports*, "Gay Power, Gay Politics," April 26, 1980, 80128 DCT 1 of 1, PAC, http://dlg.galileo.usg.edu/peabody/id:1980_80128_dct_1.

29. Halfmanhalfamazing, "Ascertainment Requirements—The Precursor of Localism?," February 23, 2009, Free Republic, www.freerepublic.com/focus/f-chat/2192302/posts. It was Charles Ferris, the FCC commissioner under Jimmy Carter, who initiated this deregulation of radio in 1981 (Mark Potts, "FCC Vote Takes TV Step Closer to Deregulation," *Washington Post*, June 30, 1983, www.washingtonpost.com/archive/politics/1983/06/30/fcc-vote-takes-tv-step-closer-to-deregulation/9e1df352-72d5-4856-a192-c9ed68c67129).

30. Waldman, *The Information Needs of Communities*.

ALLISON PERLMAN

WATCHING TELEVISION
WITH OSSIE AND RUBY

In 1970, for the third year in a row, *Black Journal*, public television's flagship black public affairs series, was submitted for Peabody consideration. The series was an important corrective to how commercial television had addressed the black freedom struggle.[1] In segments on African American culture, politics, art, and history, in analysis of contemporary events that emphasized their impact on the black community, and in its embrace of black power and black nationalism as legitimate responses to racism in the United States, *Black Journal* both countered mainstream media's images of African Americans and decentered the white spectator as the imagined audience of television programming. It was one of many black power TV shows to circulate on public television in the late 1960s and early 1970s, when the noncommercial television sector provided a platform for African Americans to recast the terms by which American racism, politics, history, and culture should be seen.[2]

The 1970 episode held by the Peabody Awards Collection exemplifies this project, as it includes segments on the Organization of African Unity meeting in Addis Ababa, singer and activist Nina Simone, and black filmmakers Ossie Davis, Melvin Van Peebles, and William Greaves. Davis had just released his directorial debut film, *Cotton Comes to Harlem*, which he also had cowritten. The film was a box office success, and film scholars have praised it for its embrace of a black visual aesthetic, its interlocking of the African American past with its present, and its presentation of Harlem as a "complete world" rather than a sociological problem.[3] But in his interview with the journalists of *Black Journal*, Davis speaks of the racism of the film industry—especially its trade unions—and his own humiliation filming a movie in an African American area, in an African American vernacular, with a white crew. It is a segment both in keeping with Davis's own political commitments and with the orientation of *Black Journal* in general, as it reveals the interrelationships between the allocation of symbolic and material resources.

This appearance on *Black Journal* was but one small instance of a much more significant relationship between Davis, his wife and collaborator, Ruby Dee, and the public television sector. As materials in the Peabody Awards Collection illuminate, Davis and Dee—much like the television auteurs of black power TV—turned to public television because it allowed for black cultural production and, accordingly, an alternate visual economy of African American life, politics, and history. In their public television work, Davis and Dee centered black voices as authorities on the African American experience and on the material and psychic consequences of racism in their lives. In so doing, they insisted on the achievements of African American artists in a culture that too often had marginalized their contributions.

This chapter focuses on two series, *The History of the Negro People* (1965) and *With Ossie and Ruby* (1981–82). The former was a prestige series of National Educational Television (NET), which produced and distributed programs for noncommercial televisions stations throughout the 1950s and 1960s, and won a Peabody Award in 1965 as part of an institutional award honoring NET and its president, John White. A Peabody Award winner, *The History of the Negro People* exemplified NET's commitment to providing alternate perspectives on controversial topics. Hosted by Davis, who penned the third episode, "Slavery," the series disrupted the representational patterns that structured civil rights discussions on commercial stations by connecting the contemporary struggle to histories of oppression, framing the African American experience within an internationalist framework and underlining the diversity of the black experience domestically and globally.

With Ossie and Ruby was first produced by KERA-TV, Dallas's public television station and aired across public television stations nationally. An anthology series whose format and look varied based on individual episode content, *With Ossie and Ruby* showcased African American artists and intellectuals, past and present, inclusive of its eponymous hosts. As the episodes submitted for Peabody consideration attest, *With Ossie and Ruby* both countered the inclusive, assimilationist thrust of post–civil rights film and television and reconceptualized the parameters of "authentic" African American representations that had taken shape in the 1970s.

ARTISTS FOR FREEDOM: DAVIS AND DEE

Davis and Dee were two of the founders of the Association of Artists for Freedom. Formed in 1963 in response to the 16th Street Baptist Church bombing, the association aimed, in the words of writer John O. Killens, to declare "a cultural revolution the purpose of which would be to undo the millions of little white lies America has told the world about herself and the African-American; to de-brainwash black people in the first instance and all Americans in the second."[4] While the association was short lived, most known for its advocacy of a Christmas boycott in 1963, the goal of which was to privilege giving the "gift of truth" by facing the injustices that marred the United States, and for a 1964 forum discussion it organized titled "The Black Revolution and the White Backlash," its mission of cultural revolution well sums up the melding of artistry and advocacy that defined the careers of Davis and Dee.[5] It was a mission they initially pursued in theatrical performances and later brought to their television work.

While Davis and Dee's political activism took many forms—Emilie Raymond dubs them as two of the "leading six" celebrities who used their position to raise money for, and raise the public profile of, the civil rights movement—their cultural productions frequently served both political and artistic goals.[6] Davis and Dee participated in a tremendous number of fundraisers for civil rights causes, and the programs of the events themselves were important political interventions, as they included dramatic readings of the works of African American poets, novelists, intellectuals, and playwrights such as Frederick Douglass, Langston Hughes, Lorraine Hansberry, and Davis himself.[7] The programs thus had the dual function of raising money for civil rights activism and educating audiences in African American history and culture.

Davis and Dee long had been instructed in the pedagogical power of the arts. While, as Davis puts it in his coauthored memoir with Dee, he "was 'red' only when I thought it a smarter way of being 'black,'" both he and Dee were part of the left in Harlem during the 1930s.[8] During the height of McCarthyite red-baiting after World War II, Davis and Dee were allies of blacklisted left intellectuals and artists and were outspoken opponents of the political repressions of the period; Dee had publicly spoken out in support of the Rosenbergs, further placing her in the crosshairs of the postwar red scare. Finding themselves victims of what Davis described as both "Red Channels [and] Black Channels," restrictions rooted in political commitment and race, Davis and Dee turned to other artistic opportunities.[9] They joined forces with former members of the Group Theater to bring theatrical performances to unions, community centers, and places of worship; as performers in *The World of Sholom Aleichem*, Davis and Dee were trained in the precepts of method acting and further came to appreciate the power of theater to educate and entertain.[10]

During this same period, Davis and Dee were involved with Local 1199, a union representing pharmacy and hospital workers that after World War II, as Cynthia Young has demonstrated, forged a coalition between the Old Left and the Third World Left.[11] The union stood in solidarity with southern civil rights activists, and both raised money for the southern campaigns and began Negro History Week celebrations in the 1950s.[12] Davis frequently wrote original plays for these events, in which he and Dee would perform. Some of Davis's plays were analogous to the "living newspapers" crafted by the Federal Theater Project in the 1930s, as they dramatized current events—from the lawsuit filed in Clarendon County against school segregation, which would be one of the cases adjudicated in the *Brown v. Board of Education* decision, to the murder of Emmett Till, to a dramatization of the union-led strike at Montefiore Hospital—and drew from them broader lessons about the fight against oppression.[13] Davis also wrote plays for Local 1199 on African American history.[14] Davis and Dee recruited African American actors to perform with them at the Local 1199 events, and through his original short plays, Davis used his art to reframe core events, historical and contemporary, in such a way as to spotlight black resistance to the myriad facets of white racism.

Davis's breakthrough as a playwright came with *Purlie Victorious*, staged on Broadway in 1961 and adapted for the screen as *Gone Are the Days* in 1963. Inspired by the humor in *Sholom Aleichem*, *Purlie* was a broad satire of racial prejudice in the segregated South in which, as C. W. E. Bigsby observes, the "Uncle Tom, the Afro-American nationalist, the race leader, the civil rights worker are all gently mocked but at the same time achieve a symbolic victory over the forces of white oppression."[15] As Christopher Sieving astutely notes about *Gone Are the Days*, the play presumes an audience widely familiar with the southern black experience and events within the black freedom struggle, mocks the behaviors and customs imposed by the customs of Jim Crow, and telegraphs black nationalism as an appropriate response to them.[16] *Purlie*, Davis notes, is "the adventures of Negro manhood in search of itself in a world of white folks only"; it highlights the liberatory potential of black laughter, as it subjects segregation to ridicule and scorn.[17] Through *Purlie*, Davis further theorizes a relationship between art and politics by insisting that African American artists must abandon white standards and create truthful works for African American audiences, a practice dubbed by Davis as "revolutionary."[18]

When Davis and Dee brought their talents to television, they brought with them not only the fame they had acquired as accomplished actors of stage and screen and not only the bona fides they had earned as dedicated civil rights activists but also their commitments to a black cultural nationalism.[19] In these shows, they translated the work they had done in theaters and community spaces for public television and, in the process, reconfigured how the fight for racial justice could be waged on the small screen.

THE HISTORY OF THE NEGRO PEOPLE: SLAVERY

Davis and Dee had worked in television since the 1950s, acting in supporting roles in series and in anthology dramas, and they continued to appear on television for the rest of their careers. In addition, as the diversity of materials featuring them in the Peabody Awards Collection attests, Davis and Dee also served as hosts on local specials on black arts and culture, narrators of documentaries on African American history, and interviewees discussing topics related to black history and culture.[20] Yet it was in their collaborations with public television that Davis and Dee most forcefully reconceptualized how television could depict the African American experience and thus operate as a technology of black liberation. The first of these collaborations was the 1965 nine-part program *History of the Negro People*.

The *History of the Negro People* was a prestige program for NET, which spent well over two years researching and producing the series. NET heavily promoted the program and partnered with community groups, religious groups, and educational institutions to utilize the series for educational and community events, a practice that continued well into the 1960s.[21] While NET had aired shows on the black freedom struggle prior to the *History of the Negro People*, this program arguably represented noncommercial television's most significant contribution to that date—its flag in the sand—as to how it was to address racial injustice.[22]

While in the main, the series focuses on the United States, it dedicates two episodes to Africa and one episode to Brazil, and its final episode, a forum discussion titled "The Future of the Negro," addresses the myriad obstacles facing Africans and African-descended people globally. Thus the series places black history within an internationalist framework and resists, in producer Arthur Rabin's words, "facile analogies between the experience of other ethnic groups and the Negro."[23] Aesthetically diverse—the *History of the Negro People*'s episodes include documentaries, dramatic presentations, visual poems/literary works, and a forum discussion—the series on whole also depicts a diverse African American community—ideologically, socioeconomically, politically, culturally, regionally—and thus resists any monolithic view of black identity, community, or history. Throughout, the series also emphasizes the perspectives and words of black intellectuals, artists, and people, who principally serve as the voices of authority as to the causes, meanings, and impact of antiblack racism.

In this, the series operates not only as a reclamation of black history and black culture by black people but as a pedagogical space that centers African American thinkers in a medium that historically had rendered them marginal or invisible. This commitment was evident in the research phase of the series during which Rabin and his team assembled a team of consultants composed of African American historians of African and U.S. history, including William Leo Hansberry, Rayford Logan, John Hope Franklin, Benjamin Quarles, and Charles Wesley.[24] Significantly, the producers sought out the advice of these historians despite the prominence at this time of white historians conducting research in this field.[25] In addition to these scholars, the series' producers also conferred with a range of African American intellectuals and read widely in African American history and literature. In this, research for the series was diverse topically, generationally, and ideologically; the intellectuals and artists consulted included integrationists, nationalists, and radicals.[26]

Yet more than any other figure, Davis is identified with the *History of the Negro People*. His role as narrator, moderator, and star was heavily promoted in the press; the first page of the series' viewers' handbook quite explicitly identifies the series with Davis; when the series' producers received discouraging letters about the show, they often mentioned Davis's participation to legitimate its content; and Davis himself in 1967,

In the *History of the Negro People*, Davis addresses the Voices as surrogates for his primary audience of African American viewers.

in an address at Howard University, commented, "My most satisfying experience, even including the plays, has been a series I hosted and acted for NET, National Educational Television."[27] As host, Davis cut a very different figure from the white news reporters who typically narrated programs on the civil rights movement. Over the course of the episodes, he shifts between offering a dispassionate voice of authority and evoking his own experiences to inform the material of the episode, directly addressing the camera as he does so. Across these registers, Davis's narration is one of "we," not "they," which grounds the subjectivity of the series in the African American experience.

The entire series but most directly the episode he wrote, "Slavery," provided Davis an opportunity to do what he had been doing throughout his career to that point: connect black liberation to cultural nationalism. It was this episode that was submitted to Peabody for consideration for an award and is the sole episode located in its archive.[28] Davis composed "Slavery" from slave narratives collected in B. A. Botkin's *Lay My Burden Down*, itself drawn from the Slave Narrative Collection of the Federal Writers' Project. Davis and Dee star in the episode alongside the members of Voices, Inc., an African American musical group who sing and act in the episode but also frequently function as the immediate audience for the stories Davis and Dee tell. This aspect of the staging of the episode is important. The Voices are often audience surrogates, suggesting that Davis primarily addresses African American viewers, that he indeed regards African American viewers as his principal audience and thus situates white viewers as secondary spectators to what is unfolding.

The episode begins with a single female voice singing "Carry Me Back to Ole Virginny," a song that evokes a "moonlight and magnolia" nostalgia for antebellum plantation life. She is drowned out first by two, then four, then six vocalists singing "Oh Freedom," an anthem underlining the wish for liberation. It is an unsubtle metaphor for what is about to take place, a debunking of the Ulrich Phillips school of slave historiography, one that presented slavery as a benevolent, if unprofitable, institution that benefited enslaved peoples.[29] In its place, Davis's episode will emphasize myriad sites of slave resistance.

Though not marked out directly, "Slavery" progresses across three thematic sections: the first focuses on slave resistance through humor and folklore, the second on slave resistance through violence, and the third on slave resistance through support of the Union army. An intermittent voiceover provides facts that complement the substance of the slave narratives. During the first section, as the stories describe forms of everyday resistance to the economic and material degradations of slavery, the voiceover stresses slavery as an economic institution. During the second section, the voiceover details the harsh punishments meted out in response to slave revolts, while the stories tell of less organized forms of violent resistance. The final section only includes one voiceover, announcing the start of the Civil War, followed by celebratory stories about the Union soldiers and the war they won.

Many of the stories Davis chose for the first section are funny, their humor punctuated by the cast's laughter at the tales being told. They include tales that illuminate how enslaved people performed ignorance as a means of outsmarting their masters and that demonstrate how white institutions, most especially the church, could be used to instruct enslaved people in survival strategies. The final story of the section is delivered by Davis and focuses on a master that "almost starved his slaves to death." Seven of his hogs died of what the enslaved people labeled "malitis." The master ordered the hogs to be scalded and cut up, but he did not intend to eat them himself for "they had malitis, and he was scared." Instead, this would be the food provided for the enslaved people. "But the slaves didn't mind. Well, they know what malitis was. Early that morning, one of the biggest of them had skidded up to the hog pen, and knocked each one of them hogs dead in the center of their heads with a great big old mallet, and that's how them hogs caught malitis. That's how all the slaves had their bellies full of pork that winter, and old master didn't have none." This story shows how enslaved people capably capitalized on masters' low regard for their welfare to outsmart them and provide for their own basic needs.

This section of "Slavery" exemplifies Davis's embrace of what he labeled "the tradition of corrective and educational humor," a tradition he had embraced in *Purlie*.[30] Part of Davis's political project in his creative work was to "give back to the Negro people the humor they themselves created" and to restore its function as a mode of resistance. "Most of the stereotypes we know about Negroes," Davis writes, "were invented by Negroes for the purposes of survival and social correction. We do this all the time. It is a way in which a society tries to control its members. It will criticize its leaders. It will state its aims, through stereotypes, through jokes and humor. But our humor has been taken away, emptied of its bitter protest content, and has been used against us. And this has led us, sometimes, to rebel against our own humor."[31] These slave narratives restore the oppositional uses of humor and reveal it to be an intelligent survival strategy, one that savvily draws on bigoted perceptions of African Americans' inferiority to *resist* the degradations of enslavement. The episode thus reclaims black humor and highlights the political utility of black laughter as it recenters black voices in the history of slavery.

The episode, however, does not shy away from discussions of the violence of slavery. The middle section verbalizes two modes of violence, that enacted *on* and that enacted *by* enslaved people. Davis and Dee narrate stories of the brutal treatment of enslaved people who in asserting their humanity and resisting at critical moments their own subordination suffer terribly for it. In addition, they tell of enslaved people who violently resist as individuals, using the literal tools of enslavement—axes and hoes—to kill their oppressors. This section is followed by joyous accounts of the Union army arriving in the South and of the liberation of enslaved people by the war.

"Slavery" counters then-prevailing depictions of African Americans and African American history. Like the series on whole, it recognizes the violence of racial oppression without depicting images of suffering black bodies, is attentive to the power dynamics that oppressed African Americans without rendering them helpless victims, and emphasizes the collective experience of African American history without suggesting the existence of a monolithic community or singular response to historical circumstance. The episode also exemplifies Davis's fusion of his creative work and his political commitments. "Slavery" honors the experiences of enslaved peoples, told in their own words, and insists that to understand the history and culture of African Americans is to respect their authority to narrate the conditions of their own lives.

WITH OSSIE AND RUBY

Davis and Dee's most sustained work in public television came in the early 1980s with their series *With Ossie and Ruby*. Davis and Dee had had a weekly radio program in the mid-1970s called *The Ossie Davis and Ruby Dee Story Hour* that was broadcast across approximately sixty stations on

Davis and Dee introduce an episode of their anthology series, *With Ossie and Ruby*.

the National Black Network, which itself had only launched in 1973.[32] A variety show, the program celebrated African, Caribbean, and African American authors, featured interviews with African American celebrities, honored moments of black history, and sponsored a writing contest for short stories and poems, the winner of which would read his or her work on the air. A 1974 episode submitted for Peabody consideration, for example, includes a discussion with Davis and Dee's musician son, Guy Davis, about African instruments, an interview with musician and composer Lloyd Price, a history of the Kwanzaa holiday, recitations of poems by contemporary African poets, and an honoring of the anniversary of the death of George Washington Carver. As evidenced in the tag that introduces it as "your folklore, your poetry, your music," the program explicitly addresses an African American audience.

KERA-TV's general manager, Bob Ray Saunders, who had heard Davis and Dee's radio program, offered Davis and Dee the opportunity to do a public television program. Produced by Emmalyn II, a production company created by Davis and Dee with their children, *With Ossie and Ruby* was a thirteen-episode anthology series devised by Davis and Dee to highlight African American arts, culture, and history that ran for an initial two seasons.[33] In 1985, Davis and Dee produced an additional thirteen episodes of the series, though this time WHMM, the television station controlled by Howard University, would be the producing station.[34] *With Ossie and Ruby*'s premiere episode, oriented around the question of the meaning of life, showcased music, poetry, humor, and drama. Additional episodes included profiles of the poet Sterling Brown, a dramatization of Samm-Art Williams's play *Kneeslappers*, an episode dedicated to Dee's poetry and prose, a staging of Davis's early 1950s play *Alice in Wonder*, and a themed episode on the topic of love.[35]

KERA-TV submitted two episodes of *With Ossie and Ruby* for Peabody consideration, one for each season the station produced the show.[36] Both programs feature adaptations of short stories by African American authors. The first, originally telecast in February 1981, adapted two lesser-known short stories by Langston Hughes, "Thank You Ma'am" and "Sailor Ashore."[37] The episode on whole is a celebration of Hughes, as Da-

In this scene from a dramatic adaptation of the Langston Hughes short story "Thank You, Ma'am," Davis narrates while Dee subdues a young man (Kevin Hooks) trying to steal her purse.

vis and Dee also recite two of his most renowned poems—"The Negro Speaks of Rivers" and "Harlem"—and provide biographical details about Hughes during intervals between the two dramatic presentations. The entire performance was filmed in a theater in front of a live audience, which the camera periodically scans over during the course of the episode. Davis narrates the short plays, and Dee stars in them alongside the father-son acting team of Robert and Kevin Hooks.

Significantly, both of the adapted stories honor African American women's strength. In the first, Dee plays an elderly woman, Luella Bates Washington Jones, accosted by a young man (Kevin Hooks) looking to steal her purse. She physically subdues him, brings him to her home, feeds him, and provides him with money to buy a pair of shoes, which had been the reason he wanted to rob her. The adaptation hews very closely to Hughes's original story, save the young man's parting words of "Thank you, Ma'am," offered with tremendous feeling in the television show but left unsaid in the story itself. In both iterations, the young man had much more to say but was stymied by the emotion that his encounter with Ms. Jones elicited.

In the second story, Dee's Azora meets a sailor (Robert Hooks) in a bar and takes him home, where the two speak of racial discrimination rather than romance. The sailor is full of rage about the inability of black men to get ahead in a "white man's country." Azora dismisses his talk as not befitting a man and insists she will raise her own son to make something of himself when he is grown. When the sailor, feeling rebuked by Azora's slight on his manhood, gets up to leave, she stops him, admits that she had lied about her job and her son, but swears to the sailor that if she had a son, she would be "making something" out of him. The story ends with Azora reiterating this pledge.

Both stories begin with a public encounter between a black man and black woman that then transition to discussions within the private spaces of the women's homes. If the public encounters are defined by the men's aggression as thieves and pick-up artists, then the private ones reveal their vulnerabilities as individuals living lives of neglect ("Thank You, Ma'am") or of simmering resentment and despair ("Sailor Ashore"). The women play a corrective role in the stories. Both Ms. Jones and Azora acknowledge the feelings of the men, their desire for what they cannot have and the frustration of being black in a white supremacist society. Yet both women refuse to succumb to weakness, to criminality, to surrender, and they refuse to sanction these impulses in the men they meet. Both stories end with the men enjoined to grow up, to "behave," and to "make something" of themselves, and both stories end with women in doorways watching the men leave, themselves unable to articulate what the encounters have meant to them.

The second Peabody submission of *With Ossie and Ruby* adapted James Alan McPherson's story "A Solo Song: For Doc."[38] Unlike the Hughes adaptations, this episode was filmed on multiple sets and does not feature a live audience. Starring Davis as Doc, narrated by Roscoe Lee Browne, and adapted by Davis and director David Dowe, this story focuses on the fall of Doc Craft, an elderly railroad car waiter reluctant to give up his job despite constant pressure from his employer to retire. Protected by union regulations and privileged by his seniority, Doc was untouchable unless he failed to provide service in accord with company rules updated within the company's black book of regulations. The story culminates when Doc nearly impeccably serves company inspector Jerry Ewell (Anthony Zerbe) but neglects to incorporate a minor change in how waiters are to serve a wedge of lemon alongside iced tea. Defeated at last, Doc is pushed into retirement.

The episode, like the story from which it is adapted, is narrated by one of Doc's coworkers, told as a pedagogical tale to a "youngblood" who lacks the experience of rail service of Doc's generation. The youngblood misunderstands what the black book means and who its authors are; for the narrator and the generation he represents, the book both codifies the labor practices they themselves had created and simultaneously is a tool that undoes their authority over their own labor conditions. The youngblood is not a character who speaks in the story or who ever appears in the television adaptation; he is the "you" of the narrator's address, whose relationship to his work and to his forebears is imagined by the narrator himself. The youngblood is someone who must be schooled about what it meant to be a "waiter's waiter," as Doc and the narrator had been, and to be edified by the parable of Doc's end and the forces that led to it.

Doc and the narrator are contrasted with a younger waiter (Bill McGhee), who laments that black waiters have lost their humility and bids Doc to submit to the will of the company. His servility serves as a foil to

Doc's dignity, his eagerness to placate standing in marked contrast to the autonomy of a "waiter's waiter" like Doc. It is a theme underlined by Davis's performance and by the differences between his Doc on and off the train. Doc is introduced in the television adaptation as a sloppy drunkard, hustled by barflies who take advantage of his compromised state. In these scenes, Davis as Doc slurs his words and is loose limbed and easy with a laugh. Doc on the train, however, is meticulously outfitted in his uniform, elegant in every step and gesture, his voice controlled and precise. When Ewell catches Doc in a mistake, his posture collapses, as he sits hunched over across from Ewell, the pride he had displayed in his erect bearing unspooled by the trap in which he was caught.

There are no black women in the adaptation to "A Solo Song: For Doc," only references to "whores" frequented by rail waiters. Work on the train was a man's world, and Doc's story is a lament for the erosion of a particular articulation of black manhood rendered anachronistic not only by changes in the opportunities for black workers—here defined by the decline of train travel—but in the changes, punctuated by the story's address to "youngblood," in the self-definition of the black working class itself.

Both Peabody episodes interrogate pressures on black manhood. They focus on characters grappling with maintaining or acquiring dignity in the face of conditions that would deny it to them. They are not stories of characters seeking integration or white acceptance, nor are they tales of overcoming and success. They are narratives in which white people are peripheral yet the impacts of white racism quite palpable. The episodes acknowledge the material and psychic consequences of discrimination but refuse the spectacle of physical suffering. They address the possibilities of solidarities among black people, while affirming how differences in gender, generation, and status can hinder them. Accordingly, the series implicitly refuses the colorblind rhetoric ascendant in the post–civil rights era and challenges its dominant representational practices on commercial television, which often offered narratives of reassurance of interracial harmony between black and white characters.

With Ossie and Ruby furthermore expands the notion of "authentic" black culture that had taken root in the previous decades, one that had shifted from an emphasis on southern African Americans marred by the violences of Jim Crow to the "brothers on the block," the northern lumpen-proletariat who lived in segregated urban spaces. If, as Amy Obugo Ongiri has argued, the valorization of the "brothers on the block" informed the cultural politics of the black power era within film and music, it also informed the "ghetto-centric" sitcoms of the 1970s and their appeal to relevance in the construction of their black characters.[39] Much as had the *History of the Negro People*, *With Ossie and Ruby* rejects a monolithic vision of African American identity and refuses to privilege a particular expression of black identity within its episodes.

CONCLUSION

If, as Manthia Diawara has asserted, "popular culture always has been where Black people theorize Blackness in America," the noncommercial television sector intermittently has offered a platform for African Americans to control the terms of their representation.[40] In the late 1960s and early 1970s, for example, public television stations circulated programming produced by and for African Americans, shows that made visible a range of strategies—political and cultural—for black liberation.[41] *Eyes on the Prize*, Henry Hampton's fourteen-part history of the civil rights movement, also has been hailed for its reframing of African American history. Across its episodes, which originally aired on PBS in the late 1980s and early 1990s, the series notably privileged the voices of movement participants, recuperated the role of on-the-ground activists whose labor was key to the movement's successes, and recalibrated nonviolence as a tactic rather than inherent moral good.[42] Marlon Riggs's *Tongues Untied*, telecast in 1989, brought to the fore a segment of the African American community ignored or derided in other sites of popular culture in its poetic interrogation of the lives of gay black men.[43] These public television texts reconceptualized how African Americans were to be depicted on the small screen and challenged constructions of African American history and identity circulating in other sites of culture.

The *History of the Negro People* and *With Ossie and Ruby* further illuminate the role of public television as a site of black authorship. Though produced in different periods in the development of noncommercial U.S. television, in dialogue with different commercial TV representational practices, and against the backdrop of different sociohistorical circumstances, both series exemplify Davis and Dee's lifelong commitment to melding their political commitments and their artistic work. The *History of the Negro People* and *With Ossie and Ruby* illustrate how public television enabled artists like Davis and Dee to change how African American history, culture, and politics were depicted on television: both programs avoid spectacular displays of suffering as key to moral suasion, emphases on interracial cooperation and integration as symbolic ameliorations of real-world divides, constructions of African American comedy divorced from its liberatory origins, and notions of authenticity tethered to particular expressions of African American identity.

These programs, importantly preserved in the Peabody Awards Collection, thus expand how we script the relationship between television history and the long-standing struggle for civil rights in the United States. Responding to a medium that often has pictured racial justice through the lens of colorblind liberalism, privileged white perspectives on questions of racial inequality, and marginalized African Americans as actors in their own history, Davis and Dee's television programs emphatically re-centered African American perspectives and told stories of resistance and resilience, of oppressions both tangible and immaterial, of a commonality of experience of racism that contained within it a diversity of responses. *The History of the Negro People* and *With Ossie and Ruby* attest to how, for artists and activists like Davis and Dee, public television could aid in the mission, in Killen's phrase, of cultural revolution, one that hinged on a necessarily pedagogical project of illuminating the power of black voices.

NOTES

1. See Devorah Heitner, *Black Power TV* (Durham, NC: Duke University Press, 2013), Tommy Lee Lott, "Documenting Social Issues: *Black Journal*, 1968–1970," in *Struggle for Representation: African American Documentary Film and Video*, ed. Phyllis R. Klotman and Janet K. Cutler (Bloomington: Indiana University Press, 1999), 71–98, Laurie Ouellette, *Viewers Like You? How Public TV Failed the People* (New York: Columbia University Press, 2002), 131–37, and Christine Acham, *Revolution Televised: Prime Time and the Struggle for Black Power* (Minneapolis: University of Minnesota Press, 2004), chapter 2.

2. See Heitner, *Black Power TV*, and Gayle Wald, *It's Been Beautiful: "Soul!" and Black Power Television* (Durham, NC: Duke University Press, 2015).

3. Vivian Halloran, "The 'Black Enough' Visual Aesthetic in *Cotton Comes to Harlem*," in *Beyond Blaxploitation*, ed. Novotny Lawrence and Gerald R. Butters Jr. (Detroit, MI: Wayne State University Press, 2016), 21–40; Melvin Donalson, *Black Directors in Hollywood* (Austin: University of Texas Press, 2003), 25–29; Paula Massood, *Black City Cinema: African American Urban Experiences in Film* (Philadelphia: Temple University Press, 2003), chapter 3.

4. John O. Killens, "The Artist and the Black University," *Black Scholar* 1, no. 1 (1969): 61. Other members included Max Roach, James Baldwin, Louis Lomax, and Odetta.

5. "The Artists and Writers Explain Their Xmas Boycott," *New York Amsterdam*

News, November 6, 1963, 24; "Black Revolution and White Backlash," *National Guardian*, July 4, 1964, 5–9.

6. Emilie Raymond, *Stars for Freedom: Hollywood, Black Celebrities, and the Civil Rights Movement* (Seattle: University of Washington Press, 2015), ix.

7. Box 1, folders 32–34, of the Ossie Davis and Ruby Dee Papers, Schomburg Center for Research in Black Culture, contain multiple flyers of fundraisers starring and created by Davis and Dee.

8. Ossie Davis and Ruby Dee, *With Ossie and Ruby: In This Life Together* (New York: HarperCollins, 1998), 117.

9. Ossie Davis, "Address at the Palm Gardens," in *Life Lit by Some Large Vision: Selected Speech and Writings, Ossie Davis*, ed. Ruby Dee (New York: Atria, 2006), 4–5.

10. Davis and Dee, *With Ossie and Ruby*, 240–43.

11. Cynthia Young, *Soul Power: Culture, Radicalism, and the Making of a U.S. Third World Left* (Durham, NC: Duke University Press, 2006), 55.

12. Leon Fink and Brian Greenberg, *Upheaval in the Quiet Zone: A History of Hospital Workers' Union Local 1199* (Urbana: University of Illinois Press, 1989), 113.

13. Young, *Soul Power*, 84–85.

14. Ossie Davis, "Negro History Week," Ossie Davis and Ruby Dee Papers, box 1, folder 29, Schomburg Center for Research in Black Culture.

15. C. W. E. Bigsby, "Three Black Playwrights: Loften Mitchell, Ossie Davis, Douglas Turner Ward," in *The Theatre of Black Americans: A Collection of Critical Essays* (Montclair, NJ: Applause Theater and Cinema Books, 1980), 156.

16. Christopher Sieving, *Soul Searching: Black-Themed Cinema From the March on Washington to the Rise of Exploitation* (Middletown, CT: Wesleyan University Press, 2011), 21–22, 34–38.

17. Ossie Davis, "Purlie Told Me," in *Life Lit by Some Large Vision*, 88, 89. This essay was originally published in *Freedomways* in spring 1962.

18. Ibid., 92.

19. See James Smethurst, *The Black Arts Movement: Literary Nationalism in the 1960s and 1970s* (Chapel Hill: University of North Carolina Press, 2011), 17.

20. For example, Davis and Dee hosted a local Philadelphia special on black arts and culture (*Now Is the Time*), narrated a PBS documentary about Mississippi civil rights struggles (*Mississippi, America*), and performed in an NBC miniseries about Martin Luther King Jr. (*King*).

21. See, for example, letters in National Educational Television Records, 1951–69, subseries 7B, box 7, folder 2, Wisconsin Historical Society.

22. Other shows in this vein aired by NET included *Take This Hammer*, *The Negro and the American Promise*, and *Louisiana Diary*.

23. *History of the Negro People: Viewer's Handbook* (New York: National Educational Television, 1965), 5.

24. Memo from Arthur Rabin to John White, October 26, 1964, National Educational Television Records, 1951–69, subseries 8D, box 46, folder 5, Wisconsin Historical Society.

25. August Meier and Elliott Rudwick, *Black History and the Historical Profession, 1915–1980* (Urbana: University of Illinois Press, 1986), 136–37.

26. Consultants included Sterling Brown, Lorraine Hansberry, Roy Wilkins, Joel Rogers, and Kenneth Clarke. Furthermore, the producers conducted extensive research, reviewing a number of newspaper and magazine articles on the southern civil rights campaigns, racial divides in the United States, and conditions in African countries as well as James Baldwin's *The Fire Next Time*, articles and poetry from the journal *Freedomways*, John Henrik Clarke's *A Curriculum Guide to the Study and Teaching of Afro-American History*, an excerpt from Carter Woodson's *Education of the Negro Prior to 1861*, Howard Thurman's *Deep River: Reflections on the Religious Insight of Certain of the Negro Spirituals*, and Margaret Just Butcher's *The Negro in American Culture*.

27. Richard L. Coe, "Ossie Davis Find a Mine," *Washington Post*, June 3, 1967, D12. Letters criticizing the program can be found in National Educational Television Records, 1951–69, subseries 8D, box 8, folder 19, Wisconsin Historical Society.

28. WNET, *History of the Negro People*, no. 3 "Slavery," October 26, 1965, 65021 EDT 1 of 1, Peabody Awards Collection, Walter J. Brown Media Archives and Peabody Awards Collection, University of Georgia (hereafter PAC), http://dlg.galileo.usg .edu/peabody/id:1965_65021_edt_1.

29. For a discussion of the historiography on slavery in the United States, see Meier and Rudwick, *Black History and the Historical Profession*, chapter 4.

30. Ossie Davis, "The Wonderful World of Law and Order," in *Life Lit by Some Large Vision*, 106.

31. Ibid., 109.

32. Frank W. Johnson, "A History of the Development of Black Radio Networks in the United States," *Journal of Radio Studies* 2, no. 1 (1993): 178–79.

33. Davis and Dee, *With Ossie and Ruby*, 384–86.

34. Ibid., 391.

35. James Brown, "'Ossie and Ruby' Makes Bow on PBS," *Los Angeles Times*, February 13, 1981, H23; John J. O'Connor, "TV Weekend: Black Experiences and Insights on Art," *New York Times*, February 13, 1981, 66; "Variety TV Series on KCET," *Los Angeles Sentinel*, May 4, 1981, B6; Clarke Taylor, "Ruby Dee Tries to Open Doors to Black Artists," *Los Angeles Times*, May 27, 1982, K1, K13.

36. KERA, With Ossie and Ruby, "Two From Langston," February 21, 1981, 81050 ENT 1 of 1, PAC, http://dlg.galileo.usg.edu/peabody/id:1981_81050_ent_1; KERA, With Ossie and Ruby, "A Solo Song for Doc," May 18, 1982, 82075 ENT 1 of 1, PAC, http://dlg.galileo.usg.edu/peabody/id:1982_82075_ent_1.

37. Both stories can be found in *The Collected Works of Langston Hughes*, vol. 15: *The Short Stories*, ed. R. Baxter Miller (Columbia: University of Missouri Press, 2002), 193–97 ("Sailor Ashore"), 299–302 ("Thank You, Ma'am").

38. James Alan McPherson, "A Solo Song: For Doc," in *Hue and Cry* (Boston: Little, Brown, 1968), 41–73.

39. Amy Obugo Ongiri, *Spectacular Blackness: The Cultural Politics of the Black Power*

Movement and the Search for a Black Aesthetic (Charlottesville: University of Virginia Press, 2009), 19.

40. Quoted in Ongiri, *Spectacular Blackness,* 18.

41. See especially Heitner, *Black Power TV,* and Wald, *It's Been Beautiful.*

42. Jon Else, *True South: Henry Hampton and "Eyes on the Prize": The Landmark Television Series That Reframed the Civil Rights Movement* (New York: Viking, 2017); Elizabeth Amelia Hadley, *"Eyes on the Prize*: Reclaiming Black Images, Culture and History," in *Struggle for Representation: African American Documentary Film and Video,* ed. Phyllis R. Klotman and Janet K. Cutler (Bloomington: Indiana University Press, 1999), 99–121; Jennifer J. Asenas, "The Political Efficacy of Nonviolence in *Eyes on the Prize*: Creating Activist, Complicating Tactics," in *American Multicultural Studies: Diversity of Race, Ethnicity, Gender and Sexuality,* ed. Sherrow O. Pinder (Thousand Oaks, CA: Sage, 2013), 85–100.

43. Rodger Streitmatter, "*Tongues Untied*: African-American Men Take the Spotlight," in *Queers in American Popular Culture,* ed. Jim Elledge (Santa Barbara, CA: Praeger, 2010), 123–38.

PART 3

REVISITING NEWS AND PUBLIC SERVICE
LOCAL COMPARISONS AND OUTLIERS

DEBORAH L. JARAMILLO

TV'S WAR ON DRUGS

LOCAL CRISES AS PUBLIC SERVICE CRUSADES

Fictionalized representations of the War on Terror and of various drug wars have shared screen time recently, and their overlap invites comparisons. At the center of both subgenres is a heavily armed, stateless enemy that neutralizes the efficacy of conventional wartime tactics and forces civilian and government actors to adapt. Circulating around this center are compromised heroes, general corruption, confusion, trauma, hopelessness, and death. A series like *Narcos* (Netflix, 2015–present), with its explicit, if abbreviated, critique of U.S. involvement in Latin America, constructs 1980s Colombia as a battlefield and introduces atrocity photographs and news footage as evidence. These still and moving images slot in comfortably beside *Homeland* (Showtime, 2011–present) and other contemporary representations of the multiple battlefields that have devastated communities since the U.S. invaded Iraq in 2003. The stylistic and thematic slippages between two ostensibly distinct types of war narrative remind us of the weight placed on TV news as a primary source.

TV news establishes discursive and audio-visual parameters around events that affect the world, the nation, and the viewer at home. These parameters can vary from region to region because local news, unlike national network news or cable news, has a responsibility to its community. By law, an unspecified amount of broadcast programming should serve the public interest. The public interest mandate compounds the indexical burden that TV news bears, and different stations interpret and articulate that mandate in different ways. It is safe to assert that the TV stations that submit their news programs and documentaries to the Peabody Awards believe their materials serve the public, so we can gain insight into how these stations understood that public service mission by analyzing these materials. To that end, this chapter focuses on ten programs in the Peabody Awards Collection about the so-called War on Drugs in the United States. All of these programs were submitted in the 1980s as the proliferation of crack, in particular, attracted national scrutiny. Eight of the programs I analyze were produced by local television stations around the country, one was distributed by a national network, and the last was distributed by a premium cable channel.

The submission categories of these programs vary. Some were submitted as news, some as public service, and some as documentary. The programs' thematic consistency renders these categories fluid. The programs' shared frame is their focus on a specific geographic place and community. Attention to the local dominates, but, significantly, the programs do not define the local exclusively as rural areas invaded by urban vice. Because their goal was to stress the scope of the drug problem, they allow the urban to join the rural in the category of local. Odessa, Texas, and Brooklyn, New York, were equals as communities and homes.

This chapter examines how the programs found in the Peabody collection construct the local, and how these constructions, in turn, define public service in multiple ways. I also explore the programs' stylized approaches to a crisis couched within the semantics of war. In a larger sense, I am interested in how the Peabody Awards as a signifier of worthwhile and important television operates as a framing device. Even though these programs were not winners, their presence in the Peabody archive is a meaningful marker of the producers' ambitions or their feelings about the quality of the program that they felt deserved recognition. In other words, this is an archive created not by the Peabody Awards but by the initiative of television makers eager for a shot at prestige. In believing they could be the best at their mission, the producers of the ten programs analyzed here inserted themselves into an ongoing dialogue about important TV.

MEDIATING THE WAR ON DRUGS IN THE 1980S

Moral and national panic about drugs predated Ronald Reagan's presidency, but President Reagan was the first to declare drug trafficking a matter of national security. In April 1986 Reagan signed National Security Decision Directive 221, which paved the way for what Ted Galen Carpenter describes as the administration's three-pronged attack on the supply of drugs entering the United States from Latin America: "drug-crop eradication projects, the interdiction of drug-trafficking routes, and crop substitution programs."[1] The George H. W. Bush administration sustained this focus on supply. Disregarding U.S. demand (and U.S. production), it created the Office of National Drug Control Policy, which did little to alleviate the deteriorating situation in the United States, as both production and consumption continued without much federal support for local law enforcement or local drug treatment strategies.

Three studies of the mediation of the Reagan and Bush administrations' war on drugs reveal how print journalism, television, and film sustained official narratives often through the use of racialized, gendered, and nationalistic frames. William N. Elwood's *Rhetoric in the War on Drugs: The Triumphs and Tragedies of Public Relations* (1994) studies print media coverage and argues that the war on drugs was a "public relations triumph" because the news media regurgitated the official language and interpretation of the war.[2] The fact that print journalism adopted the "war" frame in the first place created "expectations of winning strategies," manufactured and maintained organized enemies (primarily African American men and immigrants) in inner cities, and barred legitimate discussion of legalization and rehabilitation.[3]

Jimmie L. Reeves and Richard Campbell's *Cracked Coverage: Television News, the Anti-Cocaine Crusade, and the Reagan Legacy* (1994) uses network news coverage from 1981 to 1988 as its sample. The authors argue that a multifaceted "cocaine narrative" emerges from the 270 reports they analyzed.[4] The narrative clings to the cultural flashpoints of Reaganite politics. According to Reeves and Campbell, "the meaning of cocaine would be inflected by gender issues, it would take on racial overtones, and it would even animate myths about the sanctity of small-town life in middle America."[5] Both *Rhetoric in the War on Drugs* and *Cracked Coverage* underscore the news media's attachment to the moral failing of drug users. Reeves and Campbell attribute the creation of this narrative to the peculiar circumstances of news "packaging" and the "self-regulating system of communication."[6] They do not argue that the news offers one consistent, coherent narrative. Yes, the news is interested in "ordering the clashing voices of culture" in the pursuit of "consensus," but it cannot help but address "multiple realities," thus challenging dismissive generalizations of coverage that ignore the tensions at work within it.[7]

Finally, Camille Fojas's *Border Bandits: Hollywood on the Southern Frontier* (2008) critiques the representation of the war on drugs in films and television series. Fojas states that the crusade the Reagan and Bush administrations fed to the news was "support[ed] and extend[ed]" by Hollywood through a process of strong viewer identification.[8] In these texts the viewer as "'narc hero' is characterized by his or her deeply 'American' values of righteousness, enterprise, autonomy and initiative."[9] Fojas's analysis dovetails with Elwood's assessment of the Reagan and Bush administrations' different approaches to heroism. Whereas Reagan's heroes were "opinion leaders" and elites, Bush's heroes were "ordinary citizens" who could fight drugs on the local level without the help of big government.[10] The abundance of Latin American villains in Fojas's case studies underscores the two administrations' attention to international supply rather than domestic demand.

Each study contributes to a consequential discussion of the ways in which different media grapple with their own institutional constraints in the creation of stories, real or fictional. Absent from these studies, though, are locally produced artifacts (not distributed by national outlets) that assess the impact of drugs on their own communities. Because the Peabody Awards welcome local and national radio and television submissions, its archive is a vital repository for treatments of the local *and* the national and the work of a self-selected register of supposed quality.

ARTICULATING THE PUBLIC SERVICE MISSION

The Peabody Awards submission guidelines define public service programs as works "that address or respond to an important public problem or issue."[11] The documentary category overlaps with public service; these programs are "in-depth examinations of local, national, or international issues and/or of contemporary or historic events."[12] Even though not all the programs studied here were submitted in the public service category, all evince a public service mission in their submission forms. *Drug Wars: One Nation under Siege* (1983) from Jacksonville, Florida, station WJXT emphasized its "comprehensive look at the government's war on drugs," spanning production, distribution, consumption, and law enforcement.[13] *Inside Boston's Heroin Trade* (1985) from Boston and *Street Drug Wars* (1989) from New York City each put a community's drug crisis under the microscope. Instead of examining the problem at the level of the city, both programs opted to use neighborhoods as their units of analysis. WCVB's submission form highlighted the station's "rare investigation" that followed children, users, and police in Boston's Roxbury neighborhood.[14] WCBS underscored that its submission was a call to action. The six-part series delved into nine square blocks in the Bushwick neighborhood in Brooklyn and argued "that only when the non-drug world becomes concerned with the drug crisis, can further damage to the fabric of the community be reduced."[15] *War on Crack* (1986), also from WCBS, was the station's own declaration of war. To "curb the use of this dangerous drug" in its community, WCBS produced this documentary and, according to its submission form, installed it in a van that traveled around the metro area.[16] *Kids' Summit on Drugs* (1989) from KABC in Hollywood, California, focused specifically on educating children in a public forum with sports figures, celebrities, businessmen, and city and state officials. KABC-TV submitted the program as evidence that the station had "taken an active role in school drug education programs."[17] *Drugs: The Boom They Can't Bust* (1988) from San Francisco emphasized community involvement; KRON's submission form mentions that the station followed its program with a "live hour-long town meeting at the station with a studio audience."[18] Although a tape of the meeting was not submitted with the program, its mention in the form presumably supported the station's commitment to interactivity and public engagement. In contrast to other submissions I investigated, which highlighted educational service, *City under Siege* (1989) from WTTG in Washington, DC, located public service in authority, surveillance, and policing. The station wanted to "stop just reporting . . . and get involved as an ACTIVE force in the community."[19] The program offered the "latest information on the war on drugs" and provided viewers with a hotline through which they could reach either the police or drug counselors. Similarly, *Crack Attack* (1989) from WSB in Atlanta, Georgia, highlighted the producers' investigative skills as well as their access to all players in the drug trade. Stressing the timeliness of the program, the submission form states that "the week President Bush was ready to announce a War on Drugs, particularly on crack, our station was ready."[20] Finally, the nationally distributed programs— programs from outlets that are not licensed and are not subject to a public interest mandate—described goals consistent with these other programs. ABC's *Drugs: A Plague upon the Land* (1988) was interested in "sounding an alarm" and in calling for a war on drugs spurred not by "words" but by "actions."[21] The submission form for HBO's *Crack U.S.A.: County under Siege* (1989) latched the program's content onto its style, expressly describing the production as a "vérité" approach to overlooked stories in the war on drugs.[22] In addition to sharing public service goals with their locally produced counterparts, these national programs likewise reinforced the local consequences of a nationwide crisis.

Most of the submission forms focused on their programs' uniqueness (which they were able to achieve via access granted by the police) and on their exasperation with the status quo. Language such as "frenzy" and "chaos" (*Inside Boston's Heroin Trade*), "shocking" (*Street Drug Wars*), and "chilling" (*Drugs: The Boom They Can't Bust*) promised sensational content. These programs placed great importance on going places their viewers would never go, but the majority of the descriptions did not communicate how the programs go to those places *televisually*. Only *Crack U.S.A.* referenced style by invoking the documentary tradition of cinéma vérité. The style of the drug war programs was crucial to how they manufactured engagement with their publics. By not articulating their creative use of images and sounds, the authors of these forms actively disconnected themes and arguments from visuals and soundscapes. From the perspectives presented on all of the forms with the exception of HBO's, quality or value hinged on the exposure of crime, injustice, deaths, and institutional negligence but not on the manner of that exposure. It is left to outside analysis to ascertain how the meanings imparted by style transformed or otherwise interacted with indexical realism and the public service mission—a mission focused on local well-being.

THE LOCAL AND THE NATIONAL

Local news tells stories about home, and the proximity of these stories to the viewer creates a personal connection to a problem that may seem removed from his or her daily life. The flow of drugs was a problem that may have appeared urban, but its treatment on the programs in the Peabody collection connects it to both rural and urban localities. Consequently, the programs tend to prop up the idea of local innocence spoiled—a theme that more often than not leans on race or racial codes. *Crack Attack* establishes Glennville, Georgia, as a simpler place because, according to voiceover narration, it's "where young people can still find trouble drag racing on a Friday night." A shot of young white men explaining their racing to policemen quickly transitions to images of what the narration identifies as "the new kind of young trouble—*gang trouble*." Mugshots of black suspects clarify that gang trouble was not harmless or white. ABC's *Drug Wars* tells viewers that "mainstream Americans" are growing marijuana; the accompanying images instruct viewers that "mainstream" means white. HBO's *Crack Attack* tries to dismantle this code. Viewers see a white, female addict dispute the stereotype that crack is "a ghetto-type drug." "Clearly it's not," she argues, holding herself up as a case study in crack's pervasiveness outside of what is understood to be the black space of the urban ghetto. Crack was everywhere, but these programs had to convince viewers of that fact. In other words, local and national productions had to unmake the meanings that the press, films, and other television programs had constructed. Although many of the programs studied here were aiming to challenge entrenched attitudes, the majority of faces shown in handcuffs or in pools of blood are black faces. *Crack Attack* is the primary exception to this rule.

The theme of spoiled local innocence joined the theme of disenfranchisement that stemmed from the tension between local law enforcement and the federal government. The programs repeatedly note the dearth of federal money for drug enforcement in small towns. And one, *Inside Boston's Heroin Trade*, takes a broader view, implicating the Department of Housing and Urban Development in the neglect of Roxbury in creating the material conditions under which crime could thrive. Also at issue was the federal government's focus on foreign sources of drugs rather than domestic ones. According to *Drug Wars: One Nation under Siege*, the Reagan administration's international focus meant that allocation of funds to fight homegrown marijuana amounted to a mere $40,000 per state. Additionally, the administration's inattention to domestic production meant that the Drug Enforcement Agency had no quality intelligence on networks operating within the United States.

In addition to grappling with both international drug trafficking and domestic production, towns and cities across the country faced drug dealers, inadequate drug enforcement, lax penalties for dealers and users, corruption, and an almost complete absence of treatment facilities for addicts. The programs acknowledge these interconnected issues but approach them from different sensibilities. *Drugs: The Boom They Can't Bust* explains just how important the crack economy is to lower income communities. The income from drug deals sustained impoverished families, so the allure of a steady income outweighed the risks for some. Other programs, such as *City under Siege* and *Crack U.S.A.*, do not attempt to understand dealers' motives, painting them instead as inherently evil terrorists. In *Drugs: A Plague upon the Land*, drug gangs "swarmed eastward" like a plague of insects. Whether they describe dealers as pragmatic or evil, most programs agree that dealers benefited from a justice system ill prepared to confront the rise of drug-related crime. For the panel of industry leaders, government officials, and celebrities speaking to an audience of children in *Kids' Summit on Drugs*, the solution is to sentence dealers to death. Perhaps because most of the programs relied on local police for access to information, drug busts, and crime scenes, only two of the programs, *Drug Wars* and *Drugs: A Plague upon the Land*, argue that the corruption of public officials and community leaders exacerbated the problems in local drug enforcement.

The programs' exploration of rehabilitation reveals another dimension to the class- and race-inflected drug crisis and raises a disturbing question: who was privileged enough to receive help? *Crack Attack* explains that publicly funded treatment centers in Georgia were overwhelmed with people—mostly crack users—searching for beds. *Drugs: The Boom They Can't Bust* informs viewers that twelve thousand drug arrests had been made in Santa Clara County, but only one hundred publicly funded treatment beds were available for users. Even more troubling was the fact that, in Georgia, public treatment centers did not treat adolescents; only private options were available to juveniles. *Crack U.S.A.* interviews young, white addicts and learns that some of their parents had spent tens of thousands of dollars to send them to rehabilitation centers. The fissures between federal priorities and local perspectives become palpable in the cases of users whose fates were determined by their ability to access expensive care.

NATIONAL ENTRIES

All of the programs approached the drug crisis in local terms, but it is worth concentrating on how ABC and HBO used their national platforms to treat local concerns. ABC News anchor Peter Jennings, the host of *Drugs: A Plague upon the Land*, introduces and contextualizes each segment, transitions viewers in and out of commercial breaks, and provides closing remarks that called on the government to act. In its capacity as a national network, ABC relied on its affiliates for footage and reporting. Its first segment is composed of a rapid sequence of clips from affiliates' own coverage of drug-related crime. Each reporter explains the crisis in his town, often identifying a particular street corner or intersection—"a street corner," Jennings remarks ominously, "that may be near you." In a little over one minute of screen time we hear from fourteen affiliated local stations from New York to California.[23] For ABC News, the commu-

ABC's *Drugs: A Plague upon the Land* relies on affiliates' coverage of drug-related crime, constructing a tale of national turmoil incited by local communities of nonwhites.

nities served by these affiliates were connected to the international drug trade via immigration from the Caribbean and Latin America, although U.S.-born black and brown citizens contributed to the problem as well. Jennings cites a "national emergency" spurred by local gangs turned national drug syndicates. In one segment hosted by Bill O'Reilly, viewers learn that "organized crime that was once controlled by whites" had become "increasingly black." A later segment specifically targets Jamaicans in addition to general "urban ghetto gangs" and "foreign dealers."

ABC News's preoccupation with the national turmoil incited by local communities of nonwhites and noncitizens contrasts sharply with HBO's microexamination of Palm Beach County, Florida, in both style and emphasis. Employing an observational style of documentary interspersed with talking-head confessionals, *Crack U.S.A.* features primarily white individuals and families. Although the program begins by following the police and joining their arrests and raids, the pace and tone shifts as the narrator (actor Joe Mantegna) explains that "the hardest hit" were "the young." *Crack U.S.A.* subsequently offers profiles of a beauty queen turned addict, a sixteen-year-old champion surfer turned addict, a cop whose son was jailed because of his crack addiction, two fifteen-year-old girls also addicted to crack, a fifteen-year-old boy who confessed to stealing crack from the body of a dead user, and a sixteen-year-old recidivist addict whose family's travails take up the final segment of the program. By moving from the already limited context of a single county in Florida to the even narrower population of white, teenage crack users, HBO frames public service in terms of its ability to dive deeply into a niche, although it offers a less structured investigation of the county's drug problem than the locally produced programs in the Peabody collection. Operating with no legal obligation to serve the public interest, HBO's entry nevertheless overlaps with the public service definition offered by Peabody, thereby expanding the credibility of the channel that had already featured programs on the AIDS crisis.

Whereas HBO's entry uses voice-over narration sparingly and lets the victims tell their own stories, Peter Jennings's authoritative presence and insistence on the necessity of a true war on drugs anchors the definition of public service in a stern paternalism. That paternalism is, in turn, tied to the nation as defined by a broadcast network, that is, a nation constructed by local stations that air national programs and national commercial messages. The notable absence of these commercial messages in the Peabody submissions erases some of the context of broadcast television's construction of public service. Interestingly, at the time of my research, the Peabody collection's copy of the ABC broadcast was missing from the archive. I was able to access a videotaped recording uploaded to the Internet Archive—a recording that had eliminated all but one advertisement. Whether by design or by complete accident, the ad that remained in the recording interacts with the program in a revealing way. In the segment that airs before the ad, Jennings reports that dealers had adopted new communication technologies—beepers, cell phones—to stimulate the growth of their business: "Cellular car phones and beepers reach out and expand their drug network. They've pushed their drugs past the Rocky Mountains as far as New Jersey, tripling and quadrupling their profits." The ad that follows that segment is one for AT&T and features a woman in front of a black background speaking to a potential client off screen. To her invisible audience she says, "We can help you make money. We can help you enter new markets and have a presence. We can help you become a major player in some type of environment. You have the idea, you start it, we'll help you finish it. . . . We work with hundreds of clients annually, and I'm sure we've worked with people in the industry that you're going in. And that would allow you to understand what works, what doesn't work, to get to that market share. What's it gonna get you? Money. Isn't that what it's kind of all about in starting up a new business?"

The significance of this AT&T ad to the hour of programming can be explained by what Nick Browne calls the television "supertext."[24] Browne argues that a complete understanding of a television program can be achieved only through the inclusion of its interstitial material, which includes ads and promos. The telecommunication company's promise to make you "a major player in some type of environment" creates both a confluence and a tension with the subject of ABC's program. Distanced from this commercial context, *Drugs: A Plague upon the Land* can pretend to stand as a unified, Peabody Award–worthy program working to inform viewers and propose solutions to the drug crisis. Reunited with their ads, each of these commercial programs is complicated, contradicted, or compromised by their interstitial materials.

By contrast, *Crack U.S.A.*, a premium cable program, operates outside the commercial model of the broadcast programs. In addition, dispensing with the news-style narration and on-screen reporters that the other programs employ, *Crack U.S.A.* tries to distance itself from the conventions of a public service television program. With no local affiliates bound by a public interest mandate, HBO has never attempted to cater to the public interest as a matter of course. As cable television matured in the 1960s and 1970s, the federal government looked to it to satisfy public service goals that had more or less been abandoned by the broadcast networks. Specifically, the FCC hoped individual channels would serve a more diverse set of audiences than broadcast networks had, but as these channels were unregulated, the government could not impose a public interest mandate on them. Some channels like the Arts Channel and HBO stepped up to the plate by including socially and culturally relevant programs in their schedules, mimicking to a certain degree the programming strategies of PBS stations.

Shayne Pepper argues that HBO played a crucial role in television programming's intermixing of financial success and public service.[25] In his study of HBO's AIDS documentaries, he argues that the channel's freedom, enabled by its premium tier, allowed it to bypass concerns about controversy or "conservative sensibilities" and treat AIDS as a complex disease that had the potential to affect everyone. HBO's turn to original programming, including documentary, coincided with cable's immersion in "the discourse of public service," which was linked to its cultural offerings. While Pepper appreciates HBO's willingness to be bold at a time when the United States was mishandling the AIDS crisis, he argues that the private production and distribution of these documentaries was indicative of "broader neoliberal approaches to public service, public health, and social welfare." Faulting the government for not taking a larger role in health education, Pepper also critiques HBO for involving itself in this programming for the wrong reasons: it was cheap, it curried favor with cable regulators, and it cultivated the brand.[26] HBO launched its twenty-five years of AIDS-related programming in 1987, and two years later it released *Crack U.S.A.*. In the context of Pepper's analysis (public service as good branding), HBO's submission form is just one piece of a decade-long strategy of embracing crises for corporate gain. ABC and HBO, working under two distinct sets of circumstances, fixated on the local by latching onto two distinct genres and styles. Despite their national distribution, the shared goal of consciousness raising brings them into conversation with the locally distributed programs.

Whether the programs studied here identified as documentaries, news, or public service, each made stylistic choices that interacted with their public service tone. In *Drug Wars, Drugs: The Boom They Can't Bust, City under Siege, Crack Attack,* and *Drugs: A Plague upon the Land* the music and editing in opening montages and drug raid scenes draw attention to the construction of the war as a conventional war, a racial war, and a cultural war. The programs use popular music to convey its literal meaning, discouraging any potential intertextual irony. "Okie from Muskogee," a Merle Haggard song that begins with "we don't smoke marijuana in Muskogee," plays in *Drug Wars. Drugs: A Plague upon the Land* features two songs from Prince: "Pop Life" and "Sign o' the Times," both of which lament the havoc wreaked by cocaine, crack, and gang violence. *Crack Attack*'s eponymous title song is a blues riff describing crack's seductive high. *Drugs: The Boom They Can't Bust* uses Steppenwolf's song "The Pusher" in its opening montage. "The Pusher" distinguishes pot dealers from the pusher of harder drugs, calling the latter a "monster." Inserted into a 1980s-era news program, "The Pusher" creates nostalgia for the "love grass" of the 1960s and contributes to the dehumanization of the evil crack dealer. Haggard's song derides marijuana as the drug of hippies who dwell outside of authentic, rural America, but Steppenwolf's song idealizes marijuana, a natural drug that stands in contrast to the processed substances associated with inner city, black communities. The kind of music a TV program like these uses can complicate the interaction between culture and race as filtered through drugs, but the programs in the Peabody collection seemed to have based their musical selections on superficial thematic compatibility.

Documentaries like *Crack Attack* (*left*) and *Drugs: The Boom They Can't Bust* (*right*) begin with montages mashing together scenes of *Miami Vice*–style drug raids with images of users, dealers, and outraged neighbors.

Some of the programs' opening montage sequences combine music with frantic scenes. *Drug Wars*, *Drugs: The Boom They Can't Bust*, *City under Siege*, and *Crack Attack* all begin by mashing together scenes of *Miami Vice*–style drug raids with images of users, dealers in shadow, and outraged neighbors. In contrast, *Drugs: A Plague upon the Land* begins with a sound montage. On screen a graphic of the continental United States overlaid with the nation's flag slowly burns until the program title appears over the black space created by the fire. The sound in the montage draws from the voices of dealers, addicts, concerned citizens, and cops. Their words express despair and frustration. Opting not to reproduce an action sequence in its introduction, *Drugs: A Plague upon the Land* distances itself from the style of local news but also extracts these voices from their local contexts.

In another departure from the norm, this introduction removes these voices from their violent contexts. On the whole, these programs do not avoid depicting the sort of graphic violence that came to characterize the representation of drug violence in television series and films. *Drugs: A Plague upon the Land* regularly exploits the convention of dead bodies lying in the street, covered with sheets. *Drug Wars*, too, uses footage and photos of dead bodies, including graphic images from a murder involving the Hell's Angels. Both *Drugs: The Boom They Can't Bust* and *Inside Boston's Heroin Trade* begin with photos of dead bodies. In *Crack Attack* the camera does not flinch in the aftermath of a stabbing. The suffering bodies of addicts populate program after program. *War on Crack* shows us addicts in the process of overdosing. *Street Drug Wars* includes graphic footage of an addict trying and failing to find a vein, after which he begins convulsing.

Street Drug Wars includes graphic footage of an addict trying and failing to find a vein.

One of the traits that separates *Street Drug Wars* from the rest is its structure, which allows for the development of both a serialized narrative and a running commentary on its progression. *Street Drug Wars* aired in six installments on the WCBS nightly news, a decision that created opportunities to describe the city's reaction to the program and to allow reporter Mike Taibbi to reiterate his humanistic point of view each night. After the second installment, in which the scene with the convulsing heroin addict unfolds, Taibbi justifies the decision to air the footage by arguing that it was captured in a responsible way; it was real and not "gratuitous." The contextualization of editorial decisions, which is not atypical in controversial news programs, creates a sense of accountability to viewers. When the eruption of drug-related violence becomes normalized, a conversation about the showcasing of that violence invites viewers to interrogate that normalization.

Avoiding the TV news style of the rest of the entries, HBO's *Crack U.S.A.* vacillates between an observational mode and a more typical talking-head style of documentary. I have mentioned the different teens and parents who spoke to the camera in HBO's documentary, but I would like to turn now to the final ten minutes of the program, which eliminates the news-like aspects of public service broadcasting and embraces the dramatic techniques of a scripted series. At the start of this segment, set in the rural town of Loxahatchee, the parents of Steven Powell describe the lengths that their sixteen-year-old son would go to secure a dose of crack. The drama begins when Steven, a repeat offender, is arrested for stealing his parents' van. The camera observes his parents crying as the officers take Steven away in handcuffs. Ten days later, Steven's mom asks the judge to let her send Steven to rehab again. The judge warns that another offense will make matters worse, and a jump cut reveals that the entire family does indeed return home. Steven's father explains to the camera that this time will be different, but as the camera lingers on Steven's face, he does not express the same weary hopefulness that his parents do. He simply stares at an unseen point off camera. Another jump cut takes us to an exterior nighttime location, and a graphic tells us that twenty-four hours have passed. At some point in the night Steven's mother awoke to find that Steven had fled with the truck. Steven has violated the terms of his probation, so his parents are desperate to find him. The camera takes its place alongside the parents as they search for and finally locate their truck and begin tailing it. The parents curse and yell, "Don't lose him!" Both vehicles stop, and Steven's mother runs down the dark city street as Steven's vehicle reverses at full speed. Steven's mother screams and runs back to the van so they can resume the chase. "God, I wish I had a gun," she says. The pursuit continues. The shaky camera loses focus as Steven's parents successfully stop and confront him. The screams and cries create a soundtrack that gives way to a few chords from a synthesizer. Steven's parents are visibly discombobulated, and Steven sits in his parents' vehicle with his hand over his face. In its final moments, the program returns to a montage of silent faces from earlier in the program, but it revisits Steven's story at its conclusion. Placed back into treatment in March 1989, Steven ran away ten days later and was arrested for possession of crack. The program concludes on this note, showing only a scene of Steven hugging his mom in slow motion. No attempt is made to create closure, and viewers are left to reflect on the harrowing story that offers no prescriptions or advances, no calls to action. By employing a style unlike that of the other programs, *Crack U.S.A.* wraps public service inside the sort of reality-based drama and intrigue that seems to unfold in front of the camera. It is not packaged and presented with a television news sensibility, but in substance it is not radically different from the other programs. Even though it was produced by HBO, it is still a public service program.

CONCLUSION

The Peabody Awards Collection offers a bounty of radio and television programs that cross generic lines. The programs examined for this project are united by a crisis and a common sense of purpose rooted in local well-being. Their attention to the local reveals similar preoccupations and similar regressive tendencies. In these programs, the local serves as evidence that even though the nation was under attack , the federal government, focused on other countries, consistently ignored local needs. Race and ethnicity tangle with nationality to complicate the definition of community in drug-ravaged areas. At times, public service and policing seem interchangeable. The intimate relationship between reporters and law enforcement yields something resembling the type of war coverage created by reporters embedded with the military. The result is a fetishization of state-sanctioned action and violence to the detriment of marginalized people. The style of the programs is a reminder of the programs' industrial contexts. Information commingles with creative editing, popular music, and violent images, layering additional meanings on top of the obvious ones. The nationally distributed programs mined the local for material, while the locally produced programs went a step further by acting for their communities. The creators of these programs believed in their quality, and so the programs reside among other self-selected examples of excellence in the Peabody Awards Collection. Their worth lies not just in their complicated and fraught subject matter but also in their alignment with the values of local television and in their belief that those values could earn national recognition. For this reason, the archive itself is a useful frame for constantly changing definitions of quality, excellence, and public service.

NOTES

1. Ted Galen Carpenter, *Bad Neighbor Policy: Washington's Futile War on Drugs in Latin America* (New York: Palgrave Macmillan, 2003), 29.
2. William N. Elwood, *Rhetoric in the War on Drugs: The Triumphs and Tragedies of Public Relations* (Westport, CT: Praeger, 1994), 45.
3. Ibid., 72, 74, 76.
4. Jimmie L. Reeves and Richard Campbell, *Cracked Coverage: Television News, the Anti-cocaine Crusade, and the Reagan Legacy* (Durham, NC: Duke University Press, 1994), 15.
5. Ibid.
6. Ibid., 27.
7. Ibid., 34.
8. Camille Fojas, *Border Bandits: Hollywood on the Southern Frontier* (Austin: University of Texas Press, 2008), 111.
9. Ibid.
10. Elwood, *Rhetoric in the War on Drugs*, 53, 55.
11. "Submit an Entry for Consideration," www.peabodyawards.com/stories/story /submit-an-entry-to-peabody-awards.
12. Ibid.
13. WJXT, *Drug Wars: One Nation under Siege*, October 13, 1983, 83094 DCT 1 of 1, Peabody Awards Collection, Walter J. Brown Media Archives and Peabody Awards Collection, University of Georgia (hereafter PAC), http://dlg.galileo.usg .edu/peabody/id:1983_83094_dct_1.
14. WCVB, *Inside Boston's Heroin Trade*, July 31, 1985, 85071 NWT 1 of 1, PAC, http://dlg.galileo.usg.edu/peabody/id:1985_85071_nwt_1.
15. WCBS, *Street Drug Wars*, 1989, 89141 NWT 1 of 1, PAC, http://dlg.galileo.usg .edu/peabody/id:1989_89141_nwt_1.
16. WCBS, *War on Crack*, September 2–October 4, 1986, 1986019 PST 5 of 6, PAC, http://dlg.galileo.usg.edu/peabody/id:1986_1986019_pst_5.
17. KABC, *Kids' Summit on Drugs*, October–November 1989, 89087 PST 3 of 3, PAC http://dlg.galileo.usg.edu/peabody/id:1989_89087_pst_3.
18. KRON, *Drugs: The Boom They Can't Bust*, July 21, 1988, 88080 DCT 1 of 1, PAC, http://dlg.galileo.usg.edu/peabody/id:1988_88080_dct_1.
19. WTTG, *City under Siege*, 1989, 89078 PST 1 of 1, PAC, http://dlg.galileo.usg.edu /peabody/id:1989_89078_pst_1.
20. WSB, *Crack Attack*, 1989, 89225 DCT 1 of 1, PAC, http://dlg.galileo.usg.edu /peabody/id:1989_89225_dct_1.
21. ABC, *Drugs: A Plague upon the Land*, October 4, 1988, 88208 DCT 1 of 1, PAC, http://dlg.galileo.usg.edu/peabody/id:1988_88208_dct_1.

22. HBO, *Crack U.S.A.: County under Siege,* November 10, 1989, 89049 DCT 1 of 1, PAC, http://dlg.galileo.usg.edu/peabody/id:1989_89049_dct_1.

23. The stations included WCBD (Charleston, SC), KTVK (Phoenix, AZ), WTVM (Columbus, GA), WPVI (Philadelphia, PA), KNTV (San Jose, CA), WDTN (Dayton, OH), KBAK (Bakersfield, CA), ABC (Long Island City, NY), WTSP (Tampa, FL), KOMO (Seattle, WA), KVUE (Austin, TX), WMUR (Manchester, NH), KUSA (Denver, CO), and KMID (Midland-Odessa, TX).

24. Nick Browne, "The Political Economy of the Television (Super) Text," in *American Television: New Directions in TV Theory and Theory,* ed. Nick Browne (Chur, Switzerland: Harwood Academic Publishers, 1994), 72.

25. Shayne Pepper, "Subscribing to Government Rationality: HBO and the AIDS Epidemic," *Communication and Critical/Cultural Studies* 11, no. 2 (2014): 122.

26. Ibid., 126–29.

STRIKES, RIOTS, AND MUGGERS

HOW MAYOR LINDSAY WEATHERED
NEW YORK CITY'S IMAGE CRISIS

Virtually every major American city faced tremendous challenges in the 1960s and into the early 1970s. Riots were commonplace. White flight in the wake of *Brown v. Board of Education* and the Civil Rights Act had led to a declining tax base and urban decay. The federal government was pumping money into Vietnam, and although the war in Indochina is sometimes characterized as a "guns and butter" conflict during which citizens did not have to make the kinds of belt-tightening sacrifices they had during World War II and the United States did not strike a pose of fiscal austerity, the fact is that funding for the war had to come from somewhere. Mayors all over America knew they would be lucky to get a few crumbs of federal funding for poverty relief programs. Arguably, New York City had it the worst. It was widely referred to as an "ungovernable city," and one man was floundering at the helm: Mayor John Vliet Lindsay.[1]

If you didn't live in New York, there were several ways to learn about what was happening there in these precipitous years. Certainly, there were newspapers and the national evening news, but for those looking for less information and more entertainment there were films reveling in Gotham's squalor. Mayor Lindsay was an implicit presence in the New York productions of those years; movies like *Serpico* (Lumet, 1973) and *The Panic in Needle Park* (Schatzberg, 1971) show a sinking city, and although Lindsay is rarely explicitly mentioned, the films are obviously an indictment of the failed mayor. In a rare moment when the mayor is actually named, a reporter in *The French Connection* (Friedkin, 1971) asks, "Do you agree with the recent survey finding that showed that Mayor Lindsay was the sexiest man in the world?" The point being made by the film is not that Lindsay was a sex symbol but rather that the reporter is hopelessly out of touch for asking a frivolous question rather than honing in on Lindsay's political crises.

The city's extreme crisis even surfaced outside of overtly "realist" media. Take Richard Fleischer's 1973 *Soylent Green*, which I regularly show in my science fiction class. Most of my undergraduates quickly intuit that the film is not about the "future" but about fears of ecological devastation and overpopulation that were on people's minds in the early seventies. What they typically do not immediately perceive, however, is that the film is not simply an allegory of present or future *America* but, more specifically, a film about the *New York City* of 1973. Our antihero is a cop who steals whenever he can, and everyone he works with, from his captain to the sanitation workers who carry away dead bodies in their trash trucks, expects part of the cut. Police payoffs are simply standard practice in 2022, just like fifty years earlier. This is not the dystopian future of pragmatic cannibalism ("Soylent green is people!") but the dystopian present of pragmatic graft. Little of this resonates with college students born in the Clinton years.

So, to help them understand *Soylent Green* I explain how Serpico had attempted to expose police corruption for five years. When his tales of pervasive malfeasance finally trickled upward in mid-1969, if not to Lindsay, then to those within shouting range of him, the response from the administration was that summer was just around the corner. One could not alienate the cops at a moment when tempers raged upward with the mercury and riots were a real threat. Sidney Lumet's 1973 film conveys a compact version of Serpico's story, though it is best to consume it in conjunction with Peter Maas's best-selling book. The book relays, in painfully pedestrian prose, the tedious details of bureaucratic corruption and intransigence. The movie shows in graphic detail the crumbling police stations, rotting hospitals, and garbage-strewn neighborhoods.[2]

Dirty and decrepit, New York City suffered a national image crisis in the Lindsay years. A series of Environmental Protection Agency photos taken in 1970 shows air pollution, garbage in the streets, and a crumbling subway system. Photo by Erik Calonius, National Archives, College Park, MD.

Although any number of media texts have attempted to convey New York City's years of deep crisis, it is the films of those years that have most strongly impacted whatever public memory there may be of that era. What I'd like to do in the following pages is shift gears and focus on television and radio representations of the crisis, with a particular concentration on broadcast programs featuring John Lindsay that are held by the Peabody Awards Collection. This approach reveals a different picture than that which emerges from Hollywood films. After all, films of the late 1960s and early 1970s may have taken a harsh turn (goodbye Julie Andrews, hello Al Pacino), but they were still largely designed to speak to a general (if mostly adult) audience that would include both New Yorkers and non–New Yorkers.[3] There is only minimal room for an "insider address" in such productions. *Midnight Cowboy* (Schlesinger, 1969) would likely resonate more deeply with residents of New York City than with nonnatives, but, like most mainstream dramas of the time, it centers on the suffering of individual, flawed masculine heroes dealing with personal crises. What you "learn" from such films is that New York is a city of drugs and orgies and hustlers and hookers, but you won't learn how it got that way. The grimy films of the era show us a dying city, but, with a few notable exceptions (*Serpico*, most prominently), they convey a "structure of feeling" rather than offering an explanation of political realities. Similarly, a New Yorker watching the bigoted Archie Bunker in the 1971 premiere of CBS's *All in the Family* might recall the hard-hat riots of 1970 and, more generally, Mayor Lindsay's difficulty maintaining the support of white working-class voters. But to a wider audience the show is about *American* crisis more than it is about *urban* crisis, and to many the very fact that this was a *sitcom* would position it as a critique of interpersonal communication within the family rather than of society at large.

The Peabody archive helps us to expand our documentation of the Lindsay years, reaching beyond scripted film and television productions. Most importantly, the archive includes news and public affairs programs submitted by both local and national outlets. This is the stuff that is never rerun or released on home-viewing formats, transient material that does not linger in the popular imagination. And it often conveys an immediate, visceral picture of what was happening in the city. In local broadcasts we find that Lindsay is generally raked over the coals, either explicitly or implicitly. In national broadcasts submitted for Peabody Award consideration, by contrast, we tend to find both more formality and more sympathy.

Consider the 1967 Peabody submission *Speaking Freely*, a rather dull hour-long NBC public affairs TV program hosted by Edwin Newman on which Lindsay appeared.[4] Newman asks general interview questions about the challenges Lindsay faces, about whether or not a mayor in New York has any possible role to play in foreign policy (implicitly an opening for Lindsay to plug himself as a future presidential candidate, but the mayor does not take the bait), and about whether the city really is "ungovernable." Lindsay blandly states that if he could prove the city was governable, he could return to private life with some sense of satisfaction. He says that as mayor of New York "there's nothing you can say or do that doesn't make somebody sore," and he complains that journalists have been making fun of his description of New York as a "fun city." Newman asks about the squalor of the ghettos, and Lindsay complains that he couldn't pass a rent bill or a rat bill, but he also graciously notes that ghetto communities display "intelligence, patience, and humor." When Newman asks who he thinks might be likely Republican presidential contenders in 1968, Lindsay laughably claims to have absolutely no idea, neatly sidestepping a chance to air his opinions on New York governor Nelson Rockefeller (who would emerge as his nemesis when Lindsay could not settle the garbage strike a year later). When asked "what is your view of the hippies?" Lindsay expresses a pleasant and liberal there's-room-for-everybody-in-our-fine-city response. The image conveyed is of a tired, hard-working, well-meaning man who is certainly not "speaking freely," although he doesn't seem any more evasive than the typical politician. Newman's questions are not completely softball (no dumb questions about Lindsay's personal life), but overall this is exactly the kind of tame, neutral stuff one expects from "public service" programming. The networks produced these kinds of nationally aired shows in large part because the FCC required them to do so. They usually ran such programs on Sunday mornings, when ad rates were so low that little would be lost.

Public service radio programs had the potential to be equally dull affairs—they were also seen by many broadcasters as a duty, and they were not profitable—but they often ended up being more interesting, to my mind, because they were live, only lightly scripted, and, most importantly, the format often included phone calls from listeners. Edwin Newman's most spontaneous moment may have been when he asked Lindsay if racial disturbances had initially reflected "the revolution of rising expectations" but had now given way to a "revolt of disappointment because the expectations" had "not been met." Lindsay said, "You're using fancy language now" and floundered through an answer. Newman's less-than-fiery defense was "I was concealing thought with words." It's a stiff exchange,

Mayor Lindsay (to LBJ's left) was not only a local figure. He also received national attention for his role as cochair of the Kerner Commission and for his crafting of much of the commission's report. Photograph by Marion S. Trikosko, United States Library of Congress Prints and Photographs Division.

to say the least. On live call-in radio, by contrast, one knew that there was a real possibility of things going off the rails.

On national radio, the phone-in format seemed to work to Lindsay's advantage. If we turn our attention to the July 1968 Peabody submission *Night Call*, for example, we find that the national radio audience was incredibly forgiving.[5] Lindsay was a polished if tired politician on *Speaking Freely*, but on *Night Call* he is simply an exhausted shell of a man. The title of the episode submitted for Peabody Award consideration was "What Happened to the *Kerner Report*?" Lindsay had cochaired the National Advisory Commission on Civil Disorders and had crafted much of the commission's report; President Johnson had not followed its recommendations for governmental response to the racial crisis. In a nutshell, the report (released four months before this program aired) argued that white racism was the root source of black rioting, that America was made up of two societies, separate and unequal, and, further, that the media had failed completely in conveying the sources of black discontent.[6]

It's worth adding here that even though many New Yorkers thought Lindsay had done a terrible job as mayor, he also had won many admirers just three months before this episode of *Night Call* aired, when Martin

Luther King Jr. was assassinated. Lindsay went to Harlem in the middle of the night and walked among the emotional crowds of people in the street. Violence and looting could have easily erupted. In fact, it really seemed unlikely that there could be any other outcome. But Lindsay's presence in the streets conveyed that he cared, that black New Yorkers had good reasons to be furious but that they should not respond with destructive acts. As fires were lit and glass shattered across the rest of the country, Lindsay kept the peace, scoring a huge public relations coup among liberals both black and white, in the city and beyond. He was pictured on the cover of the May 24, 1968, issue of *Life* magazine shortly thereafter, with text reading "Cool Mayor in a Pressure Cooker: The Lindsay Style."

Lindsay's opponents made fun of his penchant for walking among the people, highlighting the pretentiousness of this Yale-educated Republican from the city's "silk stocking district" attempting to represent himself as a man of the people. Certainly, it didn't always work. When the city cleared snow from Manhattan but not Queens in the wake of the blizzard of 1969, citizens hurled epithets (and rock-hard snowballs!) at the mayor when he attempted to walk the streets of Kew Gardens and Fresh Meadows.[7] Still, his "walking tours" of all five boroughs of the city, the many schedules of which are held in his papers at Yale University, were a striking feature of his mayoralty. If he couldn't successfully fight the unions or Albany, or pass the budgets he wanted, or get federal funding to combat drug abuse and trafficking, or build sufficient public housing, he could at least hit the streets (tie tossed over his shoulder to indicate casualness or even sans tie, but rarely in sneakers) and try to show people that he really did care.

So, on a blistering July night in 1968, Lindsay appears on *Night Call* having not slept for forty-eight hours. He had spent the first twenty-four hours trying to settle a hospital workers strike and then had gone straight to Harlem to walk the streets and keep the peace, not because there had been another assassination or other obvious national crisis, but simply because it was *hot*. This was what it was like in big American cities in 1968. If you were mayor of Chicago, New York, or LA, and the weather turned sultry, you flipped your Rolodex to "National Guard," just in case. Exhausted and broken, Lindsay somehow makes it to the *Night Call* studio and seems to actually "speak freely" insofar as he appears to be wavering on the cusp of delirium.

Where the Newman interview was canned and cordial, this one is strange and free flowing, with Lindsay initially vacillating between his go-to sound bites and comments like "who knows the answer to that question?" Things turn weirdly flirtatious when a caller phones from Minnesota.

> MISS SUZIE BERKOWITZ: I'm a very, very, very liberal Democrat.
>
> JOHN LINDSAY: Well, bully for you!
>
> SB: But I would like to say, I think New York should be proud to have a great mayor like you.
>
> JL: Thank you, thank you, ma'am. I need you here.
>
> SB: I think you're fantastic.
>
> JL: I need you here, won't you move?
>
> SB: Pardon?
>
> JL: I need you here, won't you move to New York City?
>
> SB: Oh, listen, we've got [Eugene] McCarthy! . . . Do you ever plan on coming to Minnesota?
>
> JL: I was just there, how did I miss you?

Lindsay goes on to explain that he was recently in Minnesota supporting Rockefeller for president: "I made what I thought was an *electrifying* speech before the [Republican nominating] convention. I can't possibly understand how you missed it." Miss Berkowitz issues a few more compliments, and Lindsay responds, "Thank you very much, that's most kind of you. Too bad they don't feel exactly the same about me in New York." The host, Dell Shields, finally cuts Miss Berkowitz off with "thank you for calling," which was exactly the right thing to do, as the show was really not moving forward with this exchange.

On the surface there is nothing going on politically here, but the implicit lesson is that Lindsay was a mayor who could only garner strong support among people who couldn't vote for him—and he is painfully aware of the fact. The questions on this show are apparently not prescreened, which is part of why it all works. Further, the show promotes itself as caller centered: "Speak for yourself, collect, on *Night Call*!" Also, the program has a black host and features leftist guests (Stokely Carmichael, Ralph Abernathy) and liberal politicians (Lindsay, Sargent Shriver). It's not fiercely ideological or propagandistic in its approach, but it also avoids the blandness that characterizes most network public affairs shows—though it technically *is* a public affairs program, being a coproduction of the United Methodist Church, National Council of Churches, National Catholic Office for Radio and Television, and National Urban Coalition.[8]

Regardless of the quality of his performance on the show or of his performance as mayor of New York, Lindsay emerges here as a symbol of hope—and also as a symbol of the fact that hope was not enough—for black listeners. The show stood for the value of public affairs programming that was not aggressively neutral, like *Speaking Freely*. As if to drive this point home, after the earnest white caller from Minnesota signs off, Dell Shields asks his own question about whether or not whites can accept the conclusions of the Kerner Commission—for example, that civil disorder (rioting) was not the product of a "conspiracy," implicitly communist inspired. Lindsay defends the Kerner Commission's findings on this count, but he also notes that some people will simply ignore evidence and believe whatever they want to believe. The next caller, Miss Landy from New Orleans (whose voice sounds as black and southern as Berkowitz's was white and midwestern), combines elements of the Berkowitz and Shields approaches by complimenting Lindsay, then asking a procedural question about the Kerner Commission. The show from here dives into material Lindsay feels comfortable discussing, work that he has successfully accomplished. Whether or not the report had had its intended impact, at least it had been completed (unlike, say, Lindsay's public housing expansion program), and, to Lindsay's mind, its conclusions were unimpeachable. He is not boastful but rather audibly concerned. This is Lindsay—and live radio—at its finest.

Lindsay received quite different treatment on a local radio show, the 1967 Peabody submission *WMCA Reports*, during which he took questions from New York City listeners.[9] Notably, the calls are prerecorded, in what seems to be an obvious attempt to control the conversation. Prerecording the calls means that questions could be limited and shortened, and there would be no worries about profanities. It took all the fun and energy out of a "live" show. Lindsay and callers could not truly interact, and it was hard for things to heat up, although the despair of the callers and their displeasure with their mayor is plainly evident. Given the rancorous feelings of typical New Yorkers toward the mayor, one has to wonder if the prerecording was a special choice for Lindsay's appearance.

The very first question comes from Mr. Perlstein of Brooklyn, an elderly man, presumably Jewish, with a heavy eastern European accent: "I still remember when you came to Crown Heights . . . and you said, you promised, that you going to do on Montgomery Street and Utica, you promised that you going to do everything possible, you going to make a new system like they have in Chicago. Every two minutes, police is going to be around to lower the crime and mugging and robberies what's going on in this neighborhood.... Where's your promise?" Lindsay feebly responds that his promise has been kept and details changes he has made, none of which include police patrolling neighborhoods every two minutes. The reality was that all of Lindsay's attempts to improve the police force had been met with disdain and resistance by the union. For one thing, he proposed changing the hours when shifts fell in such a way that it would make it difficult for police officers to "coop," that is, hole up in a school or church basement filled with cots and sleep through most of their shift, the standard practice of those working the overnight rotation. A referendum to establish a civilian complaint review board (which many New Yorkers saw as an attempt by Lindsay to appease blacks at the expense of white police officers) was defeated by a vote of almost three to one.[10]

The bottom line is that the image of New York, both locally and nationally, was of a town run by muggers—which to many of the "silent majority" simply meant people of color. The city went so far as to run off mimeographs to help citizens better describe criminals. The ID sheets did not clearly convey the ethnicity of the generic criminal, but the ethnic divisions of the city were obvious. And Lindsay was widely perceived as being more responsive to the needs of black ghetto dwellers than middle- and upper-class whites. When he responded to calls from the black community for local control of schools, a complicated fracas ensued; the short version of the story was that a number of Jewish teachers had been fired from black schools, and the ensuing teachers' strike shut down the public schools for most of the fall of 1968. It was a public relations nightmare, with white school kids holding up signs like "Mrs. Lindsay, Clean up Your John! Revive New York City." Attempts to expand public housing into Jewish neighborhoods further strained the relationship between Lindsay and the Jewish community.[11] Lindsay won election to a second term in large part because Golda Meir visited the city and expressed obvious fondness for the incumbent—and also because the Mets won the World Series, which had absolutely nothing to do with Lindsay but simply boosted the city's morale. The Mets win made the city look good, which made the mayor look good. He was reelected less for his real accomplishments than for his success in playing the image game.

Lindsay was considered media savvy—described as "made for television" by one *New York Times* journalist—but he simply couldn't win on *WMCA Reports*.[12] For example, one caller tells Lindsay that her family of five had been approved for public housing, but there were no units

After a visit with their friend Mayor Lindsay, three congressmen sent him this "joke" photo alluding to the fact that big city politicians would say anything to get a vote but that everyone (including graffiti artists) saw right through the political performance. Photograph by Dick DeMarsico, courtesy of the John Vliet Lindsay Papers, Manuscripts and Archives, Yale University Library.

big enough, so she had been waiting for five years. Lindsay responds by explaining how great things were going with public housing, with many more units in the works. But he also acknowledges, quickly and without belaboring the point, that federal regulations have discouraged the building of larger units. On the same show, a nurse at Bellevue says Lindsay had promised hospital improvements during his campaign, but one year later Bellevue still did not have sufficient medical supplies. Lindsay explains that there was a new Bellevue building in the works and that he had gotten around some regulations so that the building would take two years less to construct than originally expected. This could offer little solace to the penniless pneumonia sufferer who found herself at a filthy and decrepit hospital lacking antibiotics. Lindsay pitifully announces that in 1967 New Yorkers should be ready for "top-grade quality government" and should seek out the "joy of living" in a city with lovely parks. This was language more suited to advertising hamburgers and air fresheners than to describing a sinking metropolis.

Another local news program also took aim at Lindsay, though this one less directly. The 1971 Peabody submission *New York Closeup* aired on WPIX and centered on the Knapp Commission police corruption hearings. The program was prepared (and reported on camera) by Anne Kaestner, under a tight deadline.[13] Anchorwoman Kaestner, sporting a mushroom cap hairdo and a plaid pantsuit with expansive, traffic-stopping lapels, opens with background commentary, noting that the question haunting the commission hearings was why it took so long for the Lindsay administration to respond to the crisis in the first place. The *New York Times*, Kaestner added, had recently noted that at the hearings it would "be almost as if the questions were being put to Mayor Lindsay himself." That is, she seemed to imply, even if Lindsay were not present everyone knew that the hearings were a symbolic referendum on his failures.

Following this introduction, most of the show consists of edited footage of the hearings. The room is crowded, stuffed with not only commission members and those testifying but also reporters with microphones, headsets, cameras, and hulking reel-to-reel tape recorders. Though we see cameras on tripods in the back of the room, some of the footage is clearly shot with handheld cameras, adding to the feeling of drama and immediacy. But this is hardly cinéma vérité reportage: as is typical of this sort of news footage, there are only two kinds of images, full shots of the room and cut-ins to speakers.

The hearing features, among others, Sergeant David Durk—friend and coworker of Serpico, the whistle-blower immortalized in Lumet's film. Durk's gripping testimony conveys the seedy decrepitude of the city:

> For me being a cop means believing in the rule of law. It means believing in a system of government that makes fair and just rules, and then enforces them.... If it's not too corny, to be a cop is to help an old lady walk the streets safely, to help a twelve-year-old girl reach her next birthday without being gang raped, to help a store keeper make a living without keeping a shotgun under his cash register, to help a boy grow up without needles in his arm.... Being a cop is a vocation or it is nothing at all. And that's what I saw being destroyed by the corruption of the New York City police department, destroyed for me and for thousands of others like me.

Toward the end of his testimony Durk suggests, voice quivering, that the Knapp Commission needs to look upward if it wants to understand the true scope of the corruption:

Those in high places everywhere, in the department, in the DA's office, and City Hall were determined not to enforce the law. . . . We wanted to serve others, but the department was a home for drug dealers and thieves. . . . I saw . . . other victims too, especially the children, children of fourteen and fifteen and sixteen, wasted by heroin, turned into street corner thugs and whores, ready to mug their own mother for the price of a fix.

Durk next shifts gears and suggests that the problem cannot be solved by simply weeding out a few bad apples:

We are not *animals*, we are not *stupid*, and we know very well, we police-men, that corruption does not begin with a few patrolmen, and that re-sponsibility for corruption does not end with one aid to the mayor or one investigations commissioner. . . . We know that there are many people be-yond the police department who share in the corruption and its rewards. So your report has to tell us about the district attorneys, and the courts, and the bar, and the mayor, and the governor, and what they have done, and what they have failed to do, and how great a measure of responsibil-ity they also bear. Otherwise, if you suggest or allow others to suggest that the responsibility belongs only to the police, then for the patrolman on the beat and in the radio cars, this commission will be just another part of the swindle.

Finally concluding, Durk fights off tears, his voice quivering:

It took five years of Frank Serpico's life and five years of mine to help bring this commission about. It's taken the lives and dedication of thousands of others to preserve as much of a police force as we have. It has taken many months of effort by all of you to help show this city the truth. What I ask of you now, is to help make us clean again [voice cracks], to help give us some leadership we can look to, . . . and perhaps one day [voice breaks] on a long summer night, we'll hear again the shout "Viva la Policía."

As a postscript, Durk mumbles "Let's get out of here" to the fellow next to him and quickly bolts, presumably to the nearest watering hole. There is nothing in the *Serpico* film or book that rivals the heartfelt intensity con-veyed on this local TV news program.

The entry digest for *New York Closeup*'s half-hour episode on the Knapp Commission describes it as "the only such special report of its kind done in the New York market by a commercial television station."[14] Translation: there was some local PBS (WNET) coverage of the Knapp hearings, but it was not a ratings grabber. Like the Army-McCarthy hearings of the 1950s on a reduced scale, the Knapp Commission was devastating but also not the kind of stuff that networks wanted to actually show uncut. In any case, anyone watching the show would learn three lessons that they really already knew: the NYPD was corrupt; New York City had an image problem; and Mayor John Lindsay had an image problem.

This had not always been the case. The city had experienced a postwar boom along with the rest of the country when Lindsay, then a congressman from the city's upper east side, was gearing up to run for mayor. At that time he was handsome and suave, looking very much like a WASP knockoff of Bobby Kennedy. In 1965, Lindsay had campaigned with the rather ridiculous slogan "He is fresh and everyone else is tired." His opponents were Abraham Beame and William F. Buckley Jr. Buckley lost terribly of course—he was running as a protest candidate on the Conservative Party ticket—but he probably helped Lindsay win by forcing a three-way race. Lindsay took office with 42 percent of the popular vote.

The new mayor was sworn in at midnight on December 31, 1965. The Transit Workers Union contract expired at exactly the same moment. Lindsay would not sit down and negotiate, believing that the union was intransigent and not operating in good faith. His strategy was poor. The union president called a press conference ten minutes after Lindsay ascended to office and made it clear exactly what he thought of the New York State Supreme Court's injunction barring a strike: he tore the injunction in half, providing a terrific photo op for the gathered reporters. The strike was on for thirteen days; the city lost at least $50 million a day (the *New York Daily News* even estimated $100 million) in income, and New Yorkers had to walk miles and miles to work. Sammy Davis Jr. quipped that after just moments in office, Lindsay had ended all crime in the subways.[15] The transit workers ultimately won and fares spiked 33 percent. By 1967, Lindsay was no longer fresh, and he was unmistakably tired. This was patently clear from every TV and radio appearance he made.

Lindsay had campaigned with charming sound bites that were apparently good enough to get him elected, but could any amount of media spin help him once he was actually in office? At a moment when interracial tension was at an all-time high, blacks sensed Lindsay's empathy for their plight, but he couldn't really fix things for them. And the more he reached out to *them*, the more he alienated white ethnics—Jews, Italians, Poles, Irish, and so forth. In February 1968 *everyone* was alienated by a sanitation workers' strike. There was no garbage pickup for nine days, and, fearing the spread of disease by one hundred thousand tons of uncollected garbage in the streets, the city declared a public health crisis. This was the stuff of nightmares; virtually every newspaper photo and news broadcast showed a city—and a mayor—at rock bottom. Sad TV news footage showed Lindsay taking one of his signature walks on sidewalks crowded with piles of trash. He pitifully leans over and sets a toppled garbage can upright, as if it would help.[16]

The strike was a national news story, and the fetid piles of refuse did nothing to help the city's image. On the other hand, it was, as I have suggested, all terrific fodder for the new generation of filmmakers, and Lindsay created the Mayor's Office of Film, Theater and Broadcasting in 1966 (the first such office in the nation) precisely to encourage media producers to profit from the city's inherent drama—and, of course, to bring money into the city. This was one of Lindsay's few successful, genuinely long-lasting political actions. In 1965, the year before Lindsay's election, New York (the actual city, not sets) had virtually no cinematic presence; two 1965 features were principally shot in New York, one of them being Lumet's grim film *The Pawnbroker*. Filmmakers were required to apply for fifty or more separate permits. Thus, in the 1950s and early 1960s, New York City was visually represented as a beautiful Hollywood soundstage, as in Billy Wilder's *The Apartment* (1960). Once Lindsay's office was set up, only *one* permit was required to shoot, which made the process much easier and, of course, more cost efficient. In 1967, forty-two feature movies were produced in New York, bringing business to the city while advertising that it was going down the toilet—notwithstanding a few more upbeat productions like *Barefoot in the Park* (Saks, 1967) and *The Producers* (Brooks, 1967). Pacino made the city look pretty bad in *Serpico*, but even worse had been his breakthrough role as a junkie in the harrowing *Panic in Needle Park*, a film showing New York as a filthy and impoverished place where the needle was the only relief for underdog residents.

Outside of New York City, Lindsay did somewhat better than in the city itself, if public service radio shows submitted for the Peabody Awards like *Night Call* are any indication. On the other hand, non–New Yorkers were well aware of Lindsay's failures. Lindsay frequently surfaced as the butt of Johnny Carson's and Dick Cavett's opening monologues. Who could resist cracking dark jokes about a city that had endured not only transit, teacher, and garbage worker strikes but also *gravedigger* strikes?[17] The material practically wrote itself. The crises of New York City were so over the top that LA's smog and Chicago's political graft could no longer be counted on as easy go-to punch lines for late night TV. As much as Carson made fun of Lindsay, he had him on the show a lot, for he was handsome and charming and only unforgivable to hostile New Yorkers. The aforementioned Miss Berkowitz on *Night Call* was emphatic about how much she enjoyed Lindsay's recent appearance on Carson, this in the high-crisis period of 1968, the year that Lindsay described as the lowest point of his entire political career.

Ultimately, Lindsay wanted to run for president, and the fact that Johnny Carson made fun of him but had him on the show all the time, the fact that outside New York people seemed to really feel bad for him, the fact that he had been elected to a difficult and, most argued, impossible job twice, the fact that he was handsome, and well-off, and considered a pleasant politician (in retrospect, more Fiorella La Guardia than Rudy Giuliani in his demeanor) must have made him think he stood a chance running for the highest office in the land. He patently did not. He quietly retired after his short-lived 1972 presidential bid.

Returning to my subtitle, "How Mayor Lindsay Weathered New York City's Image Crisis," one has to wonder, did this mediagenic, charming personality ultimately get anything right beside the film and broadcasting office? Yes, absolutely. He pushed back against the unions at a time when they had a real stranglehold on the city and were truly devastating for people of color, who were not allowed to join. If his pushback was not a huge success on a practical level, it was of great symbolic importance. He declared New York a "fun city," and even though people relentlessly made fun of this notion, there was a powerful sense of whimsy in his words. He couldn't squeeze enough money from the feds and the state to fix the slums, but he could find a budget line to create a trompe l'oeil mural to beautify a building. He opened up the parks to people, allowing them to wander on the grass and ride their bikes on the paved paths on days when traffic was scandalously barred. He staged "happenings" in Central Park, emphasizing that the park was a place for New Yorkers to get groovy; his new parks commissioner announced, "The old rinky-dink, hand-me-down stereotype of the park is out, OUT!"[18] And even though in the 1965 campaign he had mocked Buckley's strong support for bicycle paths in the city, he ended up staking a claim for the fun of cycling through the park. In an almost heartbreaking moment of nostalgia, the 2010 WNET documentary *Fun City Revisited: The Lindsay Years*, a somewhat sugar-coated retrospective on the administration, includes footage of the mayor cycling past the park while "Raindrops Keep Falling on My

Head" plays, a patently saccharine and effective quotation of *Butch Cassidy and the Sundance Kid* (Hill, 1969).

The humorless and decidedly ungroovy Rudy Giuliani would later rejoice in the replacement of peep shows with Disney stores in Times Square.[19] Lindsay didn't care if people wanted to watch dirty movies, and if films like *Superfly* (Parks, 1972) showed a city that was "dirty" in the more literal sense, at least they provided good honest work for locals. Regrettably, it is only these kinds of media productions—35mm theatrically released films—that survive in abundance, and we have only a handful of public service radio and TV programs documenting the Lindsay years.

If we step back to survey the big picture, what stands out is just how little media historians have to go on when it comes to political broadcasting; presidential election ads and TV debates have been fairly well preserved, but access to local political broadcasts is spotty at best. One might think that a city like New York would, at the very least, preserve mayoral radio and TV debates, but that is simply not the case. This is what makes the Peabody material such an invaluable resource: the collection is idiosyncratic to the extent that it contains only awards submissions, which means that it is not a collection curated to provide holistic coverage of any program or era, but it nonetheless contains both locally and nationally produced news and public service materials that provide a historical window inaccessible anywhere else. With regard to Mayor Lindsay, the extant materials held in the Peabody collection reveal a local and national audience struggling to make sense of a talented man in a thankless job.

By the time Lindsay appeared on *The Dick Cavett Show* in 1973, he had announced he would not run for mayor again, and he had completely failed in attempting to become the Democratic nominee for president. The end of his political career plainly in sight, Lindsay appeared relaxed and relieved appearing before a national audience watching "Mayor" Lindsay for one of the last times. After a reasonably spirited conversation about Watergate, Cavett disconcertingly asks Lindsay what he thought of the hard-hat, pro-Vietnam, New York City protesters who had held up signs reading "Lindsay is a fag!" Lindsay laughs and is slightly embarrassed, as Cavett had probably hoped he would be. And then, ever the pluralist and ever the liberal, he closes out the TV interview not with a homophobic defense of his heterosexuality but simply by laughing and saying "the fag vote is a very large vote!" He had perhaps been more suave in his early years on Johnny Carson, but on Cavett's show—a relatively low-rated haven for eggheads who found Carson insufficiently sophisticated—he had once again stood up for New York City as a place that was not ashamed but proud of being different.[20]

NOTES

1. As Vincent J. Cannato puts it, "John Lindsay foundered on the shoals of his unfulfilled promises" (*The Ungovernable City: John Lindsay and His Struggle to Save New York* [New York: Basic Books, 2001], x). On the financial crisis in the post-Lindsay years, see Kim Phillips-Fein, *Fear City: New York's Fiscal Crisis and the Rise of Austerity Politics* (New York: Metropolitan Books, 2017).

2. *Serpico* opens with the hero being rushed into a dilapidated New York City hospital that would have seemed completely average to New York viewers at the time. Lindsay ran a 1965 campaign commercial that resonates here; in his introduction to *America's Mayor: John V. Lindsay and the Reinvention of New York* (New York: Columbia University Press, 2010), Sam Roberts quotes a Bronx truck driver whose grandmother had recently been taken to a New York City hospital: "These are some of the things that I witnessed as I went to the hospital: cockroaches crawl all over the walls. If a person is incapable of feeding themselves, the food is just left there. If a person is dirty in their bed, they just lay there" (31).

3. See Heather Hendershot, "City of Losers, Losing City: Pacino, New York, and the New Hollywood Cinema," in *When the Movies Mattered: The New Hollywood Revisited*, ed. Jonathan Kirshner and Jon Lewis (Ithaca, NY: Cornell University Press, 2019).

4. NBC, *Speaking Freely*, September 8, 1967, 67065 PST 1 of 1, Peabody Awards Collection, Walter J. Brown Media Archives and Peabody Awards Collection, University of Georgia (hereafter PAC), http://dlg.galileo.usg.edu/peabody/id:1967_67065_pst_1.

5. Night Call Network, *Night Call*, "What Happened to the *Kerner Report*?" July 1, 1968, 68051 PSR 1 of 1, PAC, http://dlg.galileo.usg.edu/peabody/id:1968_68051_psr_2.

6. U.S. National Advisory Commission on Civil Disorders, *Report of the National Advisory Commission on Civil Disorders* (New York: E.P. Dutton, 1968), 366. For a follow-up, see Fred R. Harris and John V. Lindsay, *The State of the Cities: Report of the Commission on the Cities in the '70s* (New York: Praeger, 1972).

7. Sewell Chan, "Remembering a Snow Storm That Paralyzed the City," *New York Times*, February 10, 2009.

8. To the modern eye, it may appear strange that this coalition of forces teamed up for a nonreligious show, but the combination made sense back in the days when liberal religious groups (especially the National Council of Churches) produced and distributed a substantial amount of programming aired for free to satisfy public service requirements. See Heather Hendershot, *What's Fair on the Air? Cold War Right-Wing Broadcasting and the Public Interest* (Chicago: University of Chicago Press, 2011).

9. WMCA, *WMCA Reports*, "Mayor John Lindsay," January 8, 1967, 67035 NWR 1–2 of 2, PAC, http://dlg.galileo.usg.edu/peabody/id:1967_67035_nwr_1-2.

10. Nicholas Pileggi, "Crime and Punishment," in *America's Mayor*, 75.

11. The racial and ethnic complexities of public housing were as complicated then as they are now, and the level of discrimination was egregious. It is worth adding that the fact that Fred Trump was actually punished for keeping blacks out of his properties (with the aid of his son Donald) shows how extreme—and widely known—the Trump family's behavior was. Note also that Fred Trump was the villain in a little-known 1952 Woody Guthrie song titled "Old Man Trump" (Justin William Moyer, "The Unbelievable Story of Why Woody Guthrie Hated Donald Trump's Dad," *Washington Post*, January 22, 2016).

12. Roberts, introduction, 30.

13. WPIX, *New York Closeup*, "Off-Track Betting," November 28, 1971, 71050 PST 1 of 1, PAC, http://dlg.galileo.usg.edu/peabody/id:1971_71050_pst_1.

14. WPIX, *New York Closeup*, "Off-Track Betting," entry digest, Entry Digests, Indexes, Logs, and Card Files, carton 811, George Foster Peabody Awards Records, ms. 30000, Hargrett Rare Book and Manuscript Library, University of Georgia.

15. Richard Reeves, "The Making of the Mayor," in *America's Mayor*, 38.

16. The documentary is, as of this writing, available via Vimeo.com, but I have not found it permanently archived anywhere.

17. "Gravediggers Strike in N.Y." *Toledo Blade*, January 12, 1970.

18. James Sanders, "Adventure Playground," in *America's Mayor*, 92.

19. As Glen Corbett notes, "Despite Giuliani's frantic efforts to grab credit for it, the revitalization of Times Square actually resulted from a massive state-city development effort that began under Governor Mario Cuomo and Mayor Edward Koch and was completed by the Dinkins administration, which persuaded the Disney corporation to make a financial commitment to developing Midtown *before* Giuliani ever took office. The porn shops and theaters that Giuliani claimed to have turned out were also gone months before Rudy ever got to City Hall" ("Control" in *America's Mayor: The Hidden History of Rudy Giuliani's New York*, ed. Robert Polner [Brooklyn, New York: Soft Skull Press, 2005], 172).

20. Heather Hendershot, "Fame Is a Bee: On Dick Cavett," *The Nation*, November 22, 2010.

SUSAN MURRAY

"MEDICAL SCHOOL OF THE WORLD"

EDUCATION AND PUBLIC SERVICE
THROUGH POSTWAR MEDICAL TELEVISION

When we are first introduced to Mrs. Sollins on screen, she is sitting up-right in a metal chair, naked from the waist up, looking ahead as a doctor points at her breasts while he details her history of tumors. The doctor goes on to examine her—both by hand and by "transillumination," a technique in which a directed light is pressed into the breast while the overhead lights in the examination room are turned off, which was said to help determine the size and consistency of a tumor. In the television program, a group of male doctors in front of an audience of medical students and residents are shown the film of her exam and discuss her case and debate the various ways in which she could be diagnosed and treated. Later, another woman is examined on screen in a similar manner; her case is presented as a textbook example of how a malignant tumor manifests visually in the breast.

Image from "Lesions of the Breast and Colon."

This program, an episode of *Grand Rounds* titled "Lesions of the Breast and Colon," which never aired to a general television audience, was submitted by the Medical Radio and Television Institute for consideration by the Peabody Awards in 1957.[1] It was part of a collection of ninety-minute closed-circuit, nonbroadcast color telecasts sponsored by Upjohn Pharmaceuticals and viewed live by physicians in fifty-five cities across the United States. A number of other medical television programs had been submitted to Peabody in the late 1950s, including three local broadcasts of surgeries performed at medical schools—"Advance in Surgery," an episode of *Tulane Close-Up* (WDSU, New Orleans), "Birth," an episode of *Lifeline* (WKTK, Detroit), and *Artery Reconstruction* (KRON, San Francisco)—along with "Radiology, Blood Pressure, Hearing," the debut episode of *World of Medicine*, a thirteen-part series produced by WTTW Chicago and broadcast nationwide on educational stations covering "twenty-eight medical subjects designed to increase public understanding of medicine."[2] Although none of these local, national, or closed-circuit medical submissions won a Peabody during this period, the fact that they were submitted for consideration (in either the educational or public service categories) signals a belief by their producers that their shows adhered to the values that the organization rewards, that they were quality productions engaged in educating, informing, and serving distinct communities or publics. These series represent two interrelated developments in medical television in the 1950s: the use of color television for education (particularly surgery) within the medical world and the broadcast of medical procedures and knowledge over local stations to audiences outside of that world. Both types of programming offered a unique public service on the local and national levels while also serving commercial/industrial needs and interests. For instance, *Grand Rounds* (1956–61), one of the most visible of the closed-circuit "teleclinics," was part of a larger movement of collaborations between television networks and their research labs, pharmaceutical companies, and medical schools across the United States, in which the technology of color television was employed to expand and alter the direction and experience of medical education. In this chapter, I examine these programs in relation to the broader context of the goals of all the various industrial actors involved, the claims the programs make with regard to "quality" educational programming, their functions for local affiliates and the medical establishment, and the criticisms the programs, which were directed at a lay audience, received, criticisms that revealed the contradictory nature of their adherence to the public service mandate.

THE DEVELOPMENT OF POSTWAR TELECLINICS

As work by Kristin Ostherr demonstrates, medical education films—capturing surgeries, examinations, and other medical procedures—were used rather extensively in university hospitals and for continuing education from the 1920s into the 1960s across the United States.[3] Initially conceived of as a potential replacement for the surgical amphitheater, these films were praised for their ability to provide rich detail and to depict uniformity in technique in instructional images that could easily be transported to almost any location. However, due to how expensive these films were to produce (in 1950 the College of Surgeons estimated it paid as much as $40,000 for the filming of a single procedure) and how quickly medical advancements in techniques and tools came to pass, these films proved to be limited investments and would eventually be replaced by closed-circuit television, which promised additional advantages such as immediacy, spontaneity, intimacy, and liveness.[4] In using television, surgeons could not only employ cutting-edge techniques but also extemporaneously alter their approach, training students how to be flexible, to improvise, and to adapt to the unexpected issues that inevitably arise in the operating room. Teleclinics, as they came to be called, even provided opportunities for questions via live call-in. Conceived of as a replacement for circulating filmed procedures and examinations, television was marketed as an opportunity to widen the reach of the medical classroom, constructing a "medical school of the world" in which geography, expense, or time would not limit access to the best medical professionals and educators in the field. It was not simply a cost-effective replacement for particular forms of medical training. Medical television was also touted as an improvement for providing students and doctors "the best seat in the house," offering close-up views (taken from cameras hung above the operating table) that those watching procedures in a surgical amphitheater could never get. It also kept the audience far away from the patient, increasing the sterility of the surgical space. A total of twenty-four medical schools were producing and utilizing medical television by the end of the 1950s in their in-house television studios.[5]

Medical television was initially demonstrated at the American Medical Association using black-and-white RCA monitors, but color television quickly became the preferred medium due to its ability to reveal distinctions between bodily organs and systems and to train students how to recognize disease through color and other fine details. Sponsored primarily by pharmaceutical companies and developed by the technical labs affiliated with CBS and RCA working with major American teaching hospitals, postwar medical television brought together a range of institutions and businesses for this singular purpose. The prime example of such a relationship is that between Peter Goldmark, the designer of CBS's field sequential color television system, and I. S. Ravdin, chief of surgery at the University of Pennsylvania Hospital, along with Smith, Kline and

French, the pharmaceutical company; together they worked to develop color medical television systems for use in private and military institutions. And it was Goldmark's work with Ravdin that kept the color television project going at CBS labs long after the FCC ruled in favor of the NTSC standard (associated with RCA) over the system proposed by CBS and that also led to Goldmark being appointed a visiting professor of electronics in medicine at Penn's school of medicine. Ravdin came to believe that monochrome television had little to no use in depicting surgical procedures—in fact, he was quoted as saying that black and white should only be used when cadavers, not live bodies, were involved. He argued that one of the unique properties of color television that made it so ideal for medical use was "a sense of depth which is necessary for the adequate teaching of surgery," noting that with color television "the deep recesses of body cavities which ordinarily are difficult to discern can now be readily observed because of the various color gradations."[6]

Whether the teleclinic was in color or black and white, the overwhelming majority of them were limited to an audience of medical professionals, and many were recorded for reviewing. *Grand Rounds* was one such teleclinic, but it was also unique in terms of its scale. Submitted to the Peabody Awards in 1957 and 1960, the program, which aired from 1955 to 1962 and was hosted by a different institution and featured a different type of case each time, established itself as a televised tradition for medical schools.[7] Upjohn Pharmaceuticals covered the quarter of a million dollars it cost to produce each show (that figure would include AT&T connections, production costs of both live and filmed segments, travel expenses for doctors involved, etc.), which was aired live in color but kinescoped in black and white. The term "grand rounds" refers to a practice in teaching hospitals wherein doctors, residents, and students would gather to discuss a particular medical case, usually involving a single patient, who (during these years) was present and available to be examined.

"Lesions of the Breast and Colon."

"Lesions of the Breast and Colon," submitted in 1957, opens on a table of eminent physicians surrounded—in surgical amphitheater style—by what appear to be students and residents. Broadcast to gatherings of medical professionals, the program conveys the feeling of a very large and lavish version of grand rounds, featuring some of the most well-known experts in their fields (including Ravdin) but also at times mimics the genre of a news roundtable—as the moderator, also a doctor, leads discussion and provokes debate between the doctors at the table. It was considered to be an honor to be asked to participate in one of these events, and participants would have been very conscious of their televisual presentation to an audience of the medical profession.

The accompanying visuals attest to the limited audience for the topic of breast cancer and to the way in which it adhered to contemporary medical norms and protocols. The case at the center of the breast cancer study (presented on film) was of a forty-four-year-old white woman with a tumor in her right breast who had had two prior breast tumors removed in the preceding decade. Even for a lay viewer in the present day, the visuals are striking. A topless woman on television would have been an exceedingly rare, if not unheard of, event outside of such a medical context. It is normalized, however, through the use of distancing techniques that work to depersonalize, desexualize, and even dehumanize the human body. Certainly, we see at work here Michel Foucault's notion of the medical, clinical, or observing gaze—the belief in the observational powers of doctors to both diagnose and their ability to separate from the patient. And yet the observational is also brought to a broader and layered audience of medical professionals: first beginning with the examining physician, then the roundtable of esteemed doctors, then the residents and students in the studio, and then circling out even further to the doctors watching via closed circuit in hospitals across the country. These are assumed to be experienced professionals who are crafting a desexualized and distancing observational space outside of the typical commercial viewer/broadcaster arrangement.

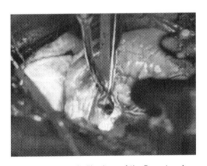

Coronary surgery in "Lesions of the Breast and Colon."

And it is not simply the desexualized/dehumanized female body that is under observation in this particular program. The doctors also explore a separate case of coronary heart disease, which is primarily focused on the viewing of and interaction with a live surgery. While viewing the type of close-up that was a hallmark of surgical training television, the group of doctors gathered in the studio and viewers watching via closed circuit listen to the surgeon narrate his movements, his mistakes, the alterations to his original surgical plan, his decision-making process, and how he chastises his assistants as he moves through the procedure. The doctors at the roundtable are able to ask him questions, shout suggestions, and even joke with him mid-procedure. In a troubling turn, the surgery does not end up going well and in the last moments of the remote broadcast from the operating room we hear the surgeon say in a tight voice, "It's bleeding like hell out of the aorta. . . . Geez, I told you fellas to go into the vena cava and you talked me out of it." The surgeon stops responding to questions from his colleagues via remote, and when we return to the roundtable the moderator remarks, "Well, listen, . . . I think that things aren't going the way that they should, and in this type of surgery you can certainly understand it," adding that while they had planned to interview the surgeon after the procedure had concluded, he would no longer be available to them. While this might make for "life hangs in the balance" television, due to a variety of ethical, moral, and even perhaps legal concerns, this is a moment that would likely only occur within the isolated context of medical institutions. In other words, this type of moment would not be available for public consumption, but it is available here because it is deemed an invaluable teaching moment that can be properly narrativized rather than spectacle ripe for exploitation.

Even though the rules about what they could show and how they could show it were different than those for broadcast television, medical schools were being trained in the processes, functions, and language of television and could also be considered early experimenters with color television production and management. There are a number of examples of articles that producers of medical television wrote for a medical audience in order to explain how to produce an interesting and engaging medical training program. One such example—a 1954 issue of the *Journal of the American Medical Association* (JAMA)—was a report on best practices by Arthur Holleb and Frances Buch, a doctor and network television director team. Buch was one of the earliest and most successful female television directors at CBS and had been asked by the American Cancer Society to produce thirty closed-circuit telecolor clinics for physicians. The JAMA article, effectively a television program production manual geared toward the highly specialized genre of medical education, instructs schools on lighting and color specifications and management, how to employ visual aids, what combination of personnel to hire, what color gowns should be worn (green), and how and when to use live models. Another example was a speech delivered by Alfred Goldsmith, former head of research at RCA, at the International College of Surgeons that provided detailed instructions on how surgeons should prepare for and act on television.[8] A downside of this level of technological management and the expectations for high production quality in a hospital studio, however, was that maintenance could be both costly and complicated. It was at least partly because investment and maintenance costs were high that it made sense for hospitals to utilize their studios as much as they could and to distribute the programs broadly. Limiting distribution locally would only increase their status and reputation within their own community.

MEDICAL PROGRAMS FOR LOCAL AND NATIONAL BROADCAST

The three general audience medical programs submitted for Peabody consideration in 1959 were all local telecasts of surgeries (open heart surgery, artery reconstruction, and cesarean section) broadcast out of area hospitals in New Orleans, San Francisco, and Ann Arbor. It might seem remarkable at first that local affiliates had this type of medical programming. However, it is more understandable when one learns that this programming was an outgrowth of closed-circuit medical education programs. Hospitals already producing teleclinics had trained staff, equipment, and surgical studios at the ready—and a desire to offset their cost. The production of local programming allowed hospitals to put their equipment to use for a secondary purpose beyond closed circuit, further justifying the significant expense of the equipment and its upkeep. A 1952 American Medical Association survey found that "77% of county medical societies and 91% of state societies use some form of radio and television" for the purposes of education and/or public relations.[9] The following year, Edward J. McCormick, the president of the association, noted in a letter to the National Association of Radio and Television Broadcasters that nonfiction medical television had "given the entire nation a better concept of good health and how to preserve it—and a better understanding of the newest techniques, discoveries, and devices which spell continual medical progress." Television, Dr. McCormick asserted, has proved "a brilliant new addition to the teaching tools of medicine."[10]

Throughout the 1950s and into the 1960s, large teaching hospitals considered the installation of a television studio to be a sign not only of their modernity but also of their increasing influence on the field of medicine. Medical television provided local stations with an opportunity both to engage in public service and, as David Serlin argues, "to transcend the geographical and technical limitations imposed by network broadcasts" by making "ingenious use of nearby resources such as teaching hospitals and clinics, local physician's clubs and medical organizations, ladies auxiliaries, and private physician citizens," which implied "a progressive democratic approach to television technology."[11] Serlin also notes that the pull to emphasize a dramatic narrative in such programming often proved too difficult to resist. This was often a "life hangs in the balance" narrative and/or a glimpse into "real life as it happens" narrative, accompanying a discourse around scientific innovation, advancements in care, and interventions into self-care and medical self-awareness. Of course, there had to be interest from audiences and stations if the broadcasting of these local programs was to continue. For their part, stations received relatively exciting or dramatic programming with decent production values to fill the time between network hours. There were a number of reasons, of course, why these programs may have engaged viewers, including the call to care for one's own body, as well as cultural and institutional factors detailed by Serlin related to the heightened interest in "medical concerns that were particular to the United States after World War II," such as obesity, cancer, and diabetes.[12]

The dramatic aspects of this type of programming are certainly on display in the three 1959 programs, although the mood and the anticipated audience response are built into their structure in distinct ways and would not cross the line into the type of "surgery gone wrong" moment witnessed in the *Grand Rounds* program. The thirty-minute premiere episode of *Lifeline* called "Birth," a series that came out of the University of Michigan Women's Hospital, aired on WJBK in Detroit, and was sponsored by Michigan Blue Cross/Blue Shield, used its first ten minutes to introduce viewers to the hospital, the doctor, the patient, and the overall context for their viewing of one woman's birth experience via cesarean section.[13] The episode opens with the following announcement: "These are medical reports that we hope will increase your understanding of the importance of doctors and hospitals to your way of life. What you will see now and in the weeks to come is *not* acting, it is *actually happening*. . . . Actually, it happens largely as a matter of chance that our cameras will witness the birth of the baby of Mrs. Del Boblitt who lives in Ann Arbor." The intermingling of claims to public service along with the promise of the sensational (functioning as a mixed appeal to viewers—allowing for pleasure without the guilt) is a familiar address to contemporary viewers of reality television. In coming to know the patient's medical and so-

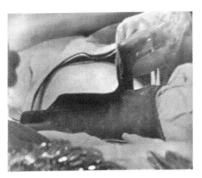

The surgeon makes the first cut in "Birth."

Cameras in the operating room recording from the mirror above the operating table in *Artery Reconstruction* (KRON, 1959).

cial background (primarily through prerecorded segments), viewers are assured that she exists within the socially acceptable frame of white middle-class heterosexual marriage and therefore must not only be in need of this particular procedure but also must be deserving of it. Her "normalness" also provides a safe and familiar body to represent on postwar midwestern television. The interaction of the patient with the doctor and nurses that viewers witness also makes them confident in the abilities and reputation of the hospital and its staff, which provides another comforting frame through which to view a live and intimate surgery.

The program switches from prerecorded to live broadcast from the hospital as Mrs. Boblitt is saying goodbye to her husband and being prepped for surgery. The camera provides an initial long shot from behind the surgeon while he arranges the drapes over Mrs. Boblitt's abdomen, but the first cut is shown in the close-up frame that is typically utilized during teleclinic operations.

For almost fifteen minutes, the camera remains in the same position as the surgeon cuts through the various layers of muscle and tissue, eventually delivering the baby. The extended scene is unrelenting in its focus and detail, and while of course a vaginal birth would not have been deemed acceptable to show on television, the surgery itself—even with all the elements in place for clinical distancing—is still quite gruesome.

The single-episode special *Artery Reconstruction* (KRON, 1959) also begins with a ten-minute explanatory setup before entering a live surgery in progress.[14] Viewers see a close-up of the open body taken from a camera recording the image reflected in a mirror over the operating table for twenty-two minutes, which is interrupted only briefly by medium shots of the surgery team and cameras. (There is also a moment in which the view is obstructed by a surgeon peering too far into the frame, and immediately we hear finger snapping and the narrator tersely shouting, "HEAD!")

The episode "Advance in Surgery" from *Tulane Close-Up*, a local series produced by Tulane University in New Orleans, opens with an extended close-up of a beating heart in an open chest during surgery before it returns to the host, who explains the significance of the image in relation to the heart-lung machine and interviews a Tulane Medical School professor of surgery about the advancement.[15] After a demonstration on a studio stage of how a heart-lung machine works, the program turns to the now familiar extended close-up (recorded) footage of an open-heart surgery in progress, narrated by the professor and interrupted only by shots of the heart-lung machine in action. Again the images of the surgery reveal the open body cavity with blood, tissue, and cutting on full display.

The first surgery on national television, sponsored by Smith, Kline and French, aired on NBC in 1951 and was an eight-minute live feed from that year's American Medical Association meeting showing the "incised abdomen of a man undergoing an operation to check hemorrhaging from a duodenal ulcer. Most of the camera work in the operating room is done close up. Especially vivid is the sight of the retractors holding back the blood vessels. Viewers also see the scissors used to cut ligatures as well as the sterile pads used to keep the incision dry."[16] A number of journalists and critics at the time were repulsed or shocked by the images and questioned the working assumption that viewers could handle such programming. The opening titles to *Artery Reconstruction* claim that the San Francisco Medical Society "feels this telecast may remove some of the fear, take away some of the mystery of a surgical procedure any of us might have to face," but critics argued that these types of programs achieved just the opposite. The press regularly reported that even doctors worried that there would be an increase in cases of hypochondria if the public was exposed to such programming, and they further argued that the average person was ill equipped to digest such strong unfiltered operating room images.

For example, influential *New York Times* television critic Jack Gould refuses to even describe the NBC broadcast's close-ups from the AMA in his review and argues that "the physician on television must recognize that the average man or child does not possess his sense of detachment." *Washington Post* critic John Crosby agreed with Gould. The 1951 broadcast of the duodenal ulcer was, he states, "conceivably the bloodiest television program of all times," adding that while he understood that it was "in its way, instructive" he was not sure how he or the average viewer would use such information. "Lie down, junior," he notes sarcastically. "Let's have a go at that duodenal ulcer."[17] In his review of a 1952 program covering a cesarean section, Crosby explains that he was relieved that it did not actually show the surgery itself, "Frankly, I couldn't have been happier. There are some things that the lay citizenry shouldn't be exposed to and I feel strongly that the birth of a baby is one of them. Too graphic a picturization of so intimate a business could easily drive a lot of young women into concluding that childbirth is not for them."[18] After describing other surgical programs that followed, such as a program by Sloan-Kettering containing close-ups of rabbits and mice whose eyes were filled with cancerous tumors and an episode of *The Search* on CBS wherein an "infant was held up in front of the cameras even before the placenta had been washed off," Gould calls for an end to such medical programming: "Much criticism has been directed at the producers of commercial horror shows and the impact that such presentations may have on the younger generation. Yet nothing seen in this reviewer's experience can compare with the potential element of shock embodied in yesterday's programs, presented on a Sunday afternoon under the guise of education.... With due allowance for the commendable objective of acquainting the lay public with the accomplishments of medicine, it is time for a halt. Medicine is not going to build confidence and faith in service to mankind by turning the living room into an operating room."[19] As a point of comparison, in the late 1920s and into the 1930s, medical *films* were forbidden from being shown to general audiences, with the Motion Picture Producers and Distributors of America (MPPDA) listing "surgical operations" not only in the Production Codes of 1930 and 1934 but also in its list of "Don'ts and Be Carefuls" in 1927.[20] As Ostherr points out, the American College of Surgeons approved of this ban, as they sought to strictly regulate the content of surgical films, only giving their seal of approval to those that followed their guidelines, which included prohibitions against commercialism, personal advertisement of the surgeon, inappropriate subjects, and nonaccepted techniques. "By restricting audiences for ACS films to medical specialists," Ostherr writes, "the college cultivated a form of medical vision accessible only to an elite, highly trained viewership."[21] This also successfully protected these films from charges of exploitation and questionable medical ethics. While the surgical television programs, both local and national, of the 1950s were encased in the distancing educational rhetoric of the medical field and worked to employ a detached medicalized vision, this wasn't enough to overcome the objections of viewers and critics to the unrelenting framing of the footage, the most common type found in medical programs aimed at professionals. The view of blood and gore could not be properly narrativized by television, in part due to the perceived intimacy of the medium and its central placement within the domestic sphere. As a result, such programming continued to be seen by many as too visceral or sensational to be educational or to serve the public in the manner the medical institutions and companies producing and sponsoring it claimed it did.

This placed the hospitals in an odd position when it came to public relations and claims to public service. In continuing to present surgical programs, they were hoping to publicize the work of their hospitals, but they also risked offending the senses and tastes of audiences and critics. Although not an institutional seal of approval like those from the American College of Surgeons for the medical films of an earlier period, a Peabody Award would certainly go a long way to validating their productions as high quality, educational, and informational, a genuine achievement in public service. None of these programs ever achieved such an honor, however.

CONCLUSION

The local medical programs began to disappear in the mid- to late 1960s as stations began to fill open timeslots with syndicated programming and the hospitals began losing interest in producing programs. Medical education via television, however, continues in various forms and is more fully integrated into the norms and daily practices of teaching hospitals. As Serlin and Ostherr note, fictional and reenactment-based medical programming became a staple of television by the early 1960s and did much of the work of medical public relations and also established itself as a certain form of public education. This glimpse into the postwar period in which nonfiction, educational, medical television was new, however, provides a rich example of the ways in which institutions and corporations worked together to construct particular genres and functions of television. The programs aired on local stations provided the type of dramatic programming thought to attract audiences; however, the gore and unrelenting close-ups into body cavities often proved to be difficult to integrate into the norms and functions of viewing for the average television audience member. These examples reveal the complicated nexus of factors that arise when programming that was originally meant for a highly specialized audience is repackaged for a general audience with the express purpose of meeting public service and educational mandates as well as the contradictory results that can ensue.

NOTES

1. Medical Radio and Television Institute, *Grand Rounds*, "Lesions of the Breast and Colon," March 27, 1957, 57020 EDT 1–3 of 5, Peabody Awards Collection, Walter J. Brown Media Archives and Peabody Awards Collection, University of Georgia (hereafter PAC), http://dlg.galileo.usg.edu/peabody/id:1957_57020_edt_1-3.

2. WTTW, *World of Medicine*, "Radiology, Blood Pressure, Hearing," 1957, 57006 ET 1 of 1, PAC, http://dlg.galileo.usg.edu/peabody/id:1957_57006_edt_1.

3. Kirsten Ostherr, *Medical Visions: Producing the Patient through Film, Television, and Imaging Technologies* (Oxford: Oxford University Press, 2013), 75.

4. "Color Television at Medical Conventions, Spring program, 1950" sponsored by SKF, "Admin," box 44, folder 4, Ravdin Papers, University of Pennsylvania Medical School Archives.

5. David Serlin, "Performing Live Surgery on Television and the Internet since 1945," in *Imagining Illness: Public Health and Visual Culture*, ed. David Serlin (Minneapolis: University of Minnesota Press, 2010), 227.

6. Ibid.

7. In addition to "Lesions of the Breast and Colon," *Grand Rounds* also submitted "Coronary Disease," November 13, 1957,57020 EDT 4–5 of 5, PAC, http://dlg.galileo.usg.edu/peabody/id:1957_57020_edt_4-5, and "Gastrointestinal Problems: Surgery or Treatment," 1960, 60028 EDT 1–2 of 2, PAC, http://dlg.galileo.usg.edu/peabody/id:1960_60028_edt_1-2.

8. "First Inter-City Consultation and Diagnosis by Pathologist in Fight against Disease" memorandum, January 19, 1955, box 67, folder 24, Ravdin Papers, University of Pennsylvania Medical School Archives.

9. "TV's Service to Medicine Extolled in AMA Letter," *Broadcasting, Telecasting* 45, no. 17 (1953): 42.

10. Ibid.

11. Serlin, "Performing Live Surgery on Television and the Internet since 1945," 229–30.

12. Ibid., 226.

13. *Lifeline*, "Birth," September 10, 1959, 59033 PST 1 of 1, PAC, http://dlg.galileo.usg.edu/peabody/id:1959_59033_pst_1.

14. WKTK, KRON, *Artery Reconstruction*, 1959, 59004 1–2 of 2, PAC, http://dlg.galileo.usg.edu/peabody/id:1959_59004_pst_1-2.

15. WDSU, *Tulane Close-Up*, "Advance in Surgery," 1959, 59015 EDT 1 of 1, PAC, http://dlg.galileo.usg.edu/peabody/id:1959_59015_edt_1.

16. William L. Laurence, "Major Operation to Save a Life Put on Network TV for First Time," *New York Times*, June 11, 1952, 1.

17. "They Sure Treat the Baby Rough," *Washington Post*, December 13, 1952, 27.
18. Ibid.
19. Gould, "Television in Review: Succession of Medical programs Rivals Horror Shows in Elements of Shock," *New York Times*, December 6, 1954, 37.
20. Ostherr, *Medical Visions*, 75.
21. Ibid., 72–75.

ETHAN THOMPSON

EVENTS DESCRIBED ARE NOT OCCURRING (AND NOT FUNNY)

SERIOUS FAKE NEWS IN THE PEABODY ARCHIVE

"Fake news" isn't what it used to be. The deliberate spread of false stories during the 2016 U.S. presidential election and Donald Trump's subsequent application of the term "fake news" to any coverage he doesn't like have effectively redefined a term that had most recently been associated with news parody. The simulated newscast has long been a dependable strategy for producing comedy from David Frost on *That Was the Week That Was* in the 1960s, to Kermit the Frog on *Sesame Street* in the 1980s, to *Saturday Night Live*'s "Weekend Update," reporting fake news since 1975. In the 2000s, news parody reached a new level of cultural caché with the satiric programs *The Daily Show with Jon Stewart* and *The Colbert Report*, lauded for critically engaging American media and political culture in informative, compelling ways. Almost immediately, there was attendant hand-wringing over what the popularity of the supposed "fake news" signified about the decline of "real" journalism. The election of 2016 put such debates in perspective. The new fake news is outright disinformation: devious entrepreneurs and foreign saboteurs concoct false stories to appeal to readers eager to have their partisan biases confirmed with a click. The more outrageously fake, the more clicks, the more profits, the better the electoral process manipulated. It's not at all funny.[1]

But broadcast history demonstrates that comedy did not previously enjoy a monopoly on the fake news.[2] There were a number of local, network, and cable "serious fake news" programs and specials prior to 2016 that were neither trying to be funny nor sabotage American politics. The most famous—arguably the most notorious episode in media history—was Orson Welles's *War of the Worlds* broadcast in 1934. Though it was clearly marked as a dramatic presentation in an introduction, the Mercury Theatre production mimicked a typical evening's flow of radio programming, interrupting musical performances and advertisements with fake news segments until entirely turning the content over to news reporting on a Martian invasion.[3] *War of the Worlds* has proven to be an outlier: a simulated newscast done explicitly for dramatic entertainment purposes. But in between Orson Welles and Vladimir Putin, there is a body of fake news specials produced not in the name of entertainment or political sabotage but public service. A search for "simulated," "fictionalized," or "dramatized" news in the Peabody Awards Collection reveals that the format has been adopted for a variety of programming about both current and historical events.

Geoff Baym argues that the distinction between real and fake news has never been as clear as many presume, and that the simplistic distinction commonly made between news (real) and entertainment (fake) obscures the conventions of the news more than it reveals.[4] The "real news" has always relied on various conventions to engage viewers and present stories about the social world. But the serious fake news programs examined here, all found in the Peabody archive, both simulate the typical news format and present themselves as a deviation from "normal" daily news—that is, they are openly "fake" in a way that does not have to do with whether or not they are funny. Though few in number, the content and history of these productions demonstrate that the fake news has been a much more versatile format than popular memory recalls. This expansion of the lineage of fake news draws further attention to the flourishing of local television production in the 1970s and early 1980s, as a number of the programs were produced by local stations, and in one case, a station group. A closer look at these programs, as well as the materials submitted along with them for Peabody consideration, shows that the simulated news format was considered a particularly useful—even legitimizing—format for representing reality, that is, dramatizing the past or future, with authority.

Two distinctive modes of serious fake news emerge: the historical, which reports past events within a contemporary frame; and the speculative, which reports on future events as the consequence of contemporary forces and conditions. By investigating these programs, including not just the texts of the programs themselves but supplementary production and publicity materials, as well as reviews from the popular press, we gain an understanding of how fake news has been (and could be) used to build civic culture, rather than break it down.

The historical mode reports past events from within a present news frame. Rather than just dramatizing events, these programs simulate a news report by including onscreen reporters and an anchor, which separates them from historical dramatizations or docudramas.[5] The most well-known example of this mode in television is *You Are There* (CBS, Radio, 1947–50; TV, 1953–57, 1971–72), which won a Peabody in 1956 and was hosted by the biggest TV news icon of them all, Walter Cronkite. The program featured Cronkite and CBS journalists "reporting" on dramatizations of past events as if they were now occurring. Unlike the other programs I discuss here, *You Are There* is regarded as canonical television that attempted to balance broadcasting entertainment with education. CBS repeatedly nominated the program for a Peabody, submitting "The Ratification of the Constitution" (radio, 1948), "Trial Run of the Tom Thumb" (TV, 1949), "The Death of Socrates" (TV, 1953), and "Mallory's Tragedy on Mt. Everest" (TV, 1954) before eventually being recognized with the 1956 win. The citation celebrated the program's unique approach to dramatizing the past: it helped to "remind us that the men who made United States history did walk and talk, and think and feel," and it made "the statues and portraits come briefly to life again."[6]

The program was revived in the early 1970s, with Cronkite again at the helm, as Saturday morning children's programming. That second iteration didn't win a Peabody (CBS tried with episodes on Susan B. Anthony and Harriet Tubman), but it closely followed the same format, which had by then been extensively parodied over the years, starting with Ernie Kovacs's "Vas you dere?" in the 1950s. It was easy to parody *You Are There* because the characteristics of the form were so simple (an anchor or reporter as straight man), and the content that could be used for it was inexhaustible (anything in the past).[7] Treating historical events like they were current news meant it wasn't necessary to create a meticulous period environment to immerse the viewer. Engagement came from the novelty of the past being treated like it was the present: not through the best costumes and acting but by simply placing the past within the frame of the contemporary news, with an anchor and one or more "on the scene" reporters. Even CBS, in its Peabody submission form for *You Are There*, emphasized the news frame, not the realism of its historical re-creation, describing it as "quite simply the recreation, in dramatic form, of significant events of history as if they were actually happening now and being described now by extremely capable reporters."[8]

Steve Anderson has noted how what he calls the "mock TV news" format of *You Are There* made it possible to address alternative perspectives on history that docudramas could not: "Alternative historical opinions or disputable facts were ingeniously qualified as being uncorroborated due to the immediacy of the live, breaking newscast. Conventions of historical speculation and investigative journalism were merged in the figure of Cronkite, who orchestrated the incoming reports and provided restrained commentary on the context and significance of the events portrayed."[9] *You Are There* thus presented discourse on historical events, not just simple re-creations. Thomas Doherty writes, "The actor-journalists brought the same level of earnest professionalism to their pretend tasks as to their real assignments, categories that television was busy collapsing anyway."[10] As Doherty further notes, this wasn't incidental, as behind-the-scenes were blacklisted screenwriters Abraham Polansky and Walter Bernstein. The episode "The Death of Socrates," which was submitted for Peabody consideration in 1953, is notable not just for the fact it featured future Hollywood star Paul Newman as Plato and was directed by Sidney Lumet but also because it was part of the shift toward critical media coverage of Senator Joseph McCarthy, which culminated in Edward R. Murrow's famous takedown on the documentary series *See It Now* in 1954. Doherty singles out the program's "Salem Witch Trials" episode from March 1953 as a "veiled commentary on the ongoing courtroom spectacle" of the Army-McCarthy hearings.[11] As Erik Barton Christiansen writes, "The subjects returned to again and again by *You Are There* writers —Galileo, Socrates, Joan of Arc, Salem—had been used and were still being used to denounce fascism, totalitarianism, and any other political system in which artists, scientists, writers, and intellectuals were forced to conform to an obnoxious political standard."[12] The fake news format, then, proved not to be just an expeditious venue on a national stage but a shield for writers that allowed them to address the oppressive elements of the political climate in postwar America that they couldn't address elsewhere.

Although *You Are There* had Cronkite and the resources of CBS behind it, the simulated newscast, as parodies showed, was a relatively easy format to adopt, thus making it attractive to those seeking to produce television on a budget. Material-wise, all that was needed was a news set and some vaguely appropriate period costumes. Throughout the history of American television, from the network era beginning in the fifties through the rise of cable and into today's era of multiple platforms, local television stations have had news sets, anchors, and reporters. What they have lacked is a reason to produce a simulated newscast. By agreement and necessity, a local affiliate broadcasts network programming whenever it can and produces its own programs when it has to. It is more cost effective (and lucrative) to fill holes in the network schedule with syndicated programs. But, to varying degrees according to the politics of the day, local stations have had to fulfill FCC localism requirements: they have to show that they serve the needs and the interests of the community. Producing local news helps to fulfill this requirement, and it also makes the station money, as covering local news is the one thing the affiliate can do better than the network. Prior to the mid-1980s, local stations often produced public service programming, usually in the form of talk shows that discussed local issues and events in fringe timeslots such as late Saturday nights and early Sunday mornings. These were produced cheaply and not expected to make money. In short, the logics of local television production have been simple: anything produced needs to help fulfill public service responsibilities, however cheap it might be.

The bicentennial year of 1976 provided an impetus for stations around the country to extend their production practices into historical television. As Lucas Hatlen and Christine Becker describe in their chapter in this book, "Broadcasting the Bicentennial," a national bicentennial commission developed a guide to encourage such productions, and funds, primarily from corporations, became available to support them. What resulted in some cases were historical documentary shorts focused on local history, such as *Minnesota Memories* from KSTP in St. Paul and *The New England Experience* from WNAC in Boston. Large-scale documentary histories and shorts with a nonregional approach were also produced, such as *A Man Named Douglass* (WNBC, New York) and *Blacks and the American Revolution* from WSB in Atlanta.[13]

At least one local television station seized the bicentennial as an opportunity to produce historical fake news: WCKT, the NBC affiliate in Miami. That program, *Sunday News Update '76*, illustrates not just that a station could produce an historical "fake news" program as public service but also how the result could cut against the grain of nationalist bicentennial celebrations.[14] As critics have noted, *You Are There* accounted for al-

Anchor Carmel Cafiero of Miami NBC affiliate WCKT reports on the news of 1776 in 1976.

ternative viewpoints on history through the figure of Cronkite and more broadly used past events as allegories for critical commentary on the present. But *Sunday News Update '76* shows how a local station, by closely simulating the news format it already followed, could produce its own more complex historical programming. Viewing the program over forty years later, the community-theater quality of the costumes in *Sunday News Update '76* seems quaint. But the program's articulation of antirevolutionary sentiment, apropos of the Florida colonies in 1776, as well as its recognition of the routine violence directed toward slaves, may surprise anyone who expects a bicentennial celebration.

Both *War of the Worlds* and *You Are There* were on the minds of reporters writing about the production of *Sunday News Update '76* for Florida papers. When WCKT came to Pensacola to shoot a segment for the program, a local news piece titled "1776: TV Takes You There" imagined a scenario where an unsuspecting "John Doe" switches the channel to a broadcast of *Sunday News Update '76*: "When the cameras cut to St. Augustine for an on the spot report of irate citizens burning John Hancock and Sam Adams in effigy—John's in real trouble. The same kind of trouble that scared the dickens out of those people who turned their radio dials in the middle of Orson Welles' Martian invasion newscast . . . in reverse. The Welles' victims thought it was happening at that moment; John is looking at events which happened 200 years ago."[15]

True to the promises of such articles and press releases, the program, which aired on July 4, did closely resemble a contemporary broadcast, with all the local news personalities on screen and all the typical segments. Carmel Cafiero, the regular Sunday anchor, opened the broadcast with a quick overview of key stories to come: representatives of thirteen colonies had announced their independence from Great Britain, the Continental army was amassing for an invasion of east Florida, and three slaves had been hanged for plotting a rebellion. There was nothing funny about her, or anyone else's, delivery. As *Miami Herald* TV editor Jack Anderson observes in a review, "Everybody plays it straight, and everybody is in costume."[16]

Right at the top, anchor Carmel Cafiero notes that the Floridas, east and west, were not represented at the signing of the Declaration of Independence. Wayne Ferris, news commentator, describes this lack of representation as unsurprising, as artist renderings of the signing are shown, mimicking the standard for news accounts of a court case, and on-screen graphics of the reporters' names and locations of the event appear in English script rather than a modern typeface. Further emphasizing that Florida was not part of the original thirteen colonies (nor did most in Florida support the revolution), the news report cuts to St. Augustine, where loyalists react angrily by burning patriots Samuel Adams and John Hancock in effigy. "Anti-patriot sentiment runs deep in east Florida," Larry Klaas reports. "Many of these people were run out of their homes in the north by rebel terrorists, and came to Florida seeking refuge." Individuals talk to the camera, praising the king, angrily denouncing the patriots. Standing on screen in a tricornered hat, Klaas closes the piece as loyalists dance around the burnt remnants of the effigies: "But today's demonstration provides ample evidence of the fact that the people of St. Augustine still feel more British than American." This antirevolutionary sentiment is echoed in the next segment from Pensacola where one woman describes the Declaration of Independence as "the most asinine thing I've ever heard of" and another warns "The king will teach them a lesson." Rather than shy away from the history of slavery, *Sunday News Update '76* draws attention to its prominent presence in Florida of 1776. Richard Whitcomb reports on the execution of three slaves in west Florida for plotting a rebellion against their masters. The plantation owner can't understand the reason for the plot: "Two of the three negroes who did this dastardly deed had never even felt the whip."

Aside from these "hard fake news" reports, *Sunday News Update '76* also includes segments on sports and weather. We hear about how an east Florida ranger beat two redcoats in target shooting and how lawn bowling continues to increase in popularity, especially in west Florida where there is a concentration of Scottish settlers. The weather report is hot and humid, as to be expected in July, but the weatherman notes that Floridians weren't the only ones who were uncomfortable. "I understand it was so hot in Philadelphia for the Continental Congress that one of the major items of debate was whether to open the windows to let [a] breeze in or close them to keep flies out."

Though much of the broadcast covers loyalist perspectives on the Declaration of Independence, the local news format of the time, which often included an editorial commentary, provides an opportunity to close the program with a more prorevolutionary viewpoint appropriate for 1976. Still, this commentary is not exactly a whole-hearted endorsement of the Declaration of Independence. Richard Whitcomb appears again, this time in the studio, and warns that "if we do not join the colonials, I have the desperate feeling that we will have chosen the wrong side." Carmel recaps the stories, and the camera pulls back to reveal cameramen in revolutionary garb.

In its Peabody submission form, WCKT claimed that two kinds of simulation contributed to the quality of the program: one was historical simulation that encouraged research and expanded the scope of the production ("Our team traveled throughout Florida, . . . researched scores of publications and talked with historians"), and the other was newscast simulation that was facilitated by the program's sticking closely to the format of the real news employed by the affiliate ("It was a soup to nuts presentation—spot news, features, sports, investigative reporting and even news commentary.")[17] The combination of historical and newscast simulation, the producers argued, created a clash between present form and past content that shocked the viewer into engagement. This approach was particularly useful for a local station in 1976; the past/present clash as well as the focus on local history in the midst of a national celebration allowed WCKT to cut through the clutter of bicentennial programming.

WCKT submitted many materials from its public inspection file to Peabody as evidence of the program's impact and significance. These materials include the press release, several newspaper clips noting the broadcast, many typed and handwritten notes from individual viewers praising the show, and a variety of letters from educational institutions thanking the station for a videotape of the broadcast. A. L. Materson of Miami Beach praised the show by contrasting it with a "sickening, cutesy, $17.76 paint commercial," implying that it was material like this that was gimmicky, not the program. *Sunday News Update '76* wasn't just novel but "interesting and imaginative," he wrote, and "a refreshing change from reporting the dull events taking place locally at that time of the day on July 4, 1976." Miss Golda R. Kortum wrote that it was "most educational and enlightening—yet entertaining too." One letter thanked the station for donating costumes used in the program to the college's theater department (and noted that the video would be one of the first viewed on the library's brand-new videocassette equipment!). The director of the St. Augustine Preservation Board wrote to ask for a copy so that the locals who participated could watch. The Broward County superintendent of schools wrote to express his congratulations and testimony that the students "found [it] not only most enjoyable but also very educational." Also included to testify to the use of the program in the schools was a memorandum from Paul S. Hanson, social studies consultant, to all principals in Dade County, advising them of the opportunity to view and consider the broadcast for classroom use. The letter accompanying the submission drew attention to this, saying it was "being distributed by the Dade County School System to 250 schools."

These various notes and letters attest to the utility—not just novelty—of *Sunday News Update '76* as fake news. WCKT included them as evidence of how the program effectively engaged the public rather than merely surprising "John Doe" by having newscasters in costume. WCKT argued that *Sunday News Update '76* was an example of excellence in broadcasting: individual viewers were moved to write to the station, educational institutions incorporated it into their curriculum, the station drew on local resources and also gave back with locally relevant content that couldn't be accessed elsewhere. All of which was delivered, as WCKT's submission noted, "in a news presentation that did not differ from the regular nightly televised newscast. From anchors to reports, all decked out in researched and appropriate costumes that might have been [worn] by newscasters and reporters in 1776.... And you are there."[18] The news format was not just the easiest and cheapest way to produce the show; the format also had the advantage of lending authority to and legitimating the production as a particularly engaging form of historical TV.

TOMORROW'S AMERICA TONIGHT: SPECULATIVE FAKE NEWS

War of the Worlds demonstrated that simulating radio news could be an effective strategy for engaging audiences, but it was fake news in the "fakest" sense: nothing reported was actually happening, nor was it reporting on something that had happened in the distant past, as *You Are There* would do. Its content was speculative: what would a Martian invasion be like? While fictional programs often incorporate actors portraying reporters, few entertainment programs have formatted themselves as simulated news reports as closely as *War of the Worlds* did.[19] However, the speculative approach of *War of the Worlds*, looking forward rather than backward, has been adopted to dramatize a near future that is the direct result of forces at work in the present. While *War of the Worlds* dramatized what an invasion of Martians would be like, the speculative mode of fake news tries to persuade audiences to consider how the future could be imperiled by human, not Martian, forces.

The Peabody collection contains a number of speculative programs, and although none of them had the impact of *War of the Worlds*, several were recognized as significant programming by critics at the time, even if they lacked a network audience. These programs from the 1970s and 1980s split neatly into speculation on two real-world concerns: nuclear war and environmental catastrophe. What if current environmental degradations continue unchecked? What if Russia—or the United States—starts a nuclear war?[20]

Though it's not as revered as *You Are There*, there is one Peabody winner among the speculative programs. *Ground Zero: Victory Road* was a special produced by WCVB-TV, the ABC affiliate in Boston, in 1982.[21] It is a prime example of how local news stations could leverage their news set,

Peabody-winner *Ground Zero: Victory Road* reports on the aftermath of a nuclear warhead detonation over Boston in 1982.

anchors, and production practices to produce compelling public service programming in a very simple, straightforward (cheap) manner. *Ground Zero* features a news anchor describing the seconds, minutes, and hours following the detonation of a nuclear warhead over a Boston suburb, supplemented by shots of an artist's rendering of what the scenes would look like. "This kind of program is not easy to watch," the Peabody Award citation read, but not because it was boring. "It is unsettling. It creates a deep sense of concern and, hopefully, spurs us to work toward eliminating the possibility that it could ever happen—anywhere."[22] The award thus recognized that the simulated news format could galvanize audiences in a simple, powerful manner. The award went to the program not for covering local content but for addressing a national concern as if it was local news.

The sole broadcast network example of speculative news in the Peabody submissions is *Special Bulletin* (NBC, 1983), which dramatizes a scenario in which leftist activists set off a nuclear warhead.[23] The submission text suggested that this entertainment program was meant as media criticism as much as a warning about the dangers of nuclear weapons. The submission form credited its fake news format for this: "By using the language of crisis news coverage," the program "encourages the audience to think about the terrible possibility of nuclear terrorism, the steps which would have to be taken to avert a disaster, and the role of the media—especially television—in covering such an event."[24] In 1984, a pay-cable network got into the nuclear fake news game. HBO (already home to the comic fake news program *Not Necessarily the News*) produced a big-budget fake news drama, *Countdown to Looking Glass*, which featured veteran newscaster Eric Sevareid and other real-life public figures such as Newt Gingrich. Program materials described it as "the story of nine terrifying days of international intrigue that propel the world to the brink of nuclear destruction. The action unfolds through the eyes of a network television news [team] whose satellite reporters dramatize the shocking incidents."[25] Besides putting real-life figures like Sevareid and Gingrich in speculative scenarios, *Countdown to Looking Glass* also alternates back and forth between the news format and a narrative presented in traditional dramatic scenes.

"Eyewitness News, Year 2000," the first episode of a series called *We the People* from KPIX, the CBS affiliate in San Francisco, is another example of a local TV station producing fake news in the bicentennial year.[26]

This 1976 fake news show from KPIX, the CBS affiliate in San Francisco, reports on the environmental catastrophes of 2000.

But as the title makes clear, it looks forward rather than backward. Segments focus on the possibility of various environmental catastrophes in the not-so-distant future. Like *Sunday News Update '76*, it sticks closely to the news format that features a central anchor and multiple segments with reporters covering food shortages, air and water pollution, and housing and energy crises. The submission form stated that "the program showed what could happen in the Bay Area 25 years from now if we do nothing about the problems of new food sources, land use, air and water pollution, education, housing, crime, energy and citizen participation in government."[27]

The earliest of the speculative fake news programs in the Peabody archive is *1985*, produced by the Metromedia station group in 1970, the year of the first Earth Day, and it is a rich example for considering how fake news programs were made sense of in their cultural and industrial contexts.[28] *1985*'s submission form described it as "a fictionalized newscast created and produced to dramatically underscore to an apathetic nation the deadly seriousness of the problems of pollution and the ever-increasing devastation of the environment."[29] Indeed, *1985* should register as one of the bleakest hours of American television ever produced. Having been produced in 1970, the program unsurprisingly begins as a psychedelic immersion into abstract video graphics. Electronic noises and swirling colors fill the screen, while years of the seventies and eighties appear in white type, then float off the screen. But the voiceover narration makes it clear this is a bad trip: "Fifteen years have swirled by and the worst of the prophecies have been fulfilled. The United States and the world are locked deep in environmental crisis. The atmosphere, the earth, and the seas are perilously polluted. For the first time in human history, a total extinction of man is possible. Even likely." The narrator's voice is calm, but the futuristic sounds are strident, and his words are ominous: "What follows is a fictionalized news special program in the year 1985. . . . The things we will describe have not actually happened. But they could."

The program's submission form explained that the simulated news format "was selected as perhaps the most effective device we might develop in an effort to blast through the modern-day façade of ignoring a problem in the belief that it will disappear."[30] After the psychedelic introduction, the program opens on Mark Evans at the news desk of WTTG in Washington, DC, where the president has just completed an emergency address to the nation. *1985* alternates between Evans as central anchor and reporters around the country who report on various ecological catastrophes in each region. Most of these include "on-the-scene" type introductions with the reporter, who then narrates stock footage taken from a real-life catastrophe. In this way, *1985* incorporates extensive actuality footage within a "fake news" context.

For example, George Putnam reports from KTTV Los Angeles, "nature's perfect trap for smog," where eleven thousand are already dead. Footage shows us classic shots of LA smog but also people in hospitals breathing into respirators, then bumper-to-bumper freeway traffic, visually amplified by the superimposition of the footage of the cars on top of itself. Although there are thirty crawls during the program identifying it as *1985: A Fictionalized News Program* or *1985: A News Dramatization*, these alternate with onscreen crawls used as part of the dramatization. These say things like "Members of all 'D' section military reserve units must report to the nearest staging areas" and "Residents of cities in the 'double a' areas are reminded to boil all water used for drinking or cooking."

Coverage of water pollution especially draws on reports from affiliates around the nation. Maury Povich reports from the edges of the Potomac to report on pollution of rivers, showing off polluted shores, closeups on trash and dirty foam rather than Washington monuments. Plenty of footage could be found to show refuse on shores of bays and rivers. Bill Jorgensen also reports from New York with similar scenes. "Today as the tides ebb and flow in the estuary of the great river the accumulated garbage and filth sloshes back and forth, like an obscene ballet. This is Bill Jorgensen along the Hudson River." In this way, Metromedia successfully emulates a network's national news broadcast, cutting from region to region. As the program winds up, there is another round in which we hear from each anchor. Evans, the central anchor, remains doggedly optimistic up until the end, when he loses connection with each anchor. All through the program there has been a "televisual" approach, exaggerating TV manipulation visually with superimpositions and rapid editing. At the end, the framing changes to a TV set, as if we are now in the home of a viewer watching. That TV set goes completely blank, and the program ends.

1985 was neither a local production nor a production of a major broadcast or cable network, and this can be seen both in its content and its distribution. A look at the program's production history and critical reception suggests that, like *Sunday News Update '76*, it is significant in ways that might be overlooked due to its dated look. In 1970, Metromedia owned a chain of independent television stations around the country. When the year 1985 actually did roll around, those stations were purchased by Rupert Murdoch and formed the initial core of the new Fox Network. In the industrial context of 1970, *1985* offered a chance for Metromedia to assert its strength as a network of independent stations, as well as promote Metromedia as a producer of television content at a

George Putnam anchors *1985* from Washington while reporters from Metromedia stations around the country relate local catastrophes.

time when the prime-time access and financial syndication rules were being negotiated but had yet to go into effect. Metromedia took out ads in *Broadcasting* magazine to promote the program and offered to share it free of charge to any station who wanted to broadcast it. This made sense as an altruistic public service gesture that not only promoted Metromedia and its stations but also independent television production at a crucial time in regulatory history. William Tusher's review of *1985* in the *Hollywood Reporter*, which praises the program, begins by raising a general question: "Does off network television really hold promise? Is there any evidence that if the prime-time siphoning goes through, the public won't be cheated, as critics claim? The implications for the multiple program source doctrine of the FCC couldn't have a more persuasive friend in court than Metromedia's absolutely shattering, Orwellian documentary on the ecology crisis, '1985.'"[31]

This review signals how obscure programs like *1985*, which now appear dated and seem to have had little impact on television culture, were at the time considered very significant in ways that can escape us. Evidence shows that many stations took Metromedia up on its offer to distribute the program for free. *Broadcasting* reported that more than twenty outlets had played it in its initial telecast, and within months it had been broadcast on seventy-nine non-Metromedia stations.[32] The letter written to accompany the submission to Peabody described how a number of station groups had banded together to reach stations in thirty-two different states. "Group W, Taft, Gilmore, Storer, Capital Cities, Cox, U.S. Communications and King broadcasting groups all joined the special 'network'" as well as a number of educational channels.[33]

Judging by these numbers and the critical reviews, *1985* was successful as entertaining dramatic content, not just as programming that fulfilled public service requirements or promoted Metromedia's profile. *1985* filled a need for programming, but the critical response suggests that was not just because so many stations wanted to air an ecological documentary. The airwaves had been inundated with ecological documentaries in 1970. Few network documentaries were produced during the 1960s on the topic, with the notable exception of the Peabody-winning "Poisoned Air" (*CBS Reports*) in 1966. The years 1969–70 were a different story. In March 1969, two episodes of the CBS series *The Twenty-First Century* titled "What Are We Doing to our World?" reported on the dangers of pollution, nuclear power, hydraulic fracturing, and the possibility of another Dust Bowl.[34] Examples in 1970 included a series of reports on environmental pollution titled "Can This World Be Saved?" that aired as part of the CBS Evening News with Walter Cronkite.[35] NBC's flagship documentary series *White Paper* aired "Pollution Is a Matter of Choice" in April 1970, a program that won two Emmys. Starting in May, NBC aired a weekly documentary series titled *In Which We Live,* which was composed of nine episodes dealing with the root causes of overpopulation, air and water pollution, noise pollution, and auto traffic.[36] ABC's series *Now* ran an episode on various ecological problems as a prelude to Earth Day in April, then another in July on insecticides and other forces creating "the poisoned planet."

This barrage of eco-programming didn't strike the TV critics as evidence of a collective social enlightenment on the part of the networks. Instead, critics complained about the lack of creative approach in them. Tusher's review of *1985* notes that there had recently been "television warnings coming out our ears on the encroaching dangers of polluting ourselves to extinction."[37] Cecil Smith's review of *1985* in the *Los Angeles Times* calls the topic of ecological disaster the "new gold rush": "Everybody's doing shows on it. Not that this is bad, but TV so often falls into the trap of not covering the stories so much as flogging them to death."[38]

Before broadcast, and well before submission for a Peabody, Metromedia's *1985* ad in *Broadcasting* had visually signaled its news format, with half of the ad constituted by the headline "14,000 DIE IN L.A. KILLER SMOG". Further previewing the unflinching, bleak tone of the program, the ad described Metromedia's intentions for *1985*: "The unusual format—a 'fictionalized' newscast—was selected as perhaps the most effective method of blasting through today's public apathy." Although the ad did not mention the clutter of ecological documentaries on the air being produced by the networks and independents, Metromedia's production team, however, was explicit that the format was adopted because it was different from what the networks were doing. Zev Putterman, executive producer, explained: "All the networks are working doubletime on ecology documentaries and we knew we couldn't compete with them so we tried another approach. We got to talking of George Orwell and of Orson Welles and came up with this."

Although it may look bleak and stylistically dated now, Putterman's choice of format paid off in 1970, according to the reviews. Tusher argues it "exceeded in impact anything done by the networks" and calls it "a smasher from every point of view." He lays the reasons for the success squarely on the program's successful mimicking of real news, saying that all the Metromedia correspondents "heighten the illusion of actuality in performances impossible to distinguish from their daily news-casts." By projecting the crisis fifteen years forward, the program gives it "such immediacy and impact as to defy any lingering pocket of indiffer-ence or skepticism."[39] Cecil Smith also credits the hybrid nature of the program: "I feel that a steady diet of gloom-doom documentaries is of less purpose than the use of docudrama—the weaving of a documentary theme through a dramatic presentation. . . . It would be unfair to reveal the ending, but let me say if you simply shrug, your stomach is stronger than mine."[40] While noting that the program was short on rational solu-tions while opting for the most pessimistic projections, George Gent's re-view in the *New York Times* credits the power of the program's "bleak vi-sion": "The aim of '1985' was to frighten and it did. . . . The program was a frontal assault on complacency, and in terms of its limited objective it was brilliantly successful."[41]

CONCLUSION

This project began as an inquiry into the history of a subgenre of comedy: news parody. I hoped to find examples in the Peabody Awards Collection that had escaped mainstream attention in order to illuminate the histori-cal antecedents for contemporary television satire. While I did find a few comedies that were funny, and a few that were trying to be funny, the pro-grams that I decided were the most interesting were those that weren't try-ing to be funny at all. *You Are There* was the only series, and aside from it and the Peabody for *Ground Zero: Victory Road*, they were not programs that had received much attention, and none of them was canonical TV by any means. In other words, none of these "fake news" programs have registered as historically "significant" in the way *War of the Worlds* has be-cause of the furor (real or imagined) it created, or the way *You Are There* has by being remembered as an innovative approach to merging entertain-ment and education. In comparison to the comic fake news, they weren't cult TV originators like *That Was the Week That Was*, much less ongoing successes like *Saturday Night Live* or *The Daily Show*. As one-off specials, those chances were negligible to begin with; because they were on local TV stations (or in the case of Metromedia, a station group) they never stood much of a chance of receiving widespread recognition.

The producers thought they stood a chance of being awarded a Pea-body, though, and so they are preserved in the Peabody Awards Collec-tion. By expanding our understanding of what television culture has been in the past, they can help us reimagine possibilities that have been forgotten with the ebbing of the FCC's public service expectations and the consolidation of station ownership. We recover a history in which simulated news was not synonymous with comedy but was a viable option for creating educational programming with dramatic value. That format leveraged resources available to local stations to economically produce the kind of content that local stations needed to produce and that individuals working at those stations felt they could use to creatively educate their audiences and meet public service expectations.

We also must acknowledge that the simulated news format, whether used to journey into the past or future, has been adopted as a legitimating strategy, not just for simple budget reasons. In the programs themselves and in the responses from the critics and the public, we find evidence of effective and authoritative representations of reality. These programs openly embraced their simulation, effectively saying that although this particular newscast was simulated, the content mattered: this is, was, and will be our reality. By 2018, Americans had grown accustomed to hearing a president cry "fake news" at anything he didn't like. A station group acting as his ally, Sinclair, even made newscasters at all its stations read the same identical "fake-news" warning on-air.[42] That the news format still holds the same legitimating power seems unlikely.

NOTES   1. Robert M. Faris, Hal Roberts, Bruce Etling, Nikki Bourassa, Ethan Zuckerman, and Yochai Benkler, *Partisanship, Propaganda, and Disinformation: Online Media and the 2016 U.S. Presidential Election* (Cambridge, MA: Berkman Klein Center for Internet and Society, 2017).

2. Other well-known comedy-news programs include the Canadian *This Hour has 22 Minutes* (CBC, 1993–), the British *On the Hour* (BBC, 1991–92), *The Day Today* (BBC, 1994) created by Chris Morris and *Brass Eye* (Channel 4, 1997, 2001). Other well-known antecedents include *Not Necessarily the News* (HBO, 1982, 1983–90), *That Was the Week That Was* (BBC, 1962–63; NBC, 1964–65), and *Monty Python's Flying Circus* (BBC, 1969–74), which frequently made use of a newscaster as a narrator or formatted segments as news reports. *Laugh-In* (NBC, 1968–73) occasionally did as well. In addition to sending Kermit the Frog into the field for reports, *The Muppet Show* (ITV and Syndication, 1976–81) and *Sesame Street* (PBS, 1969–present) have both utilized a "newsman" Muppet. Of course, there were other, more short-lived programs and segments on variety shows, and others that never got beyond the pilot stage.

3. This chapter provides further evidence that the impact of the *War of the Worlds*

broadcast is best measured not by the real public panic that ensued but by the impact of the broadcast on subsequent program development. The radio play has also served as a handy framing device for journalists, TV producers, and promoters. See A. Brad Schwarz, *Broadcast Hysteria: Orson Welles's War of the Worlds and the Art of the Fake News* (New York: Hill and Wang, 2016) for a fascinating examination of public response to the broadcast that focuses on letters to the FCC and Welles himself.

4. Geoffrey Baym, *From Cronkite to Colbert: The Evolution of Broadcast News* (Boulder, CO: Paradigm, 2010), 7.

5. An important antecedent of the fake news format was the radio series *The March of Time* (CBS, 1931–37; NBC Blue, 1937–42, NBC Red, 1942–44, ABC, 1944–45). The alternation between the narrator's voice and those of actors performing in the historical dramatizations can sound quite like a newscast, even though the scenes are also heavily supplemented with sound effects and dramatic score. Though *The March of Time* never won a Peabody, Welles did perform on it, and he must have drawn inspiration from it for the *War of the Worlds* broadcast.

6. Citation for 1956 Peabody award, www.peabodyawards.com/award-profile/you-are-there.

7. For an extensive consideration of how Kovacs adopted parody as a useful method for producing early live television, see the chapter on Kovacs in my book *Parody and Taste in Postwar American Television Culture* (New York: Routledge, 2011).

8. WCBS, *You Are There*, 1952, entry digest, Entry Digests, Indexes, Logs, and Card Files, carton 108, George Foster Peabody Awards Records, ms. 3000, Hargrett Rare Book and Manuscript Library, University of Georgia.

9. Steve Anderson, "Loafing in the Garden of Knowledge: History TV and Popular Memory," *Film and History: An Interdisciplinary Journal of Film and Television Studies* 30, no. 1 (2000): 14–23.

10. Thomas Doherty, *Cold War, Cool Medium: Television, McCarthyism, and American Culture* (New York: Columbia University Press, 2003), 131.

11. Ibid.

12. Erik Barton Christiansen, "History Limited: The Hidden Politics of Postwar Popular Histories" (PhD diss., University of Maryland, 2009), 164.

13. All of these programs are in the Peabody collection. In its overview of bicentennial programming, *Broadcasting* noted *Sunday News Update '76* as an example of how local history was reported ("Bicentennial Eyes and Ears," *Broadcasting*, July 12, 1976, 19). Other local bicentennial productions included *Historical Western New York* in Buffalo and *Centennial Nuggets*, a series of fifty-six shorts produced by Colorado Springs KKTV commemorating both the bicentennial and Colorado's centennial.

14. WCKT, *Sunday News Update '76*, July 4–5, 1976, 76036 BCT 1 of 1, Peabody Awards Collection, Walter J. Brown Media Archives and Peabody Awards Collection, University of Georgia (hereafter PAC), http://dlg.galileo.usg.edu/peabody/id:1976_76036_bct_1.

15. Dot Brown, "1776: TV Takes You There," *Pensacola Journal*, May 6, 1976.

16. Jack Anderson, "Relive July 4, 1776, with Ch. 7," *Miami Herald*, June 3, 1976.

17. WCKT, *Sunday News Update '76*, entry form, clipping, and presentation, box 97, folder 76036 BCT, George Foster Peabody Awards Collection, Series 2: Television Entries, Peabody Awards Collection, ms3000_2b, Hargrett Rare Book and Manuscript Library, University of Georgia (hereafter HAR).

18. Ibid.

19. I could not find any "fake news" radio programs in the Peabody collection, despite using a variety of search terms such as "simulated," "dramatized," and "fictional."

20. Of the two, nuclear war was treated far more often on television in both fictional and nonfictional formats. Programs that specifically dramatized nuclear war or war between the United States and Russia and that were submitted for Peabody consideration include the well-known TV movie *The Day After* (ABC, 1983) and the miniseries *Amerika* (ABC, 1987).

21. WCVB, *Ground Zero: Victory Road*, June 19, 1982, 82023 EDT 1 of 1, PAC, http://dlg.galileo.usg.edu/peabody/id:1982_82023_edt_1.

22. Citation for 1982 Peabody Award, www.peabodyawards.com/award-profile/ground-zero-victory-road.

23. NBC, *Special Bulletin*, March 20, 1983, 83038 ENT 1–2 of 2, PAC, http://dlg.galileo.usg.edu/peabody/id:1983_83038_ent_1-2.

24. NBC, *Special Bulletin*, entry form, production credits, booklet, and clippings, box 127, folder 83038 ENT, George Foster Peabody Awards Collection, Series 2: Television Entries, Peabody Awards Collection, ms3000_2c, HAR.

25. HBO, *Countdown to Looking Glass*, October 14, 1984, 84004 ENT, PAC, http://dlg.galileo.usg.edu/peabody/id:1984_84004_ent_1-2; HBO, *Countdown to Looking Glass*, entry form and press kit, box 131, folder 84004 ENT, George Foster Peabody Awards Collection, Series 2: Television Entries, Peabody Awards Collection, ms3000_2c, HAR.

26. KPIX, *We the People*, "Eyewitness News, Year 2000," January 6, 1976, 76014 BCT 1 of 1, PAC, http://dlg.galileo.usg.edu/peabody/id:1976_76014_bct_1.

27. KPIX, *We the People*, "Eyewitness News, Year 2000," entry form, box 97, folder 76014 BCT, George Foster Peabody Awards Collection, Series 2: Television Entries, Peabody Awards Collection, ms3000_2b, HAR.

28. KTTV, *1985*, 1970, 70003 PST, PAC, http://dlg.galileo.usg.edu/peabody/id:1970_70003_pst_1.

29. KTTV, *1985*, entry form, box 77, folder 70003, George Foster Peabody Awards Collection, Series 2: Television Entries, Peabody Awards Collection, ms3000_2b, HAR.

30. Ibid.

31. William Tusher, "Television Review," *Hollywood Reporter*, June 3, 1970.

32. In 1971, the rights to the program were sold to McCann-Erickson, which dubbed the show in Japanese and aired it in Japan as a public service of the National Cash Register Company of Dayton, Ohio ("*1985* Going to Japan," *Broadcasting*, November 1, 1971).

33. KTTV, *1985*, letter from Reavis G. Winckler to dean of Grady School of Journalism, December 30, 1970, box 77, folder 70003, George Foster Peabody Awards Collection, Series 2: Television Entries, Peabody Awards Collection, ms3000_2b, HAR.

34. Daniel Einstein, *Special Edition: A Guide to Network Documentary Series and Special News Reports, 1955–1979* (Metuchen, NJ: Scarecrow Press, 1987).

35. "Hottest New Program Topic: Ecology," *Broadcasting*, March 16, 1970.

36. Einstein, *Special Edition*, 309.

37. Tusher, "Television Review."

38. Cecil Smith, "Docudrama Tells Paralyzing Story," *Los Angeles Times*, June 1, 1970, 18.

39. Tusher, "Television Review."

40. Smith, "Docudrama Tells Paralyzing Story."

41. George Gent, "TV: A Frightening Look at the Problems in '1985,'" *New York Times*, June 2, 1970.

42. Emily Price, "Sinclair TV Group Requires Local News Anchors to Echo President Trump in Bashing 'Fake News,'" Fortune.com, March 8, 2018, fortune.com/2018/03/08/sinclair-media-group-fake-news.

CONTRIBUTORS

CHRISTINE BECKER is an associate professor in the Department of Film, Television, and Theatre at the University of Notre Dame; she specializes in film and television history and critical analysis. Her book *It's the Pictures That Got Small: Hollywood Film Stars on 1950s Television* (2009) won the 2011 IAMHIST Michael Nelson Prize for a Work in Media and History. She is currently working on a research project exploring issues of cultural taste in contemporary American and British television. She also cohosts and coproduces the *Aca-Media* podcast for the *Journal of Cinema and Media Studies*.

SUSAN J. DOUGLAS is the Catherine Neafie Kellogg Professor of Communication Studies at the University of Michigan. She is the author of six books, including *Celebrity: A History of Fame* (2018), *The Rise of Enlightened Sexism: How Pop Culture Took Us from Girl Power to Girls Gone Wild* (2010), *Listening In: Radio and the American Imagination* (1999), and *Where the Girls Are: Growing Up Female with the Mass Media* (1994). She served on the board of the Peabody Awards for six years and served as its chair in 2010.

HERMAN GRAY is an emeritus professor of sociology at the University of California, Santa Cruz, and has published widely in scholarly journals in the areas of black cultural theory, politics, and media and television studies. His books on jazz, television, and black cultural politics include *Producing Jazz* (1988), *Watching Race* (1995), *Cultural Moves* (2005), and *The Sage Handbook of Television Studies*, which he coedited. His latest book is *Racisms, Postrace* (2019), coedited with Sarah Banet Weiser and Roopali Mukherjee.

JONATHAN GRAY is a professor of media and cultural studies at the University of Wisconsin, Madison. He is the author or coeditor of numerous books, including *Television Studies* (2018, with Amanda Lotz), *Television Entertainment* (2008), *Show Sold Separately: Promos, Spoilers, and Other Media Paratexts* (2010), *The Companion to Media Authorship* (2013, with Derek

Johnson), and *Keywords in Media Studies* (2017, with Laurie Ouellette). He is a member of the board of jurors for the Peabody Awards.

LUCAS HATLEN is a doctoral student at the University of Georgia in the Grady College of Journalism and Mass Communication and a former research fellow with the Peabody Awards. He received his MA from the University of Texas, Austin, and his undergraduate degree from the University of North Texas. His research interests include the intersection of local media histories and American identity.

HEATHER HENDERSHOT is a professor of film and media at Massachusetts Institute of Technology. Her most recent books are *What's Fair on the Air? Cold War Right-Wing Broadcasting and the Public Interest* (2011) and *Open to Debate: How William F. Buckley Put Liberal America on the Firing Line* (2016).

ERIC HOYT is an associate professor of communication arts at the University of Wisconsin, Madison, and director of the Media History Digital Library (http://mediahistoryproject.org), which has digitized 2.3 million pages of film and media publications for broad public access. He is the author of *Hollywood Vault: Film Libraries before Home Video* (2014) and coeditor of the anthologies *Hollywood and the Law* (2015) and *The Arclight Guidebook to Media History and the Digital Humanities* (2016).

DEBORAH L. JARAMILLO is an associate professor of television studies at Boston University. She is the author of *The Television Code: Regulating the Screen to Safeguard the Industry* (2018), which examines how the National Association of Broadcasters, the Federal Communications Commission, the United States Congress, and television viewers sought to police early television programs. Her first book, *Ugly War, Pretty Package: How CNN and Fox News Made the Invasion of Iraq High Concept* (2009), analyzes the style, narrative, and marketing of cable news war coverage.

JEFFREY P. JONES, PhD, is executive director of the George Foster Peabody Awards, director of the Peabody Media Center, and Lambdin Kay Chair for the Peabodys at the University of Georgia. He is the author and editor of six books, including *Entertaining Politics: Satiric Television and Civic Engagement* (2010), *Satire TV: Politics and Comedy in the Post-Network Era* (2009), and *The Essential HBO Reader* (2013). His research and teaching focuses on popular politics, or the ways in which politics are presented and engaged through popular culture. His research subjects include media figures and programs such as *Saturday Night Live*, Jon Stewart, Stephen Colbert, Bill Maher, and Michael Moore, as well as examinations of Fox News as a form of political entertainment television.

DEREK KOMPARE is an associate professor and chair of film and media arts at Southern Methodist University, where he teaches courses on media histories, industries, and cultures. He is the author of *Rerun Nation: How Repeats Invented American Television* (2004) and *CSI* (2010) and coeditor of *Making Media Work: Cultures of Management in the Entertainment Industries* (2014).

SUSAN MURRAY is a professor of media, culture, and communication at New York University. She is the author of *Bright Signals: A History of Color Television* (2018) and *Hitch Your Antenna to the Stars! Early Television and Broadcast Stardom* (2005) and coeditor of *Reality TV: Remaking Television Culture* (2004, 2009).

ALLISON PERLMAN is an associate professor of film and media studies and history at the University of California, Irvine. She is the author of *Public Interests: Media Advocacy and Struggles Over US Television* (2016) and coeditor of *Flow TV: Television in the Age of Media Convergence* (2010).

LYNN SPIGEL is the Frances Willard Chair of Screen Cultures at Northwestern University. She is author of numerous books, anthologies, and essays, including *Make Room for TV: Television and the Family Ideal in Postwar America* (1992) and *TV by Design: Modern Art and the Rise of Network Television* (2009). Her book *TV Snapshots: An Archive of Everyday Life* is forthcoming from the Duke University Press.

ETHAN THOMPSON is a professor of media arts at Texas A&M University, Corpus Christi. He is the author of *Parody and Taste in Postwar American Television Culture* (2010) and coeditor of *How to Watch Television* (2013) and *Satire TV: Politics and Comedy in the Post-Network Era* (2009). He also directed the documentary *TV Family* (2015), about a forgotten forerunner to reality television. He is coeditor of the Peabody Series in Media History from the University of Georgia Press.

INDEX

1985, 216–21, 224n32

ABC (American Broadcasting Company): and bicentennial programming, 104; and fake news, 215, 220, 223n5; and gay and lesbian representation, 120, 131, 134n15; and Vietnam coverage, 26; and war on drugs, 161–67
accents, discernable in local television, 6, 106, 181
activism: and civil rights movement, 82–93, 137–42, 149–50, 151n20, 152n26; and fake news, 215; feminist, 62, 118–19; and gay rights movement, 119–23, 127–33; in histories of local television, 15n13; and U.S. bicentennial, 98–100
The Adams Chronicles, 104
Adorno, Theodor, 61
"Advance in Surgery," 193, 201
Adventuring in the Hand Arts, 71
advertising on television: and bicentennial celebrations, 98, 103, 111; and children, 26; and local markets, 36; and mediated war on drugs, 166; and sexism, 119
affect and emotion: affective ties to local television, 8, 12, 72, 124; "feeling America," 101, 104, 111, 113; representations of, 39, 43, 86, 146–47, 176
African Americans: in children's media, 63–64; in Madison, WI, local media, 33, 57; reframing history, 136–53; and representation in bicentennial media, 98, 110–11; and representation in

media archives, 31n15. *See also* black subjects
Agué, Marc, 5, 15n11
AIDS crisis programming, 116–17, 134n15, 165, 167
Allen, Craig M., 51
All in the Family, 47, 176
Almost Grown, 29
American exceptionalism, 8, 96. *See also* nationalism
American Forces Radio and Television Service, 110
American Revolution Bicentennial Administration (ARBA), 97–99
American Revolution Bicentennial Commission (ARBC), 97, 100
"American Rock," 105
Anderson, Steve, 209
Annenberg School of Communication at the University of Pennsylvania, 66
antigay backlash. *See* homophobia
The Apartment, 187
archives, 14n4, 14n5, 14n7, 15n15, 31n12, 134n14; and blackness, 80–82, 92–93; and discourse of quality television, 28–30, 171–72; funding, 31n15; and gay, lesbian, and transgender representation, 130–32; and the local, 5–10, 15n15, 158–60; and media histories, 10–14, 20, 34–35, 116–17, 128–30; Peabody Awards Collection overview, 1–5, 21–25; Peabody Awards Collection search tools, 30n3, 30n5, 31n8, 59n1; size of, 20, 42, 48–49, 134n14. *See also* Peabody Awards Program; preservation

Printed in the United States
By Bookmasters